Accounting Theory and Standards

Second Edition

Mike Harvey

*Dean of the School of Accounting and Finance,
City of London Polytechnic*

Fred Keer

*Director of Studies,
Accountancy Tuition Centre Certified School*

Prentice/Hall PHI International

Englewood Cliffs, New Jersey   London   New Delhi   Rio de Janeiro
Singapore   Sydney   Tokyo   Toronto   Wellington

British Library Cataloguing in Publication Data

Harvey, Mike
  Financial accounting theory and standards.—2nd ed.
  1. Accounting
  I. Title   II.Keer, Fred
  657'.48   HF5635

  ISBN 0-13-314211-6

ISBN 0-13-314211-6

Prentice-Hall International, Inc., *London*
Prentice-Hall of Australia Pty, Ltd., *Sydney*
Prentice-Hall Canada, Inc., *Toronto*
Prentice-Hall of India Private Ltd., *New Dehli*
Prentice-Hall of Japan, Inc., *Tokyo*
Prentice-Hall of Southeast Asia Pte. Ltd., *Singapore*
Prentice-Hall Inc., *Englewood Cliffs, New Jersey*
Prentice-Hall do Brasil Ltda., *Rio de Janeiro*
Whitehall Books Ltd., *Wellington, New Zealand*

HARVEY

Typeset by MHL Typesetting Ltd, Coventry
Printed and bound in Great Britain by A. Wheaton and Company Ltd, Exeter

10 9 8 7 6 5 4 3 2 1

Contents

Preface

A book on accounting theory, especially one aimed specifically at practising accountants and those who hope to be admitted to the profession in the near future, may appear somewhat paradoxical. Surely accounting is an essentially practical exercise, intended to serve the needs of businessmen, through a workable series of rules and conventions evolved over many years in response to problems confronted by its practitioners. Not so many years ago this would have been a commonly held view. However, in recent years the increasing variety of demands made of published accounting statements and reports has revealed serious deficiencies in such data. In fairness, though, accounts as understood today were neither intended nor designed to meet demands currently placed upon the accounting profession. Thus those deficiencies are hardly surprising.

Accounting as understood today was evolved to meet the needs of an expanding economy which was becoming commercially complex. A particular development which probably gave the greatest impetus to the establishment of a comprehensive system of accountancy was the formation of the Joint Stock Companies. Once the divorce between ownership (i.e. the provision of risk-taking capital) and control (i.e. the taking of decisions) had become a fact there was clearly a need for the controlling decision-takers to account to the owners of capital as to how their funds had been deployed. Accordingly accounting procedures were developed to meet this need, which is frequently referred to as the 'stewardship function'. Current accounting conventions, notably the basing of accounts on historic cost, are the legacy of early considerations and developments.

Inevitably accounts were eventually required to show not only how, but how wisely, funds had been used. This resulted in the shift from the balance sheet to the profit and loss account as the primary accounting statement. Increasingly greater demands have been placed on accounts until the situation as outlined in *The Corporate Report** has been reached whereby financial statements are expected to assist the various user groups

---

* *The Corporate Report*, Accounting Standards Steering Committee, July 1975.

in making decisions about the entity. It is not surprising then that certain deficiencies have emerged in today's conventionally prepared accounts.

Recognising the need for a re-evaluation of the traditional principles and conventions, the Profession set up the Accounting Standards Committee to consider those areas of practice that produced the greatest anomalies and to make recommendations as to how they should be dealt with.

At the time of writing the ASC has produced some 30 exposure drafts, some two-thirds of which have become Statements of Standard Accounting Practice. Furthermore, prodded by the EEC, the Government has introduced a range of detailed requirements for published accounts in the 1981 Companies Act.

The effect of all this is that accountants are now hemmed in by a considerable range of legal and quasi-legal requirements. Clearly they need a framework within which to interpret these requirements. Furthermore, notwithstanding the details of the rules, the overriding principle remains the need to give a true and fair view. This is the context in which the need for an understanding of accounting theory must be seen.

We feel it would be useful to point out at the outset that in our view the central concepts of value and income on which all accounts are based are artificial abstractions invented by accountants and economists. Accordingly in considering different ways of accounting for economic events we will not be concerned with whether the varying treatments take the accountant closer to or further from the 'real' or 'true' profit figure, since in our view the quest for 'true' profit has much in common with the quest for the holy grail. Rather, we will be interested in whether the accounts that are the results of the various treatments are more or less useful in achieving the objectives of financial accounting. Even in theory we remain pragmatists.

The Second Edition

This new edition represents a major revision of our first edition of this book— *Financial Accounting Theory*. While retaining the overall objective of explaining accounting theory and demonstrating its relevance to practitioners, we have shifted the emphasis slightly to illustrate more clearly the link between accounting theory and the Statements of Standard Accounting Practice. All of the chapters have been updated to incorporate the requirements of recent standards and the latest Companies Act as appropriate.

Chapter 1 has been substantially modified to consider alternative approaches to theory construction and their significance for the development of accounting standards. The introduction of SSAP 16 has made the problem of accounting for price level changes too big to cover in one chapter. Therefore we have split the coverage of this into two chapters with Chapter 6 providing an introduction to the subject while Chapter 7 considers the development of Current Cost Accounting. Chapter 8, 'Towards Accounting Standards', has also been extensively rewritten to incorporate recent developments and also to reinforce the new theme of the book, i.e. the relationship between theory and standard.

A new chapter on stock valuation, Chapter 4, has been included to provide a fuller coverage of areas that both students and practitioners find difficult to understand. For justification of a chapter on the valuation of inventory and work-in-progress we need hardly look further than the introduction to SSAP 9 which says 'No area of accounting has produced wider differences in practice than the computation of the amount at which stocks and work in progress are stated in financial accounts.'

We would like to thank our many friends and colleagues who first inspired and then encouraged and helped us to produce this book. In particular we would like to thank Bernard Alexander, Doug Richardson and Albert Slow for commenting upon earlier drafts of both the first and second editions, and Paul Rouse for his remarks on the classification of SSAPs and EDs in Chapter 8. We are grateful to Giles Wright of Prentice-Hall International for his encouragement with the project; to Ronald Decent and Ruth Freestone for the arranged layout and production of the book; and to our publisher's anonymous reviewers for painstakingly reading earlier drafts and making many useful suggestions for improving the text. Needless to say any remaining errors are entirely ours. We would also like to thank Edna Gambie for her considerable efforts in converting a succession of barely decipherable manuscripts into typescript.

We would also like to thank: The Institute of Chartered Accountants in England and Wales, for information contained in Exhibits 4(b) and 5(c); for Allied Breweries PLC, British Airways, British Gas Corp., Coats Patons PLC, Currys PLC, Debenhams PLC, Imperial Chemical Industries PLC, Marks & Spencer PLC, Record Ridgway PLC, Redman Heenan International PLC, Samuel Osborn & Co. PLC, Thorn EMI PLC and Tube Investments PLC for the use of their accounts; and Phillips & Drew for the use of their table on p. 131.

Finally, we thank our respective wives, Maureen and Linda, for their encouragement and understanding as we deserted them during our many discussions in the preparation of the text.

M.H.
F.K.

CHAPTER 1

The Construction of Financial Accounting Theory

1.1 INTRODUCTION

As with many areas within the social sciences the study of financial accounting can be restricted to a more or less detailed description of current practice or it can attempt to understand practice in the context of an underlying theory. The aim of this chapter is to consider the need for a coherent theory of accounting and look at various approaches to the development of an appropriate theory. It is hoped that readers will be better able to understand current developments in accounting practice if they can relate these through an understanding of their theoretical underpinnings.

1.2 ACCOUNTING METHODOLOGY AND THE NEED FOR THEORY

Accounting theory can be defined as

> a cohesive set of conceptual, hypothetical and pragmatic propositions explaining and guiding the accountant's action in identifying, measuring and communicating economic information.*

This statement, while couched in language that might seem a little pretentious to the average practitioner, would appear to provide a reasonable enough definition. Few would doubt the need for such a set of propositions, although many would suppose that they existed. Few indeed would see any immediate practical relevance in such a statement.

The difficulty arises in that if a number of competent and professionally qualified accountants were presented with the basic data concerning a series of economic transactions undertaken by an organisation and asked to prepare sets of accounts reflecting the progress and current position of

---

* This definition has been culled from the definitions for 'theory' and 'accounting' found on page 1 of *A Statement of Basic Accounting Theory*, American Accounting Association, 1966.

that organisation, it is more than likely that they would produce a number of differing sets of accounts. This apparently odd behaviour is the result of two factors. First, in the preparation of any set of accounts a certain number of subjective estimates have to be made and some predictions of future events are required. For example, in calculating the appropriate depreciation provision it is necessary to make estimates of the useful life and terminal value of an asset. Not surprisingly, indeed inevitably, different estimates of these are likely to be made by different accountants even from the same data.

A second, and more disturbing, cause of the discrepancies amongst the various accounts will be conflicts in the principles applied by various accountants.

The concepts of value and profit with which accountants deal are neither clear nor unambiguous. Accordingly, accountants have developed a number of principles or postulates over the years to reduce the ambiguities associated with these concepts in the accounts that they produce. The problem is that these principles have been built up in a piecemeal fashion over a long period to meet the difficulties of the time during which they were developed. When confronted with a difficult situation the accountant has traditionally asked questions such as 'What do others do?' or 'How was this done in the past?' rather than 'How should this problem be resolved today?' Hence accounting principles would be better described as conventions which have largely been developed without reference to any coherent theory. In consequence, the conventions on which traditional financial accounts are prepared are frequently inconsistent and definitely incomplete. For example, accountants value stock at historic cost because of the need to be objective, yet they cheerfully estimate useful life and terminal value of capital assets subjectively, because of the need to spread the cost of these over a number of accounting periods due to the matching principle. Conservatism or prudence tells accountants to 'anticipate no profits and provide for all possible losses', yet the 'going concern' assumption enables them to include highly specialised machinery in the accounts at amounts far in excess of the realisable value of this machinery.*

It cannot be surprising, therefore, that such conventions are open to a variety of interpretations and hence a variety of accounts can be produced to depict a given set of economic events. Conventional accounts have always suffered from these problems. However, the increasing complexity of the economy has resulted in increasingly greater demands being placed upon published accounts. This, in conjunction with the special problems associated with high and sustained rates of inflation, has resulted in the defi-

---

* This, for example, applies to much of the BL PLC plant and machinery, which is unlikely to be purchased by other vehicle manufacturers if BLMC went out of business.

ciencies of conventional financial accounts becoming more apparent and has accordingly strengthened the demands for reform.*

Many of these demands came to a head as a result of a number of controversial take-over bids and unexpected business collapses during the middle to late 1960s. A particular example that illustrates this is the GEC/AEI take-over battle during the latter half of 1967.[1]† The facts of the case are as follows. In September 1967 GEC made a take-over bid for AEI. The bid was unacceptable to the AEI board and on 20 October 1967, which was within two months of the end of their financial year, they published a formal defence to the GEC offer. A central plank of the AEI defence was a profit forecast which predicted a £10 million company profit for 1967, which a major accounting firm declared to have been prepared in a fair and reasonable way. However, in spite of the opposition the GEC bid was successful. Ultimately the results of AEI for 1967 turned out to be a £4.5 million *loss* as against the forecast profits of £10 million. The discrepancy of £14.5 million was the subject of a joint investigation by Deloittes, the AEI auditors and Price Waterhouse, the GEC auditors. In this investigation the discrepancy was analysed as those elements substantially relating to matters of fact being £5.0 million, and those of judgement, £9.5 million.

This sort of thing continues: for example, early in 1982, Sir Freddie Laker's airline crashed. The Insight column of the Sunday Times on 14 February 1982 pointed out that, 'Put bluntly, Laker Airways was made to appear much more profitable, and much more valuable than it really was by some obvious manipulation of the figures!' It then gave examples including that of a change in the company's 'depreciation' policy. Until 1973 planes appeared to have assumed a life of around seven years but from then on a 'minimum structural life basis relative to flying hours' was assumed. Insight says that 'In other words Laker's planes only lost value when they flew' and continuing that 'In practice, this appears to have doubled the "expected" life of the planes'.[2]

Such occurrences[3] caused widespread public concern and undoubtedly undermined confidence in published accounts. However, the widespread

---

* As a result of concern over the ambiguities and inconsistencies in published accounting statements the Accounting Standards Steering Committee (ASSC), later to be called the Accounting Standards Committee (ASC), was set up during 1970. The Committee's function is to consider problem areas in accounting reports and produce recommendations as to how these problems should be dealt with. Its procedure has been to produce an Exposure Draft (ED) which outlines the problem being considered and suggests a possible way of dealing with it. The ED invites written comments on the proposals from interested parties by a set date. After considering comments on the ED, the Committee produces a Statement of Standard Accounting Practice (SSAP) which sets out how the area is to be dealt with in the future. In 1976 the International Accounting Standards Committee (IASC) was established to perform a similar function in the international context. The IASC issues exposure drafts and International Accounting Standards (IAS).

† Superior figures denote end-of-chapter references.

and fundamental reform that appears necessary cannot properly be undertaken without reference to a coherent underlying theory.

1.3 APPROACHES TO THE CONSTRUCTION OF A THEORY OF ACCOUNTING

Most of what passes for financial accounting theory as accepted by the majority of accountants today appears to be little more than rationalisation of what is considered to be good practice. For most accountants in the UK the theoretical reference framework is provided by the Statements of Standard Accounting Practice issued by the Accounting Standards Committee. However, the work of the ASC in issuing standards has been piecemeal in nature. It can hardly be otherwise as the ASC has so far declined to make a definitive statement on the nature and purpose of published financial accounts. The closest it has come is in the discussion document 'The Corporate Report':[4] in the foreword to this document, Ronald Leach who was the Chairman of the Accounting Standards Steering Committee at the time, emphasises that *the Report does not necessarily represent the views of the ASSC nor of any individual accounting body*.[5]

Significantly there has been no further comment from the ASC since the publication of the Corporate Report in 1975, although it should be noted that the ASC has recently published the research it commissioned into a conceptual framework.[6] Evidence of the lack of a coherent underlying theoretical base for the standards may be found in the faltering steps of the ASC to producing a system of accounting that is suitable for use in an economic environment that is characterised by significant inflation.[*]

An example of the way in which widespread practice has become acceptable theory is to be found in the valuation of stock and work-in-progress. The practice of valuing stocks at the lower of cost or Net Realisable Value was common in Italy in the 15th century.[7] It gained further acceptance in the UK during the 19th century and in the USA in the early 20th century because it produced a conservative balance sheet. With the increasing importance being attached to the profit and loss account and the variety of uses to which published financial statements are now put the approach has come under increasing criticism. Nevertheless it has been enshrined in SSAP 9, as a method of stock valuation. More recently it has been given the blessing of the UK Parliament in the 1981 Companies Act. However, its attributes are lost in the mists of time and certainly SSAP 9 makes no

---

[*] Chapter 6 discusses the current 'state of play' in this area. The lack of a coherent, underlying theoretical base for the standards currently being used in the preparation of financial statements is bound to lead to changes in the future.

attempt to offer a justification for the basic lower of cost or market value rule* beyond a restatement of the need to match costs with revenues.

However this somewhat pragmatic approach does have certain advantages. Given that the objective of accounting is to provide information which is useful to its recipients, procedures that have passed the practical test of time may be assumed to have some merit. Furthermore, practice will inevitably be a compromise to some extent between the attributes of ideal information and the costs associated with getting it. 'Purer' approaches to the construction of theory may overlook the costs of the principles advocated which although resulting in marginally better information may produce this at a disproportionate increase in cost.

The disadvantages of such an approach are twofold. Firstly, lacking as it does a clear statement of objectives the resulting propositions will inevitably be inconsistent. Secondly, it will be unable to respond to changing environments or circumstances without a considerable time lag. Furthermore the response to changing circumstances will undoubtedly be to tack new propositions onto the existing set,† which will reinforce the tendency towards internal inconsistency.

The Deductive Approach to Theory Construction

A deductive approach to the construction of theory involves a clear statement of objectives, the identification of a number of assumptions or postulates about the environment in which the theory is to function and the development of a number of principles and ultimately rules or laws which have been logically derived from the objectives and postulates. The principles and laws may be descriptive or normative. That is, they may state what does happen or what should happen to achieve a given objective. It is often suggested that the essence of a theory is the explanation of observed phenomena and that a measure of its success may be found in its ability to predict future events.[8] Therefore, in formulating a theory of financial accounting, one needs to know first, who wants to make the prediction and, second, what it is they want to predict. In answer to the first question the issue of who are the legitimate users of financial statements must be considered. As will be seen in later chapters, the most authoritative statement on the identities of the various user groups of financial accounts is to be found in *The Corporate Report*. This publication identifies a wide range of user groups including employees, existing and potential shareholders, suppliers, customers and the State.[9] The Corporate Report concludes that

---

* It should be noted that SSAP 16 gives a different rule, with the lower of Market Value or Net Realisable Value having to be used in CCA.
† For example in practice most companies have 'tacked on' supplementary statements for CCA to historic cost accounts.

the primary function of published accounts is to assist the various user groups in making decisions concerning the business.*

In considering what the users wish to predict it must inevitably be concluded that all users of financial data are concerned with the value, vulnerability and likely future success of the organisation. But how do we define success? In this context the reader may usefully consider Harold Edey's article 'The nature of profit'.[10] In this article, Professor Edey suggests that the successful company is one which is able to maintain and increase the cash payments made to the various factors of production that it employs. Hence the critical factor in determining success becomes the ability to ensure that long-run cash flows are, on balance, positive. In this context profit may be judged in terms of how successful a surrogate it is for the firm's ability to generate these positive net cash flows. Professor Edey rightly points out that a major failing of conventional accounts based on historic cost is that it is possible for reported profits to be shown as increasing in a period in which the organisation's capacity to generate positive cash flows in the long run has deteriorated. For example, if a firm delays investment in some new and necessary capital project it may benefit in the short run from reduced depreciation charges, which enables it to report higher profits. However, in the long term its competitive position may be damaged and its ability to survive may be placed in jeopardy.

Hence the accounting conventions selected in the production of accounts must ensure that an accurate reflection is made of the company's success or failure in terms of its ability to produce positive net cash flows in the long run. However, it should be noted that the acceptability of a profit definition will not be enhanced by its ability to aid in the prediction of future profits. To accept a definition because it aids in the prediction of itself is tautologous. If the resultant figure has no intrinsic meaning its use will be limited. Therefore, in considering various theories of income and value the critical question is: 'Does this measure aid in the prediction of the long term success or failure of the organisation?'

An Inductive Approach to Theory Construction

An obvious problem with a deductive approach to accounting theory is that it presupposes agreement on the objectives of accounting and entails acceptance of a set of postulates or assumptions about the world which may turn out to be false. In contrast an inductive approach proceeds from the specific to the general. Developing a theory using induction entails making a number of observations and seeking a common characteristic which will

---

* *The Corporate Report*, page 31 Section 3.16 states: 'In our view the fundamental objective of corporate reports is to communicate economic measurements of and information about the resources and performance of the reporting entity useful to those having reasonable rights to such information.'

enable a general principle applicable in all cases to emerge. The difficulty of course is in deciding what to observe. One possibility would be to observe the financial data associated with business transactions. A danger in this is that knowledge that the observation is taking place may influence the nature of the event, i.e. because there is an observer the observation is affected.

One of the major problems in using an inductive approach is that the observer may have a preconceived bias about what he is to see and he may already have developed ideas about the relationships he believes to exist. Furthermore as there is obviously a limit to the number of observations that can be made there may be a danger in ascribing general applicability to the generalisations derived.*

In consequence it is usually necessary to test generalisations derived inductively by deductive reasoning.

Validation of a Theory

In the physical sciences it is frequently possible to carry out experiments to test a theory; in the social sciences this is rarely possible. This means that it is often necessary to test the theory by using historical data to predict the known outcome of events. Thus it is possible to compare the predictions of the theory with what is known to have occurred. The major problem in this is that in the complex economic world it is not always possible to segregate cause and effect. Nevertheless it is important to collect data both to enable theories to be constructed and also to enable the testing of the validity of any hypothesis developed, remembering that different sets of data must be used for each stage to avoid circular reasoning.

The discussion as to what constitutes a 'good theory' has raged for many years. An insight into the nature of the debate may be had by considering the arguments regarding the development of economic theory since economics is the traditional 'academic' discipline which is the source of much of the methodology of modern accounting. Stated crudely the issue is whether the test of a theory should be based on the validity of its assumptions and the logic with which its conclusions proceed from them or the accuracy of predictions made by the theory—its predictive ability.

The controversy relating to the importance of assumptions in economic theory goes back nearly as far as the foundation of the discipline itself. In the nineteenth century there was an argument between economists interested in their subject historically and those who were in favour of developing it from a purely theoretical viewpoint. Lord Robbins, writing in the 1930s stated that pure economic theory should be used to enable absolute truths

---

* For example observations of bird life in the UK might have given rise to the generalisation 'all swans are white'. That it did not have general applicability was demonstrated when black swans were discovered in Australia.

to be established from pure assumptions.[11] Following from this, empirical evidence could then be used to see whether the theory accorded with the real world. He thereby suggested a methodology which could be established for the development of economic theory. Lord Robbins also stated that economic theory should be normatively neutral so that value judgements are removed from it. Inherent in his thinking was a tendency towards simplifying the assumptions underlying economic theory.

However, since World War II, a new stream of economists has become interested in economic theory. In many senses they have been dominated by the Chicago School and Milton Friedman in particular. Basically they have stressed the importance of positive economics, and even more importantly they have questioned the usefulness of making the assumptions used to develop economic theory more realistic. No longer, suggests Professor Friedman, should economists hold to the idea that the validity of a theory depends upon the reality of any assumption made in its development. He states that the simple answer to the question about whether a theory should be accepted or rejected is to judge it by the validity of any predictions made using it, especially when the circumstances under which the predictions are made change.

Most theories in the social sciences will result from simplifications of the real world, and obviously will have to be based upon assumptions—some of which may not be very realistic. Questions arise as to the number of assumptions that should be used to build a theory and as to the realism of these assumptions. It may be that a surrogate can be used to replace a number of assumptions to simplify even further. The question becomes one of degree. In his important article on the role of assumptions in the development of a theory[12] Professor Friedman refers to the natural sciences. In mechanics it is established that the acceleration of a physical body due to gravity, in a vacuum, is 9.81 ms^{-2}. However, on earth bodies rarely fall in a vacuum. Nevertheless, when it is wished to predict the acceleration that a body would achieve on earth the approximation of 9.81 ms^{-2} may be used.

Professor Friedman suggests that assumptions are not important because any descriptive accuracy they provide may have little connection with analytical usefulness. The major problem associated with his view is that the usefulness of a theory can only be judged on observation. However, in the complex real world observation is difficult. Furthermore, a theory in the social sciences which worked in the past may not work in the future. Hence, although his views are persuasive, the argument that the true test of a theory lies in the reasonableness of its assumptions, and the precision with which its conclusions follow from those assumptions, cannot easily be rejected.[13]

From Theory to Standard

As has been already observed, for most accountants the theoretical framework within which they operate is provided in the main by the various accounting standards issued by the ASC. Therefore it is necessary both to consider the transition process which moves 'pure' theories to standards and to reconcile the existing standards with the underlying theory.

Accounting research and literature has provided many theories for various areas of accounting some of which have had an effect on the rules issued by various accounting bodies in different parts of the world. For example, it was in the early 1940s that the Institute of Chartered Accountants in England and Wales began to issue 'recommendations', and the American Institute of Certified Public Accountants have issued research bulletins, opinions and principles since the late 1930s. Throughout the remainder of this book, theories for the various subjects being discussed will be related to the development of accounting standards for the areas concerned.

1.4 ARE STANDARDS NECESSARY?

Before discussing this point it is important to define clearly what the accounting profession appears to mean by the word 'standard'. Essentially a standard in accounting is a method of or an approach to preparing accounts which has been chosen and established by the bodies overseeing the profession.*

Thus it can be seen that a standard is some form of rule. The word 'standard' is preferred to that of 'principle' because clearly a standard is pragmatic and it also has a less permanent connotation than principle. Therefore the use of the word 'standard' in itself can only do good because it will remove any inhibition about its replacement with a better standard if this becomes appropriate.

In a discussion on whether accounting standards are necessary it will be beneficial to consider the advantages and disadvantages they are said to provide.

Advantages of Standards

The following advantages, except the last, will be baldly stated without comment.

---

* Part of the definitions provided in two dictionaries, which seem appropriate to the use of the word 'standard' in accounting are as follows: *The Shorter Oxford English Dictionary*, 3rd ed. (1950): 3a: Something that is established by authority, custom, or general consent as a mode or example to be followed. b: A definite level or degree of quality that is proper and adequate for a specific purpose. 7a: A carefully thought out method of performing a task (auditing standard).
Webster's Third New International Dictionary (1961): A 11 2. An authoritative or recognised exemplar of correctness, perfection, or some definite degree of quality. B 1 3. Serving or fitted to serve as a comparison or judgement.

(a) Provide the profession with a manual of useful working rules.
(b) Force improvements in the quality of the work of the accountant.
(c) Strengthen the accountant's resistance against pressure from directors to use an accounting policy which may be suspect in the circumstances.
(d) Ensure that the users of financial statements get more complete and clearer information on a consistent basis from period to period.
(e) Help in the comparisons users may make between the financial statements of one organisation and another.
(f) Direct financial statements towards establishing the economic truth of the entity's performance—however this must be considered an extremely dubious benefit for standards may provide rules based on current practice rather than taking another accounting theory for the area which would lead to greater economic reality.

On this last point Professor William Baxter says that 'the estimation of wealth is probably closer to judging in a beauty competition than to physical measurement'.[14]

Disadvantages of Standards

(a) The working rules are bureaucratic and lead to rigidity.
(b) The quality of work of the accountant is restricted because firms and industries differ, and change, as do the environments within which they operate. Standards which are based on averages lead to rigidity and reduce the scope for professional judgements. In fact they make the accountant a technician rather than a professional.* An extension of this point could be that standards may adversely affect accountants' education and development by stultifying critical thought as they tend to be accepted and applied rather than thought about.†
(c) Official acceptance reduces the accountant's strength to resist the application of an inappropriate standard when the directors wish to follow it.
(d) Users are likely to think that the financial statements produced using accounting standards are infallible.
(e) Although providing formulae, standards still allow for the figures

---

* It has been suggested that financial statements provide a record of how man sees the enterprise in financial terms, this is best encapsulated by Mr R.M. Morison who said '. . . an accountant is an artist. He finds a subject; he studies it; he must be moved; and then endeavours to portray his subject faithfully. The main principle involved is one of truth . . .', Morison, R.M. 'A critical review of recognised accounting conventions' *The Accountants Magazine*, September/October 1962 page 661, which implies giving the accountant scope to use his professional judgement rather than constraining him with rules.
† Professor W.T. Baxter makes this point in his article 'Accounting standards—boon or curse?', *Accounting and Business Research*, Winter 1981.

used as inputs to be selected with some subjectivity,* which reduces the possible benefits of comparison between firms when the input base may not be known.

(f) They have been derived through social or political pressures which may reduce the freedom or lead to manipulation of the profession.†

(g) They stultify the development of critical thought.

(h) The more standards there are the more costly the financial statements are to produce.

Professor Baxter writing his 'Recommendations on accounting theory'[15] said that 'the development of working regulations was to make things easy', and he continued that 'working regulations are required in accounting'. However, Professor Baxter further argued that 'working regulations need not necessarily be the basis for a theory'. He provided the example of the government of a nation having to make a decision on which side of the road cars should drive. There could be no real theory to help solve this problem.‡ Yet to enable the government avoid chaos on their roads they need to have a working rule which states that vehicles must stick to one side of the road or the other.

The accounting profession can learn from Professor Baxter by being more careful in distinguishing between rules and theory, and remembering that it is the former, the need for rules, which has led to the development of SSAPs. However, the ASC may perhaps be criticised for failing to make the distinction between rules and theories—on a number of occasions, where the issues have not been of great theoretic importance and where theory did not help in deciding between possible alternative courses of action the ASC has been prepared to leave a variety of options open. For example, SSAP 4 *The Accounting Treatment of Government Grants*, considers two possibilities which appear to have equal merit. On the one hand, it would be possible to credit the asset account with the amount of the grant, reducing the depreciation charges accordingly. Alternatively, the grant could be held in a reserve, being released to the revenue account over the asset's useful life. The effect of both systems in terms of the profit measurement is identical. Furthermore, there is no theoretical basis on which to make a choice between the alternatives. Following Professor Baxter's

---

* This point can be compared to the use of the DCF model, where although the model itself is provided by a precise formula, its inputs permit considerable subjectivity in their selection as for example, in the choice of the discount rate.

† A possible example is when the ASC switched their recommendation for the use of CPP to deal with the effect of changing price levels on financial statements, to the use of CCA, based on the recommendation of the Sandilands Committee which was set up by the Government.

‡ It could be hypothesised that passing on the left in a country with right-handed warriors is more natural because they are better positioned to do battle!

analogy, the ASC might well have decided to enforce an arbitrary rule that only one of these methods for dealing with the accounting treatment of government grants should be followed. This could be justified on the grounds that it could do no harm and might reduce the amount of confusion that a variety of treatments of similar events can produce. In fact SSAP 4 leaves both options open—creating the possibility for further confusion.

In stark contrast to this, in an area of much theoretical debate and confusion the profession has preferred to make definitive statements. This is in the question of how accounts should be prepared to allow for the effects of inflation. Here, in an area where there is considerable debate and theoretical discussion as to the appropriate procedure the profession was, in effect, prepared to say, 'Drive on the left only' through the issue of (P) SSAP 7 for CPP accounting. The fact that it subsequently changed its mind and now instructs us to 'Drive on the right only' by issuing SSAP 16 for CCA, serves to emphasise the danger of an overtly authoritarian approach to important issues of theory and principle.*

Perhaps Professor Baxter sums up the unspoken view of the majority of the profession about whether standards are necessary when he says that some feel that 'there is even something to be said for the view that it is better if all firms issue second-rate figures on the same basis than first-rate figures on conflicting bases.'†[16] However, whatever an individual's views are either on the debate for and against standards, it is quite clear that accounting standards are here to stay.

1.5　SEMANTICS AND FRAMEWORK

It should be possible for accountants with common backgrounds and shared professional experiences to be able to understand the language that each uses because they have become familiar with the definitions of the words and contexts within which they are used.

All this should help in the development of an acceptable body of accounting theory and techniques. However, the frequently found vagueness in definitions of objectives, words and usage render this more difficult than it may at first appear. The two major problem areas of semantics and the provision of a conceptual framework will be briefly discussed.

Semantics

Problems of semantics hinge on the coding of definitions used in accounting and the communication of these. Frequently writers on accounting use

---

* IAS 6, by giving two options had indicated that it was alright for different groups of people to drive either side of the road at the same time.

† This is not Professor Baxter's own view.

words which can have different shades of meaning and rely upon the context in which they are used to help the reader understand what is meant. Often this leads to misunderstandings about what had been written. At the extremes there are even problems defining some terms used because there is no agreement amongst accountants as to what is meant. A good example of this was seen in the inflation accounting debate that culminated in SSAP 16 on current cost accounting. Much of the debate was about maintaining 'capital' or the 'substance of the business', but accountants have rarely agreed on what they meant by these terms. Having considered such definitions as the equity interest, capital employed, and so on, the conclusion is finally reached that the definition of this phrase still has to be agreed amongst accountants. Peter Bird discusses communication problems such as the possibility of the semantic coding used by a writer for his message losing something in the coding, transmission and decoding processes.[17]

A Conceptual Framework

There have been a number of attempts to develop a conceptual framework for financial accounting and reporting. In 1976 the US Financial Accounting Standards Board (FASB) produced a discussion memorandum on this which ran to 360 pages.[18] This document stated that

> Perhaps because accounting in general and financial statements in particular exude an aura of precision and exactitude, many persons are astonished to learn that a conceptual framework for accounting and reporting has not been articulated authoritatively.

Hence the reason for trying to establish such a framework.[19] During 1981 the ASC published a report[20] that they had commissioned

> with a view to forming preliminary conclusions as to the possibilities of developing an agreed conceptual framework for setting accounting standards.[21]

The emphasis was to be on such a framework for financial accounting and reporting.

A problem in the development of a conceptual framework to be used by the accounting theorist is that it still has to be decided whether such a framework should be the means or the end. In the development of accounting theories there appears to be confusion about which way the relationship goes in the induction–deduction cycle. Because any such interaction may not necessarily be trivial those developing accounting theories must ensure that they are aware of any such inter-relationships. However, whether the move is from theory to observation or observation to theory is of less importance than the ultimate match between the two. Sometimes a theory will be developed from observing the real world, while, at other times the theorist will hypothesise and look for evidence to validate his theory.

1.6   CONCLUSION

In this text interest centres around accounting theories that are likely to provide rules or standards for the accountant. Even where a theory appears to enable a reasonable prediction to be made, the ultimate acceptance of the theory, and its conversion into an acceptable standard, may well depend upon the professional bodies, and in some cases the members of the profession. *

A problem in the development of an accounting theory is that subjectivity and value judgements may enter into the final stage of selection of the theory to be developed into an acceptable standard. Individuals, groups of individuals and the professional bodies, will frequently prefer one method to be used in the preparation of financial statements to another. So it is important that in their education and training, prospective accountants are taught to place the various accounting theories and techniques in their proper perspective. For in order to understand why certain standards have become accepted as preferable to other rules that may have appeared as equally good, the accountant must have a knowledge of how theories are developed and have been turned into standards. Thus it is important for accountants to become involved in trying to understand all sides of the various debates about accounting rules that occur from time to time. The eventual result of the current upsurge of interest in the development of accounting theories may be that accountants are progressively being guided towards more exact hypotheses, and it appears that this process will progress at an ever increasing rate.

REFERENCES

1. A more detailed description of the GEC/AEI case will be found in Latham J., *Take over the Facts and Myths of the GEC–AEI Battle*, Iliffe, 1969.
2. 'Is Freddie Fit to Fly?' *The Sunday Times*, 14 February 1982, p. 17.
3. For examples of other similar occurrences see Stamp E. and Marley C., *Accounting Principles and the City Code: The Case for Reform*, Butterworth, 1970.
4. *The Corporate Report*, Accounting Standards Steering Committee, July 1975.
5. *Ibid*, page 7.
6. Macve R., *A Conceptual Framework for Financial Accounting and Reporting*, Accounting Standards Committee, 1981.
7. See Vance L.L., 'The authority of history in inventory valuation', *Accounting Review*, Vol. 28, July 1943, p. 219.
8. For example see Friedman M., *The Methodology of Positive Economics, Essays in Positive Economics*, University of Chicago Press, 1953, p. 8.

---

* A large number of grass roots membership of the Institute of Chartered Accountants in England and Wales did not like ED 18s total rejection of historic cost accounting (HCA), and pressed for a special meeting, which ultimately rejected the ED.

9. *The Corporate Report*, *op. cit.* Section 2, pp. 19–27.
10. Edey H.C., 'The nature of profit', *Accounting and Business Research*, No. 1, Winter 1970.
11. Robbins L., *An Essay on the Nature and Significance of Economic Science*, Macmillan, 1932.
12. Friedman, M., *op. cit.*
13. See Nagle E., 'Assumptions in economic theory', *American Economic Review*, May 1963 for useful discussion on this topic.
14. Baxter W.T., 'Accounting standards—boon or curse?', *Accounting and Business Research*, Winter 1981, p. 8.
15. Baxter W.T., 'Recommendations on accounting theory', *The Accountant*, 10 October 1953.
16. Baxter W.T., 'Accounting Standards—boon or curse?', *op. cit.*, p. 7.
17. Bird P., 'Standard accounting practices', in Edey H.C. and Yamey B.S. (eds), *Debits, Credits, Finance and Profits*, Sweet and Maxwell, 1974.
18. 'Conceptual framework for financial accounting and reporting: elements of financial statements and their measurement', *Financial Accounting Standards Board*, 2 December 1976.
19. *Ibid.*, p. 2.
20. Macve R., *op. cit.*
21. *Ibid.*, p. 3.

QUESTIONS AND DISCUSSION PROBLEMS

1. 'The conventions from which traditional financial statements are prepared are frequently inconsistent and definitely incomplete.' Do you agree with this statement? Give reasons for the stance you take.
2. Briefly explain the major stages followed in the development of an accounting theory. Reference your answer to any accounting theory with which you are familiar.
3. '. . . the belief that a theory can be tested by the realism of its assumptions independently of the accuracy of its predictions is widespread . . .' (from 'The methodology of positive economics' in *Essays in Positive Economics* by Milton Friedman).
   Discuss the importance of assumptions in the development of accounting theories.
4. Consider the problems that are likely to be encountered in the development of an accounting theory and suggest ways of minimising the effects of these.
5. Carefully distinguish between accounting theory and accounting standards. Is the former (i) always likely to lead to, and (ii) necessary to the development of the latter?
6. In 1976, the FASB and in 1981 the ASC, published reports on a conceptual framework for financial accounting and reporting. (i) What do you understand by a conceptual framework in this context. (ii) Discuss the likely advantages and disadvantages of having a conceptual framework for financial accounting and reporting. (iii) How likely is it that such a framework will be established in the near future?

CHAPTER 2

Theory of Accounting: Income – Capital – Value

2.1 INTRODUCTION

Stated simply the function of financial accounts is to report , in money terms, on the current position of an organisation and to show its progress in the preceding accounting period. To this end, for a business organisation two main statements are utilised—a balance sheet and a profit and loss account. These statements are the basis of financial reports to external users.

The balance sheet, sometimes referred to as a position statement, reports on the position of the business in terms of its value at a given point in time. The profit and loss account reports on progress in terms of the income and profit for the period, and is sometimes called an income statement.

Many of the problems in the preparation of financial reports stem from the inherent complexity of the two central concepts of income and value. If it is desired to convey information about the size of a physical body, the concepts of height, length, width and weight used to convey the impression of size are relatively clear and unambiguous. There may be problems in measurement, particularly if the object in question is very big or very small, and there may be certain difficulties in the choice of the unit of measurement, e.g. pounds or kilograms, yards or metres, and so on. However, the basic ideas of height and weight are understood by all.

Unfortunately, this happy state of affairs does not prevail with respect to the notions of value and income. For example, a second-hand motor car may be said to have a value of £3000 but what does this mean? It could mean that the car could be sold for £3000. Alternatively, it could mean that a similar motor car could be purchased for £3000. However, in the real world resale value and replacement cost will rarely coincide; in this case it is largely because of transaction costs. Furthermore, it could mean that the car cost £5000 two years ago and is expected to be worth £1000 in two years time. Hence the portion of original cost as yet unexpired is £3000. Finally, it could mean that the owner has made an attempt to assess the money value of the benefits in terms of convenience, comfort and time saved that he derives from ownership of the car. If all these problems arise in the valuation of a basic, easily tradeable and general purpose asset such as a motor car, imagine the problems of trying to assign a money value to a highly specialised piece of industrial machinery or a partially completed research project. In order to understand the nature of the accounting information and the problems that arise in the preparation of financial accounts it is necessary to consider the theoretical concepts of income and value in rather greater detail.

2.2 THE NATURE OF INCOME

The problem of defining income has taxed the minds of lawyers, economists and accountants for over two hundred years. A major impetus was given to the study of the problem in the UK by the introduction of income tax to finance the Napoleonic Wars. If a government wishes to tax income it is obviously incumbent upon it to define the basis of taxation. Those early legislators took an extremely pragmatic approach to the definition of income. They made no attempt to arrive at an all-encompassing general definition but simply defined income, for taxable purposes, in terms of revenues yielded by certain specified sources. This resulted in the so-called schedular definition of income which is still used in the UK. While this approach is clearly unsatisfactory in that it makes no attempt to answer the fundamental question of 'what is income', it does highlight the relationship between income and value, or capital. This is because the approach implicitly defines income as revenues flowing from certain specified capital sources (including human capital).

Fisher's Income Concept

One of the earlier attempts to produce a more general definition of income was that of Irving Fisher.[1] Fisher's fundamental idea was that income is a series of events. In his view income was concerned with consumption; money has no value until it is spent.* Ultimately, although wages are paid in the form of money, it is the enjoyment that money buys which is worked for. Clearly, it is not possible to make a direct measure of this psychic enjoyment. Thus it becomes necessary to approximate to it by measuring the physical events of the outer world that provide the inner satisfaction. It is these physical aspects of consumption which are what Fisher calls 'real income'. Finally, in order to measure the real income, called 'living' by

---

* Fisher does not accept that money has any intrinsic value and thereby ignores that satisfaction derived by the miser from his store of wealth and even the sense of security which the average person gets from having a reasonable amount of money saved.

Fisher, it is necessary to approximate even further by measuring the monetary cost of goods and services. It is this, the money value of goods consumed, that Fisher calls income.

The relationship between income and capital is quite clear. Capital is a stock of wealth existing at a given instant in time; a flow of benefits from wealth through a period of time is called income. Capital, including human capital, is a stock of wealth which generates income. The value of capital depends upon the income that the stock of wealth generates. The apparent circularity of the argument is overcome by consideration of a simple example. A field is a stock of wealth, the crops grown in the field represent the flow of benefits from the stock of wealth and therefore represent the 'real income'. However, the value of the field will depend on the expected money value of the income, i.e. the value of crops. Therefore, the value of capital is the discounted present value* of the flow of net benefits derived from it. The essential prerequisite for understanding Fisher's concepts of capital and income is this recognition of the distinction between capital and the value of capital. Capital is a stock of assets capable of generating the power to consume. The amount of goods and services consumed in a period represents the real income. The money value of the stream of net benefits discounted to a present value gives the value of the initial stock of assets, i.e. the capital.

Fisher's income concept does not recognise or make allowance for saving, although through the use of his phrase 'even when he "lives beyond his income"' Fisher implies the possibilities of borrowing or dissaving. He recognises that individuals receive cash in exchange for goods and services during the course of a period. This money received he calls 'money income'. However, he remains adamant that income depends upon consumption and not the receipt of cash. For him 'all one spends on his living measures real income, even when he "lives beyond his income" (beyond his *money* income)'. Fisher concludes:

> Thus we have a picture of three successive stages, or aspects of a man's income:
> Enjoyment or psychic income, consisting of agreeable sensations and experience;
> Real income *measured* by the cost of living;
> Money income, consisting of the money received by a man for meeting his cost of living.
> The last—money income—is most commonly called income; and the first—enjoyment income—is the most fundamental. But, for accounting purposes, real income, as measured by the cost of living, is the most practical.[2]

The rate of interest provides the link between income and capital. As we have already seen, the value of a stock of wealth depends upon the money values of the flow that it generates. Since most of the benefits are likely to be received in the future, they are qualitatively inferior to immediate con-

---

* Appendix A to this chapter discusses discounting and value.

sumption. The measure of their relative inferiority is the rate of interest. Fisher defines the rate of interest as *'the per cent of premium paid on money at one date in terms of money to be in hand one year later.'*[3] Hence the rate of interest provides the bridge between income and capital by providing the basis on which future benefits are discounted back to present capital value. One of the consequences of this definition of income and capital is that capital gain, or loss, cannot be incorporated in the measure of income for that period. Capital gains and losses represent improvement or deterioration in income prospects for future periods and must be excluded from the measurement of income for the present period. Fisher's concept of income, while perhaps appearing somewhat confusing, is important in that it differs strikingly from other, later, definitions which tend to define income in terms of changes in capital values. While it can be criticised, the idea that income is best defined in terms of events within a period could be important in subsequent considerations of what constitutes the best definition of business income. As to the more immediate difficulties with Fisher's definition, two are obvious.

Firstly, it has been argued that as companies are inanimate they are incapable of feeling satisfaction and therefore cannot have any real income! The acceptance of this view would make Fisher's definition inappropriate as a measure of corporate income. However, Taylor[4] has argued that Fisher's definition of income can be interpreted in a way which would allow it to be used as a measure of corporate income. He quotes from Fisher that 'The income of a community is the total flow of services from all its instruments' and further ' . . . any adequate concept of income must leave room . . . for the income rendered by a factory or a bank . . .' Hence he suggests Fisher is clearly implying that his income concept is applicable not just to individuals but also to corporate entities of inanimate or collective bodies as well.

The critical feature of Fisher's theory as identified by Taylor lies in the relationship between income and capital. Capital is a stock of assets capable of generating future benefits, income is the flow of benefits generated by capital. Hence 'where capital exists so must income and vice versa.'[5] From this it can be concluded that where business assets, including human assets, exist, so must business income. Quoting again, Taylor notes that Fisher says: 'Income always implies (1) capital as the source, and (2) an owner of capital as the beneficiary.'

Since under the present system of Company Law the income of business capital belongs to the shareholders this suggests a weakness in the application of Fisher's theory in the measurement of corporate income. However, Fisher resolved this problem by noting that business income is an inter-

---

* Another way of thinking about this is that current consumption gives more satisfaction than the expectation of future consumption and the rate of interest is the premium received for deferring consumption from now into the future.

mediate flow coming before the ultimate enjoyment of income by the owners of the business. The only difficulty in employing Fisher's theory in the measurement of business income is concerned with the necessity to avoid double counting in the preparation of national income accounts when the business income is ultimately enjoyed by the shareholders.

Secondly, when saving and dissaving are excluded from the definition of income the difficulty remains, which Professor Kaldor has expressed so succinctly:

> if we reserved the term income for consumption we should still need another term for what would otherwise be called income; and we should still be left with the problem of how to define the latter.[6]

Hicks' Basic Income Concept

An alternative view on the definition of income, i.e. income seen as consumption adjusted for changes in the value of capital (which may be through either appreciation or depreciation), is perhaps best expounded by John Hicks.[7] In defining income Hicks goes back to the basic purpose of measuring it. He states that 'The purpose of income calculations in practical affairs is to give people an indication of the amount which they can consume without impoverishing themselves.'[8] Thus Hicks arrives at his *ex-ante* definition of income as being the amount that a man can consume in a period and expect to be as 'well off' at the end of the period as he was at the beginning. Central to this definition is the concept of 'well-offness.' In this sense Hicks again, like Fisher, defines the value of capital as the discounted present value of the income flowing from the capital. In some senses Hicks' definition involves even more circular reasoning than Fisher in that incorporated in his definition of income is the value of capital which in turn depends upon the level of income. However, it has the advantage of providing a definition of income which takes account of saving and dissaving as well as consumption. This definition of income is highly subjective in that it depends upon expectations of both consumption and future receipts. As a partial remedy to the problem of subjectivity Hicks offers his *ex-post* definition of income as being consumption plus appreciation, or less depreciation, in the value of the capital over the period.

Therefore the basic definition of income is given as consumption in the period plus changes in the value of the capital stock. The difficulty in this approach lies in the causes of changes in capital value. Essentially there are three factors that can cause the value of capital to change within a period. These are investments made by the firm or business; changes in the interest rate; and changes in expectations about the future. Of these, only the first can truly be considered to affect the income of a period. Where a business or individual gives up consumption by deciding to invest in assets in order to increase consumption potential in the future, the amount given up this year might reasonably be included in the income for the period. However, where the present value of the prospect of future earnings increases due to changes in the interest rate, it is hard to see how this can be considered as income for the period. Consider the capital appreciation position in which an investor holds a security which guarantees income at a fixed rate of £100 per annum into perpetuity. When prevailing interest rates are at 10 per cent then the present value of that security will equal £1000.* Now suppose that within an accounting period the investor receives his £100 but in addition interest rates fall to 5 per cent. In these circumstances the value of the security is likely to rise to £2000. However, it is hard to see that the income for the period is the receipt (£100) plus the capital appreciation (£1000). For even if he sold the asset for £2000 all that he does is to change the form of his capital from that of a bond into cash. If income is to have any meaning in Hicks' terms as an indication of the amount that can be consumed without impoverishing oneself then clearly to consume the whole of the interest (£100) plus the whole of the capital gained (£1000) will result in the future income prospect on the remaining £1000 being reduced from £100 to £50 per annum.

The capital depreciation situation can also be examined if, instead of assuming that the interest rate had halved to 5 per cent, it had doubled to 20 per cent. Then, the value of the capital may be reduced due to revisions in the estimates of the flow of future benefits that are to be received from alternative assets.

This can be analysed a different way. Assuming a constant interest rate of 10 per cent a security with anticipated returns of £10 per annum will have a current market value of £100. However, if during the period expectations are revised and it is now anticipated that the security will yield returns of £12 per annum then the market value at the end of the period will be £120. Notwithstanding this it is hard to see that the income for the period is truly represented by adding actual receipts (assumed to be £12) to the increase in market value of £20 which is entirely due to changes in expectations. It might reasonably be suggested that what has been done is to overstate income as a result of understating the initial values of the security due to imperfect knowledge.

The easiest way to understand the nature of Hicks' income concept is to utilise Macdonald's analysis.[9] In the determination of income, both *ex-post* and *ex-ante*, six variables are relevant. Using a simple symbolic shorthand these can be represented as:

---

* Using the perpetuity formula of $V = D/i$ the value of the security is 100/0.1 or £1000. All this means is that the minimum sum necessary to produce an indefinite income of £100 per annum when interest rates are at 10 per cent is £1000.

C_0^0 the capital value at time 0 as estimated at time 0 (current estimate).

C_0^1 the capital value at time 0 revised in the light of additional information coming to light in period $t_0 - t_1$ (*ex-post* revision).

C_1^0 the capital value at time 1 as estimated at time 0 (*ex-ante* forecast).

C_1^1 the capital value at time 1 revised in the light of information discovered in time $t_0 - t_1$ (*ex-post* revision).

R_1^0 receipts in period $t_0 - t_1$ *as estimated at time 0 (ex-ante* forecast).

R_1^1 actual receipts in period $t_0 - t_1$ (actual position).

Using these symbols Hicks' *ex-ante* income measure (I) is seen as:

$$I_1 = R_1^0 + (C_1^0 - C_0^0)$$

that is, anticipated receipts in period $t_0 - t_1$ plus anticipated increases in capital value. And Hicks' *ex-post* income measure (I^*) would be:

$$I_1^* = R_1^1 + (C_1^1 - C_0^1)$$

that is, actual receipts plus increase in the capital value between t_0 and t_1. The capital value, C_1 and C_0 have been revised utilising information, including that regarding changing interest rates, which has emerged during period $t_0 - t_1$.

The effect of this procedure is to exclude from current income those changes in value due to both changing interest rates and changing expectations as to the future. This is because changes in the capital value resulting from these are excluded from the measure of income by revising the values of C_1 and C_0 used in the income calculations to allow for them. The increase in wealth at the end of the period due to these factors is treated as an increase in future, rather than current, income and the *ex-post* increase in initial wealth is assumed to be the income of prior periods.

The Fisher and Hicks Income Concepts Compared

The two classic approaches by Fisher and Hicks to the theory of income appear to differ widely. Fisher insists that income is simply consumption. Hicks argues that income is consumption plus capital appreciation. However, he is careful to eliminate from his income measure those components of capital appreciation attributable to changing expectations and changing interest rates. The fundamental difference between the two refines itself to the question of how savings and dissavings are to be treated in the measurement of income. Fisher excludes saving, but includes dissaving, in his definition as has been seen by insisting that income is measured by the money value of the goods and services actually consumed. Hicks includes saving and excludes dissaving by focusing his attention on the amount that *could* be consumed while leaving capital intact. Hence Hicks bases his income definition on the concept of capital maintenance which is notable by its absence in the Fisherian definition. Before moving on to a consideration of how these income concepts are, or could be, incorporated into financial accounts it is necessary to consider complementary ideas about capital and value.

2.3 CAPITAL AND VALUE

As has already been noted, the concept of value is anything but clear and furthermore is closely related to the definition of income chosen—the more important definitions of income have already been discussed. The example of the value of a motor car discussed in the introduction to this chapter gave some insight into the nature of the problem to be solved. In essence there are four reasonably objective concepts of value that could be used. These are historic cost, replacement cost, realisable value and the discounted present value of the expected benefits from ownership of the particular asset. This section will consider the merits of these alternatives and discuss the relationships between them.

Historic Cost 'Value'

Although historic cost has been the basis of valuation in published accounts for many years it has few theoretical merits. In anything other than a perfect market and with anything less than a completely stable price level historic cost is unlikely to bear much relationship to realisable value, replacement cost or the value of the asset in use. The principal, perhaps only, advantage of historic cost is that it is capable of being objectively determined where adequate accounting records are maintained. It is this attribute of historic cost that has ensured that it has remained the basis of conventional finacial accounts for many years.

The shortcomings of valuing assets using historic cost are obvious. To know that a particular piece of machinery cost £20,000 ten years ago tells very little about its value now. Furthermore as it is usual for the asset to be shown in the accounts at its net book value, i.e. original cost less accumulated depreciation, and because the depreciation charges have been based upon estimates of the useful life and the terminal value (both of which are highly subjective) even the objectivity of the historic cost valuation can be questioned. The limitations of historic cost as a valuation method have been recognised for many years. However, it has been only recently because of rapid changes in price levels, that the probems resulting from its use have become so apparent that the accounting profession has been prepared to sacrifice its spurious objectivity for other, more useful, although more overtly subjective, valuation techniques. A more detailed discussion of both the problems and the proposed changes are contained in Chapter 6.

Market Value

Both replacement cost and realisable value are market based valuation methods. *Replacement cost* is the cost of replacing an asset with an exactly similar one taking account of any costs associated with the time lag necessary to affect the replacement. For example, the replacement cost of a new motor car will be the price of an exactly similar car plus any additional transport costs such as taxi and train fares incurred while waiting for delivery of the new car. *Realisable value* is the price the asset could be sold for taking account of any transaction costs necessary to complete the sale. Except under perfect market conditions the results obtained from the two methods are unlikely to coincide. For general purpose assets such as motor cars the difference will be the result of transaction costs. However for specialised assets any discrepancy is likely to be correspondingly greater. Both of these valuation methods present problems in use.

It is often difficult to make reasonable estimates of the value of used, highly specialised machinery where markets for such equipment do not exist or are limited. In the latter case, the use of the prices recorded would be invalid as a basis for valuation. Furthermore, replacement cost would be an inappropriate basis for valuing an asset where there was no intention of replacing the asset. For example, if a business owns a highly specialised piece of machinery which was originally acquired to manufacture a product which has gone out of fashion and is no longer made it would probably prove extremely expensive to replace the machinery concerned. However, since the product it was designed to manufacture is no longer marketable it is unlikely that the firm would wish to replace it anyway! In consequence, the replacement cost of the specialised machinery would not seem an appropriate measure of its value.

Similar problems exist in the utilisation of realisable value as the basis for valuation. One example of this would be the valuation of partly finished goods such as engine components produced by a motor car manufacturer. While there is a market for parts of car engines as spares and replacements, the market is so small relative to the total output of engines by motor manufacturers that prices therein are completely inadequate for the valuation of the parts in the hands of the vehicle manufacturer. Similarly, where a business has just acquired a highly complex and specialised piece of industrial plant for the manufacture of one of its more profitable products, at the time of acquisition the realisable value will not provide a reasonable indication of the 'true' or economic value of that equipment. For due to its highly specialised nature it is presumably worth little more than scrap if sold. However, since the firm has no intention of selling the equipment its realisable value does not represent an acceptable valuation base.

Discounted Present Value of Benefits from Ownership

It would be possible to value an asset by discounting to a present value equivalent the benefits derived from the ownership of the asset as a result of it being put to the use for which it was acquired. This necessitates the use of the discounted cash flow (DCF) approach and is the valuation method most closely associated with the earlier discussions on income. Because it relates most clearly to theoretical discussions on the nature of income it is extremely attractive. The principle difficulty in the application of this method is in the estimation of the variables needed to establish it, i.e. the size and length of the expected flow of benefits and the appropriate discount rate. Inevitably, estimates of these variables will be subjective and hence the resultant valuation must also be subjective. However, today it is frequently argued that in an uncertain world, subjectivity is the price that may have to be paid for relevance and usefulness. It is relatively simple to obtain an objective valuation, namely historic cost, but for all purposes other than the stewardship function this is virtually useless. Furthermore as time passes individuals and businesses will gain reputations as reliable (or unreliable) predictors of the future benefits likely to accrue from the ownership of its assets and the market will modify the subjective estimates of the owners accordingly. Hence despite its subjective nature the discounted present value, or value in use, of the asset remains a serious possibility as a valuation concept.

Deprival Value

In a perfect market with no transaction costs and perfect knowledge, realisable value, replacement cost and value in use will all be equal. In the real world, however, they are likely to diverge substantially: in the simplest case traders' profits will cause discrepancies between realisable value and replacement cost. As has already been observed with highly specialised machinery the difference is likely to be correspondingly larger. The discounted present value of future benefits will rarely equal either of the valuations obtained using market based methods for a variety of reasons. For example, most assets cannot be used in isolation and frequently many of the necessary complementary assets are not readily available in the market. As an illustration consider the value of a new industrial knitting machine bought by a reputable manufacturer of high class fashion garments. The value to the owner i.e. the discounted value of future receipts, depends upon the contribution derived from the manufacture of garments using the machine. However, a single factor of production, in this case the machine, used in isolation is not sufficient to produce these benefits. The additional requirements are the flair of the designer, the skill of the operator, and the reputation of the manufacturer and his contacts with appropriate retail outlets who will take his product. Typically, it is not easy to buy and sell these latter requirements in the market. This example demonstrates two important points. Firstly, the value in use of any asset will depend upon the other assets owned by the user, some of which may be intangible, and may well be unique. So it certainly need bear little relationship to their market value (however defined). Secondly, it illustrates the difficulty in valuing the assets of a business piecemeal where they are used as a whole in the generation of benefits for the business.

In considering the relationship between replacement cost, value in use and realisable value, for most businesses it is convenient to divide assets into fixed assets, such as machinery, and current assets, notably stocks. For fixed assets under normal conditions, replacement cost will be greater than realisable value and, where the business is operating successfully, both will be less than the discounted present value of future benefits. For the current asset stock, replacement cost will be less than realisable value as long as the inventory can be sold at a profit, and this will be approximately the present value of future receipts since the future receipts are likely to be the sales revenue. Any minor deviations between realisable value and the discounted present value will be due to the time lag in selling and collecting the cash from the sale.

The most important attempts to draw together these various ideas of value into a single, cohesive concept was made in 1937 by Bonbright in his 'value to the owner.'[10] Bonbright defines the value of an asset to its owner as follows:

> The value of a property to its owner is identical in amount with the adverse value of the entire loss, direct and indirect, that the owner might expect to suffer if he were to be deprived of the property.[11]

Bonbright's approach to valuation was subsequently developed by Baxter as 'deprival value'.[12] The loss could fall into one of three categories: the loss in revenue resulting from being unable to sell the asset; the increase in costs due to the need to acquire a replacement asset; and the loss of the benefits resulting from owning and using the asset. As we have seen, for a successful business this latter category will represent the greatest amount. However, it will only rarely represent the deprival value. This is because where an asset can be replaced with a similar asset then the greatest loss that can result from the destruction of the original asset is the cost of replacing it, including any costs associated with the time needed to effect the replacement. Hence an asset can never be worth more than the cost of replacing it. Consequently the deprival value can never be more than replacement cost. However, occasionally deprival value may be the discounted present value of future benefits from the asset (sometimes referred to as the value of the asset in use) where this is greater than the asset's realisable value but less than its replacement cost. Similarly it may be realisable value where this is greater than value in use but less than replacement cost. Hence Baxter defines deprival value as 'the lower of replacement cost or expected direct benefits' and continues 'Replacement cost must be interpreted in the light of cost avoidance or postponement and "expected direct benefits" means the higher of services in use and of scrap value.'[13]

The idea of deprival value has recently attained considerable significance since it is the basis of the definition of 'value to the business' which is the valuation method required by SSAP 16 *Current Cost Accounting*.[14] 'The "value to the business" of an asset is to be equated with the amount of the loss suffered by the company concerned if the asset is lost or destroyed.'[15]*

The following table† considers the six possible relationships between Net Replacement Cost (NRC), Net Realisable Value (NRV) and the value in use which is the economic value (EV) of the asset and indicates the appropriate deprival value or value to the business under each set of circumstances.

Relationship between value concepts						Deprival value or value to the business
NRV	>	EV	>	NRC		NRC
NRV	>	NRC	>	EV		NRC
EV	>	NRC	>	NRV		NRC
EV	>	NRV	>	NRC		NRC
NRC	>	EV	>	NRV		EV
NRC	>	NRV	>	EV		NRV

2.4   INCOME AND VALUE CONCEPTS IN FINANCIAL ACCOUNTS

As we have seen, the major issue in the definition of income is whether it is to be treated as consumption, a current transactions approach, or whether it should incorporate in its definition an allowance for changes in the value of the capital stock. The first definition, that of Fisher, makes no allowance for capital maintenance. The second, Hicks' definition of income as consumption plus capital accumulation, has been incorporated in financial accounts. This definition has been accepted by accountants and the acceptance of the broad principles has not been affected by recent debate on financial accounts, notably in Sandilands and SSAP 16. However, while the accounting profession has accepted the Hicks definition in principle it has adopted a fairly strange definition of value and taken a very rigid position on how and when it will recognise changes in the value of the capital

---

* A decision tree showing the approach to deprival value is provided on p. 124.
† Although this approach has become associated with Sandilands, where similar tables have been provided in paragraphs 212 and 218 of the report, it can be traced back through *Readings in the Concept and Measurement of Income* edited by R.H. Parker and G.C. Harcourt (Cambridge University Press 1969) in the editor's introduction, page 17, and to David Solomons 'Economic and accounting concepts of cost and value' in *Modern Accounting Theory*, edited by M. Backer (Prentice-Hall 1966) page 125.

stock. This section will consider the concepts of income and value as portrayed in conventional financial statements. In addition it will look in more detail at the profession's position on the definition of value and its attitude to possible changes in that definition.

When Changes in Value are Recognised

Traditionally the basis for valuing all assets in financial accounts has been historic cost. For fixed assets the original cost is spread over the estimated useful life using one of the techniques of depreciation, and the value reported in the balance sheet is net book value, i.e. historic cost less accumulated depreciation. Current assets are valued at the cost of manufacture except where the realisable value has fallen below cost when the lower of cost or realisable value is usually taken as the value of the stock. Changes in the value of current assets, notably stock, are only recognised where there is objective evidence of a market valuation through a business transaction. For most businesses this is at the point of sale. This is the realisation principle. Accountants require objective evidence of increases in market values if they are to recognise an increase in the value of an asset in the accounts. This is usually provided by evidence of sale for current assets although external, unbiased valuations by professional valuers may be accepted in the case of fixed assets, notably property.

However, because of the conservatism or prudence concept accountants are prepared to recognise diminuation in the value of an asset where no such objective evidence exists. The most obvious example of this process is in the calculation of depreciation charges for the use of fixed assets. Here the accountant spreads the original cost of the asset over the estimated useful life reducing the value of the asset in successive balance sheets by a predetermined amount. However, while unrealised increases in the value of fixed assets may be recognised in the accounts, SSAP 6[16] is quite categoric* that they shall not be included in profit. Instead of being credited to the profit and loss account any unrealised gains in fixed assets are to be credited directly to the appropriate reserve account.

Hence, accounting profit becomes:

	Increases in the value of stock, only recognised at the point of sale
plus	Realised increases in the value of fixed assets
minus	Decreases in the value of fixed assets, based on arbitrary and largely subjective allocation of historic cost; and decreases in the value of stock as a result of the application of the lower of cost or market value rule

---

* SSAP 6 para 13 states 'The profit and loss account for the year should show a profit or loss after extraordinary items, reflecting all profits and losses recognised in the accounts of the year other than prior year adjustments and unrealised surpluses on revaluation of fixed assets, which should be credited direct to reserves'.

with appropriate adjustments made for injections and withdrawals of capital. Thus to measure the accounting profit in any period the following steps are necessary:

(a) Establish the size and value of the capital including all fixed and current assets at the start of the period.
(b) Determine the extent of all increases in the size of the capital stock in the period including all additions made to fixed assets.
(c) Calculate the increases in the value of the capital stock only recognising increases in the value of the current assets where satisfactory market evidence (usually shown by a sale) is available.
(d) Estimate all decreases in the value of the fixed and current assets in the period.
(e) Make the appropriate adjustments for the introduction and withdrawal of capital.

The Conventional Approach to Valuation: The Stock Valuation Example

Perhaps the best example of conventional thinking on valuation was provided by the Accounting Standards Committee when they issued SSAP 9.[17] Here the issue is not seen to be about which basis stocks shall be valued on, for historic cost is taken as given. The issue resolves itself to a fairly technical discussion as to which element of historic cost should be incorporated in the value of inventory and which should be written off directly as an expense in the profit and loss account. SSAP 9 recognises that the measurement of profit entails matching costs with related revenues. It further recognises that firms carry stocks and work in progress forward from one period to the next in anticipation of generating revenues in future time periods. Accordingly, it concludes that in these circumstances it is inappropriate to write off the costs of closing stocks of finished goods and work in progress in the periods in which they are incurred. However, in determining the value of these closing stocks to be carried forward it does not consider the possibility of valuing inventory at anything other than historic cost.* Other possibilities such as value in use, replacement cost or realisable value are disregarded except where realisable value has fallen below historic cost. In this case, since the benefits to be expected in future

---

* Perhaps this is not surprising as a departure from the historic cost treatment in the valuation of the asset stock could not be made in isolation from the way in which other assets were dealt with. Also, accounting for price level changes by way of some form of current cost accounting is being considered by the ASC to cover all aspects of financial accounts, especially the value of assets to the business, including stock. In any event the first-in first-out (FIFO) basis for valuing stocks, which is the method most used within the UK, provides a closer approximation to replacement cost than the accounting basis currently used for dealing with the valuation of other types of assets.

periods are less than the costs thus far incurred it is recommended that the stock be valued at realisable value.

The bulk of the discussion in SSAP 9 is concerned with which costs shall be included in the value of stock. It concludes that the cost of stocks should include the cost of purchase together with such costs of conversion as are appropriate to bring inventory to its current conditions and location. These are:

(a) costs which are specifically attributable to units of production, e.g. direct labour, direct expenses and sub-contractor work;
(b) product overheads;
(c) other overheads, if any, attributable in the particular circumstances of the business to bringing the particular product or service to its present location and conditions.

The requirements of SSAP 9 have, in the main been incorporated in the 1981 Companies Act.[18]

They remain a good illustration of conventional thinking on valuation. A more detailed consideration of the problems of stock valuation is contained in Chapter 4.

Determination of Additions to Capital Stock: the Research and Development Example

An allied problem to the determination of the value of increases in the capital stock is to decide what constitutes an addition to the capital stock. This obviously involves making the time honoured distinction between capital and revenue expenditure. Capital expenditure results in the creation of an asset. Sprouse and Moonitz define an accounting asset as follows: 'Assets represent expected future economic benefits, rights to which have been acquired by the enterprise as a result of some current or past transaction'.[19] Based upon this definition the attributes of an accounting asset can be listed as:

(a) It must convey a future benefit to the business.
(b) It must be specific to the particular business.
(c) Rights to the benefits must have been acquired as a result of some past or current transaction and be capable of being measured in money terms.

In applying these criteria a major difficulty exists with respect to intangible assets such as research and development (R and D) expenditure. The ASC considered the conditions in which R and D expenditure could be capitalised in SSAP 13.[20] In the USA similar deliberations of the Financial Accounting Standards Board were summarised in their Statement of Financial Accounting Standard (SFAS)2. Broadly speaking the statements are similar. Both agree that capitalisation of R and D expenditure is undesirable because of the uncertainty associated with it. An initial UK Exposure Draft on the subject, ED 14, favoured charging all R and D expenditure as an expense in the year in which it is incurred. It was withdrawn, apparently under pressure from the electronics and aerospace industries, and replaced by ED 17, from whence SSAP 13 came. This states that R and D expenditure should be capitalised when specific conditions are fulfilled, otherwise it should be charged as an expense. The conditions for capitalising R and D set out in SSAP 13 are:

(a) There is a clearly defined project.
(b) The related expenditure is separately identifiable.
(c) The outcome of the project is reasonably certain on technical and commercial grounds.
(d) The aggregate costs of the project are reasonably certain to be more than covered by related future revenues.
(e) Adequate resources are available to complete the project.

Furthermore, SSAP 13 is quite categoric that 'Deferred development expenditure once written off should not be reinstated even though the uncertainties which had led to its being written off no longer apply'.[21]

The 1981 Companies Act states that development costs should only be capitalised under special circumstances. While it does not state it explicitly it is to be presumed that the special circumstances are those set out in SSAP 13. SSAP 13 envisages that R and D expenditure, if capitalised, should be included in the balance sheet at its historic cost. However, SSAP 16 on current cost accounting recommends that expenditure, when carried forward, should normally be revalued on a current cost basis. The practical effect of SSAP 13, given the stringent conditions for capitalisation and the naturally conservative tendencies of auditors, is that most R and D expenditure will be written off in the year in which it is incurred. This may be considered unfortunate in that ongoing R and D projects presumably meet the requirements set out by Sprouse and Moonitz.[22] Certainly information about the extent of a business's investment in R and D would be useful to users of the financial statements.

Possibly in recognition of this Directors' reports are now expressly required to contain information on R & D expenditure.[23]

The problem could be mitigated by providing the information as a note in the accounts. However, there is a danger that a proliferation of notes concerning relevant information omitted from the main body of the accounts will make accounting reports even more difficult to analyse.

Determination of the Value of a Business: The Goodwill Problem

Another question with respect to the determination of the size and value of a business's capital stock has vexed accountants for many years is that of the valuation of goodwill. The difficulty usually arises on the acquisition of one business by another. Earlier attempts to place a value on goodwill, notably by P.D. Leake,[24] put their emphasis on the observation that many businesses were able to earn an above normal return on their tangible assets. Surely, then, it was argued, this super-normal return must be attributable to some unseen, intangible asset, i.e. goodwill. The valuation approach frequently taken for goodwill when businesses were changing hands during arm's length transactions was to subtract the return normally expected from the assets from the business's actual profits based on some past years average, and then multiply the resultant 'super-profit' figure by a number of years normal for the trade or industry concerned. Other approaches were used, such as simply multiplying total profits (adjusted by some computation for costs not registered in the organisation's books, such as interest on capital employed, use of owner's services, etc.) and then multiply this figure by a smaller number of years. This figure was then added to the value of the tangible assets to arrive at a total price or valuation for the business.

A more modern refinement of the same basic technique would be to discover the size of the anticipated super-profit and then to discount this back to a present value at an appropriate discount rate. Leake himself implied that the discount rate applied should be greater than the normal expected rate of return since super-profits, by their very nature, are more risky. For example, the very existence of super-profits within an industry is likely to attract new entrants into that industry, resulting in the competing away of these super-profits.

The discounting process used would depend upon the expected life of the stream of super-profits. If they were expected to continue indefinitely then the perpetuity approach would be taken. Otherwise the appropriate section of the annuity table would be used.

While for some time writers on goodwill have accepted the general idea of its nature, and Hinton defines goodwill as 'that part of the value of a business which arises from all of its advantageous circumstances which generate unusual earnings[25] the process of its valuation during recent years has changed significantly. Today the earning power concept of goodwill recognises that many intangibles contribute to any enhanced earning power of a business. Such intangible factors will include good staff and industrial relations, a well-trained workforce, good relationships with and the loyalty of customers, and so on. As the effects of these individual components cannot be separated they need to be valued as a whole. The current procedure for valuing goodwill is to define its value as the difference between the purchase consideration given to acquire the business and the fair values of the separable net tangible and identifiable intangible assets acquired.

It is important to note that this value of goodwill is very often different from that revealed in conventional post-acquisition accounts. There are two reasons for any discrepancy between these two valuations. Conventional accounts usually value goodwill as the difference between the purchase consideration and the value of separable tangible and identifiable intangible assets acquired. The value of the tangible and identifiable intangible assets taken into the accounts of the acquiring company can be the book value of the assets acquired. This book value, of course, need bear little relationship to the 'fair value' of those assets. However, many acquiring companies do, in fact, revalue the acquired company's assets to accord with their own view of the value of the assets concerned and thus reduce the price paid for goodwill. Secondly, where part or all of the purchase consideration is in the form of shares then, where the purchase consideration is shown at the nominal value of the issued shares, this may well result in understating the value of the purchase consideration and thereby the purchased goodwill.*

Having identified and valued goodwill the remaining problem is how to account for it. There are two choices: to write it off immediately against shareholders' equity or to capitalise it and show it as an asset. If the second choice is adopted it gives rise to a second question: should the goodwill be held in the accounts indefinitely or amortised as an operating expense over its estimated life or some arbitrary period?

The most persuasive argument appears to be that goodwill should be written off against shareholders' equity at the time of acquisition. The basis of this approach lies in the nature and function of the conventional balance sheet which is primarily to provide information about the nature and magnitude of a business's tangible and identifiable intangible assets. Thus the balance sheet as it is conventionally prepared cannot show the total value of the enterprise. This means that any party interested in determining the total value of a business can only do so by reference to its balance sheet earnings record and the general market conditions. Goodwill on acquisition is perhaps best thought of as the price paid in terms of tangible assets to acquire the expectation of enhanced future earnings. That these expected earnings can be incorporated in the valuation of a business by the investor or analyst is beyond doubt but the very vagueness of the nature of the asset 'goodwill' denies it a place in the conventional balance sheet. If a radical reform of accounting comes about, where perhaps the balance sheet purports to provide a more meaningful total value of a business, it may be necessary to revise this view.

A recent development with respect to accounting for goodwill is the legal requirement that purchased goodwill *must* be written off over a fair estimate of its useful life.[26] The ASC issued an exposure draft on goodwill

---

* This is referred to as the 'merger' or 'pooling of interest' method of consolidation which has only been adopted by a minority of companies, the majority following the acquisition method. A debate has ensued as to whether the development of merger accounting contravenes S56 of the Companies Act, 1948, although the issue of ED 3 *Accounting for Acquisitions and Mergers* on 20 January 1971 recognises merger accounting, it has yet to become a standard, the delay in itself an indication of the differences of opinion involved.

in 1982.[27] Basically, it says that any *non-purchased* goodwill must have no amount attributed to it in a company's financial statements. Any amount attributable to *purchased* goodwill (which should include the value of intangibles such as patents and trade marks, these being included under appropriate headings elsewhere in the accounts) should only be the difference between the fair value of the consideration given and the separable net assets received. However, any purchased goodwill *must not* become a permanent item on the balance sheet, but either removed through *amortisation* or *immediate write-off*: the former policy concerning amortising this systematically over its estimated useful economic life through the profit and loss account; the latter, writing it off immediately against any reserves of realised profits.

Diminution of Capital Stock: Introducing Depreciation

The problem of estimating decreases in the value of fixed assets is considered by the ASC in SSAP 12.[28] In the explanatory note they observe that 'Depreciation is a measure of the wearing out, consumption or other loss in value of a fixed asset whether arising from use, effluxion of time or obsolescence through technology and market changes.' To enable the appropriate annual depreciation charges for a particular asset to be computed, it is necessary to know the asset's original cost and to estimate its useful life and residual value in order to allocate the cost of an asset over its life.

Although SSAP 12 was produced in the context of a historic cost accounting system its requirements are equally applicable to current cost accounting.

In particular, SSAP 12 makes it clear that it is not appropriate to omit charging depreciation because market value is greater than the net book value. Where the value of the asset is written up to reflect the increased market value, as it may be under current cost accounting, then the depreciation charge will have to be increased accordingly. Similarly, where it becomes apparent the net book value is not recoverable in full, then the value of the asset should be written down immediately to the amount likely to be recoverable and that amount should be spread over the remaining useful life of the asset. Finally, where for any reason the estimate of useful life is revised then the amount to be depreciated should be charged over the revised remaining useful life.

It is important to recognise that conventionally depreciation has always been a process of allocating historic cost rather than an attempt at valuing partially used assets. With the introduction of current cost accounting the position becomes rather more confused since assets are to be regularly revalued at their 'value to the business' which will usually be replacement cost. As replacement costs rise then appropriate depreciation charges, which are to be calculated by apportioning replacement cost over the estimated remaining useful life, rise in harmony. Therefore, although the principle that depreciation is a process of allocating costs over useful life is preserved, as the concept of value used becomes more meaningful and the need to revise this concept regularly is accepted, then net book value will approximate more closely to the 'true' value of the assets. In Chapter 5 this subject will be dealt with more fully.

The Appreciation of Capital Stock: Extraordinary Items

One of the difficulties Hicks is concerned with in defining income as consumption plus appreciation is that certain categories of capital appreciation, notably those associated with changing interest rates and changing expectations, cannot properly be included in income for the current period. It is suggested that increases in the value of the capital stock associated with falling interest rates are the results of changes in the level of income for future periods and more properly should be included in the income of those periods. Increases in capital value due to enhanced expectations with respect to future income prospects imply an undervaluation of capital value at the start of the period and should be thought of as income for prior periods. The profession's concern with value changes brought about by unforeseen changes in circumstances is reflected in SSAP 6 and ED 16 which provides a supplement to this.[29] Extraordinary items 'are those items which derive from events or transactions outside the ordinary activities of the business and which are both material and expected not to recur frequently or regularly.'[30] Examples could be profits or losses arising from:

(a) discontinuance of a significant part of the business;
(b) sale of an investment not acquired for resale;
(c) writing off assets because of unusual developments;
(d) expropriations of assets.

SSAP 6 recommends that extraordinary items should be shown separately in the profit and loss account and their size and magnitude disclosed. However, they are apparently to be included in the profit for the year. The statement is careful to distinguish between extraordinary items and abnormal items. The latter are the result of unusually high profits or losses resulting from the ordinary operations of the business and are to be included in the profit before allowing for extraordinary items. SSAP 6 distinguishes prior year adjustments from extraordinary items and defines them as: 'those material adjustments applicable to prior years arising from changes in accounting policy and the correction of fundamental errors. They do not include the normal recurring corrections and adjustments of accounting estimates made in prior years.'[31] It is recommended that prior year adjustments are accounted for by making the appropriate adjustment to the opening balance of the profit and loss account. That is, they are not to be reflected in the calculation of profit for the current period.

An interesting anomaly emerges in ED 16 which reinforces the statement in SSAP 6 that unrealised gains on fixed assets should not be included in the profit for the period but rather should be credited directly to the appropriate reserve. However, unrealised losses on revaluation of fixed assets should be debited to the profit and loss account to the extent that they exceed any surplus held in the reserves relating to previous revaluations of the same assets. All realised gains and losses both realised and unrealised on fixed assets will be credited or debited to the profit and loss account.

2.5   THE CONFLICTS BETWEEN HICKS' INCOME CONCEPT AND SOME SSAPS

The parallels between Hicks' discussion on those changes in value which may or may not be included in profit for the current period and the ASCs treatment of extraordinary items and prior year adjustments are obvious. Yet there are significant differences. The greater measure of agreement is in the treatment of prior year adjustments. The proposal that corrections of fundamental errors, presumably principally in valuation, should be effected by adjustment to the opening balance of the profit and loss account is obviously in harmony with Hicks' assertion that increases in value resulting from revised expectations imply an error in the estimation of value at the beginning of the period and should properly be treated as income of prior periods.

The discrepancy exists in the treatment of extraordinary items. The ASC are apparently content to include all profits and losses from extraordinary events in the profit and loss account for the period with the proviso that they are separately identified and their magnitude stated.* It follows quite clearly from Hicks' definition of profit that certain profits from extraordinary events are not part of current income at all. He is clear that where an asset increases in value due to changing interest rates then to treat the whole appreciation as income is at variance with the basic propositions that income is the amount that can be consumed without impoverishing oneself. Any appreciation in an asset's value, whether realised or not, due to changing interest rates relates to changes in future income not to income for the current period.

Ironically the roles of Hicks and the ASC are reversed in the treatment of Government grants. SSAP 4[32] distinguishes two categories of grants, namely revenue based grants and capital based grants. It was not thought necessary to prescribe a standard for the treatment of revenue based grants since they should clearly be credited to revenue for the period in which the expenditure was incurred. However, capital based grants should be credited to revenue over the expected life of the asset. Two possibilities exist for achieving this. Firstly, the grant could be credited to the asset account to which it relates, reducing the value of the asset in the balance sheet and the annual depre-

---

* Extraordinary items are required to be shown below the line of the net (after tax) profit for the year so are not expressly shown in the calculation of profit for the year.

ciation charges accordingly. The second possibility is to treat the grant as a deferred credit releasing a proportion to revenue annually. If this second course is adopted the deferred credit, if material, should be shown separately and not included in shareholders funds.

In fact, this treatment of capital based grants does not follow from Hicks' definition of income. To illustrate this, consider a firm with no fixed assets which operates entirely for cash. In a year in which no new investments are made and no dividends paid the profit will be reflected in the increase in the cash account. If subsequently some of the cash balance is used to acquire some fixed assets, then the increase in the value of the firm will be transferred from the cash account to the fixed asset account. However, the total increase in the value of the firm will not change as a result of the acquisition and, as there is no consumption, i.e. dividends paid by the firm, the profit of the year will not be affected either. If the Government then pays a grant to the business as a result of its decision to invest there is no obvious reason why this should not be included in income for the year. The result of payment of the grant will be to increase the firm's cash balance and thereby increase the appreciation in the value of the firm over the period. As payment of the grant does not represent mis-valuation at the start of the period there is no case for including it in the profit of previous years. Similarly since the payment of the grant does not in any sense jeopardise earnings in later years in the way that the consumption of an increase in asset value resulting from falling interest rates would, there is no reason for including it in the profit of subsequent years.

2.6   CONCLUSION

It is obviously difficult, if not impossible, to incorporate all of the discussion in this chapter in a comprehensive definition of income and value which could form the basis of financial accounts. Hicks wrote 'We have seen eminent authorities confusing each other and even themselves, by adopting different definitions of saving and income, none quite consistent, none quite satisfactory.' He continued that 'When this sort of thing happens, there is usually some reason for the confusion; and that reason needs to be brought out before any further progress can be made.'[33] Later Hicks put the problem in its real perspective when he wrote that he felt

> rather strongly nowadays that most economic controversies about definition arise from a failure to keep in mind the relation of every definition to the purpose for which it is to be used . . . We have to be prepared to use different definitions for different purposes; and although we can often save ourselves trouble by adopting compromise, which will do well enough for more than one purpose, we must always remember that compromises have the defects of compromises and in the final analysis they will need qualification. It is not profitable to embark on the fine analysis of definition unless we have decided on the purpose for which the definition is wanted.[34]

Thus any recommendation for a compromise solution which provides a comprehensive definition of income* should be considered in the light of Hicks' comments. Although it is extremely doubtful as to whether it is even desirable to try and attempt to produce a single comprehensive definition of income based on compromise.

REFERENCES

1. *See* Fisher, I., *The Theory of Interest*, Macmillan 1930, Chapter 1.
2. *Ibid*, p. 11.
3. *Ibid*, p. 13.
4. Taylor, P.J., 'The nature and determinants of income: some further comments', *Journal of Business Finance and Accounting*, Vol. 2, No. 2, Summer 1975.
5. *Ibid*, p. 234.
6. Kaldor, N., *An Expenditure Tax*, Allen and Unwin 1955.
7. *See* Hicks, J.R., *Value and Capital*, Clarendon Press 1946, Chapter XIV 'Income'.
8. *Ibid*, p. 172.
9. Macdonald, G., *Profit Measurement: Alternatives to Historic Cost*, Accountancy Age Books 1974, Chapter 5, 'Economic concepts of income'.

---

* One of the most powerful analyses of income theory and recommendation as to the nature of business income is that of Edwards and Bell in their book *The Theory and Measurement of Business Income* (University of California Press 1970). As well as being regarded as a classic by academic accountants for many years their work has obviously had a profound influence on the thinking of the Accounting Standards Committee in their preparation of SSAP16. Edwards and Bell subdivide business profits into four categories. These are: (a) current operating profit; (b) unrealised cost saving (which they refer to as realisable cost savings); (c) realised capital gains: (d) realised cost savings. Current operating profit is the excess over a period of the current value of products sold and the current cost of the inputs used in the production of the products sold.

Unrealised cost savings, realised capital gains, and realised cost savings together constitute what Edwards and Bell describe as holding gains. Holding gains represent the increase in the value of the firm's assets as a result of increasing replacement costs. Cost savings, both realised and unrealised, are the savings the firm enjoys as a result of holding assets which are necessary to generate output and whose cost has appreciated.

Capital gains are increased values resulting from sales of assets not held with the intention of resale. Thus unrealised cost savings are the increase in the current period of the cost of assets held by the organisation which are to be used in producing the future output of the firm. On page 115 of their book cited above Edwards and Bell provide the following definitions:

Realised capital gains — the excess of proceeds over depreciated historic costs on the irregular disposal of assets.

Realised cost savings — the excess of the current cost over the historic cost of inputs used in producing output sold.

An example describing the Edwards and Bell approach is provided in Appendix B to this chapter.

10. *See* Bonbright, J.C., *The Valuation of Property*, republished by the Mitchie Company 1965, Vol. 1 Part 1, 'Concepts of value' Chapter IV, 'Value to the owner'.
11. *Ibid*, p. 71.
12. *See* Baxter, W.T., *Depreciation*, Sweet & Maxwell 1971 and *Accounting Values and Inflation*, McGraw Hill, 1975 and also Edey, H.C., 'Deprival value and financial accounting' in Edey H.C. and Yamey, B.S. (eds), *Debits, Credits, Finance and Profits*, Sweet & Maxwell 1974.
13. *Depreciation, op. cit.*, p.36.
14. SSAP 16 *Current Cost Accounting*, Accounting Standards Committee, April 1980.
15. *Inflation Accounting: Report of the Inflation Accounting Committee*, Cmnd. 6225, HMSO September 1975 (popularly referred to as 'Sandilands' after its Chairman) p. 161, para. 529.
16. SSAP 6 *Extraordinary Items and Prior Year Adjustments*, Accounting Standards Committee, revised April 1975.
17. SSAP 9 *Stocks and Work-in-Progress*, May 1975.
18. Companies Act 1981, Schedule 1, para. 20(1).
19. Sprouse, R.T. and Moonitz, M., *A Tentative Set of Broad Accounting Principles for Business Enterprises*, Accounting Research Study No. 3, American Institute of Certified Public Accountants, 1962.
20. SSAP 13 *Accounting for Research and Development*, Accounting Standards Committee, December 1977.
21. *Ibid*, para. 26.
22. Sprouse, R.T. and Moonitz, M.,*op. cit.*
23. Companies Act 1981, Section 13(3)(iii).
24. *For example see* Leake, P.D., *Commercial Goodwill its History, Value and Treatment in Accounts*, Pitman 1921, Chapter 2, 'The value of goodwill'.
25. Hinton, P.R., 'Accounting for goodwill', *Accountancy*, February 1973.
26. Companies Act 1981, Schedule 1 (para. 21(2)).
27. ED 30 *Accounting for Goodwill*, Accounting Standards Committee, October 1982.
28. SSAP 12 *Accounting for Depreciation*, Accounting Standards Committee, December 1977.
29. SSAP 6 *Extraordinary Items and Prior Year Adjustments*, Accounting Standards Committee, April 1974.
30. SSAP 6 *op. cit.*, para. 11.
31. *Ibid*, para. 12.
32. SSAP 4 *The Accounting Treatment of Government Grants*, Accounting Standards Committee, April 1974.
33. Hicks, J.R.,*op. cit.*, p. 171.
34. Hicks, J.R., 'Maintaining capital intact: a further suggestion', *Economica*, 1942, p. 175.

QUESTIONS AND DISCUSSION PROBLEMS

1. Many attempts have been made to define 'the nature of income'. Critically discuss the major income concepts with which you are familiar.

2. 'The value of property to its owner can be stated only by reference to the conditions under which the ownership interest shall be assumed to cease' (from *The Valuation of Property* by J.C. Bonbright). Briefly consider Bonbright's proposition and relate it to current developments in valuation concepts.

3. SSAP 9 paragraph 4 states 'The methods used in allocating costs to stocks and work-in-progress need to be selected with a view to providing the fairest possible approximation to the expenditure actually incurred in bringing the product to its present location and condition'. Do the requirements of the Standard ensure that this objective is achieved?

4. SSAP 13 appears to be reluctant for all R & D expenditure to be capitalised. SSAP16 suggested dealing with all assets at their 'value to the business' with exceptions for goodwill. Why do you think that these stances have been taken?

5. Consider whether if purchased goodwill is no more tangible than the goodwill generated by an organisation it should be written off. In your discussion relate your views to those of current accounting theory and practice in the area of goodwill.

6. Discuss how three SSAPs with which you are familiar may have either drawn upon, or departed from, accounting theory as far as the areas of income, capital and value are concerned.

Appendix A

DISCOUNTING AND VALUE

An obvious possibility for valuing any possession would be to consider the benefits that possession was likely to bring over its useful life. Therefore it is possible to say that the value of any item is a function of the benefits to be derived from its ownership. However, the value of the asset is a concept of the present, whereas the benefits to be derived from it lie further into the future. It is easy to demonstrate that the timing of the receipt of benefits is as important as their magnitude. Most people if asked whether they would prefer £100 now or in a year's time would opt for the immediate payment. The reasons for this assumed preference can be summarised as:

(a) *Investment*. If a person has £100 now he could invest it and because of the interest would have more than £100 in a year's time.
(b) *Inflation*. £100 will buy more now than it would in a year's time during a period of inflation.
(c) *Risk*. There is always a risk associated with future receipts. The risk may be connected with whether the payment will actually be made or with the ability of the recipient to be able to accept the payment.
(d) *Liquidity preference*. Even in the absence of the first three preferences for having money now rather than in the future, most people would still prefer to have the money immediately. Keynes suggested that an individual's preference for liquidity is attributable jointly to precautionary transactions and speculative motives, and for these reasons, if for no others, a person is likely to prefer immediate to future·money.*

Hence it is possible to assert that money or, indeed, benefits ensuing from money have a time value and that normally immediate receipts will be preferred to deferred ones. Furthermore, it is possible to express this time value or rate of time preference in a percentage form as:

---

* This is discussed in Chapter 13 'The general theory of the rate of interest', J.M. Keynes, *The General Theory of Employment, Interest and Money*, Macmillan 1936.

$$\frac{\text{equivalent future value} - \text{value now}}{\text{value now}} \times 100$$

It has been established that most individuals will prefer £100 now to £100 in a year's time. Assuming this, by progressively increasing the amount offered in the future it should be possible to establish a point of indifference. The point of indifference would be the situation in which the individual would be equally satisfied with £100 now and (say) £125 in a year's time. In these circumstances the individual's preference for money now rather than in the future can be expressed as a percentage using the ratio given above: in this case $(125 - 100)/100 = 25$ per cent. Having established the concept of a time value for money it is relatively easy to convert future money benefits to their present value equivalent. The process is called discounting and is best thought of as being a mirror image of the more familiar concept of compounding. Given a rate of interest of i per cent, then in n years' time £1 will be worth:

$$£1 (1 + i)^n$$

Similarly, £1 accruing n years from now with a rate of discount of d per cent will be worth now:

$$\frac{£1}{(1 + d)^n}$$

Using this simple algebraic formula it is possible to convert a stream of net benefits in the future to their present value equivalent and thereby place a present value on an asset by discounting expected future receipts at an appropriate interest rate. To facilitate the computations most books on financial management and investment appraisal include sets of discount tables.

An important extension of the basic formula shown above is with respect to perpetuities, that is income streams or flows of benefits stretching into the indefinite future. In this case we have the valuation formula for a security which gives an income of £1 a year for ever as

$$V = \frac{1}{(1 + i)} + \frac{1}{(1 + i)^2} + \frac{1}{(1 + i)^3} \cdots + \frac{1}{(1 + i)^n}$$

As n tends to infinity we can simplify this rather messy equation by using the formula for the sum of a geometric progression with a first term $1/(1 + i)$ and a common ratio $1/(1 + i)$ to give $V = 1/i$.

REFERENCE

For a more detailed discussion of discounting, see Wright, M.G., *Discounted Cash Flow*, McGraw-Hill 1967, Chapter 5 'DCF problems and solutions'.

Appendix B

AN EXAMPLE OF THE EDWARDS AND BELL APPROACH

A firm commences business on 1 January by purchasing fixed assets for £1000 which are expected to have a useful life of five years and no terminal value at the end of that period. It also purchases stock for £500 on the same date. On 31 December the firm sells half of its stock, which would now cost 10 per cent more to replace, for £1200. At that date the fixed assets now have a value of £1500.

In these circumstances the different categories of business income can be computed for the period as follows:

(a) *Current operating profit*
The difference between the current cost of inputs consumed and the current value of output produced.

		£
Current value of output		1200
Less cost of stock consumed (£250 + 10 per cent)	275	
Current cost of depreciation (20 per cent of £1500)	300	575
Current operating profit		£625

(b) *Unrealised cost saving*
The increase in the current cost of the assets held by the firm during the period.

	£
Stock (£275 − £250)	25
Fixed assets (80 per cent of £500)	400
Unrealised cost saving	£425

(c) *Realised capital gains*
The excess of proceeds over the historic costs on the irregular sale or disposal of assets.
In this case since none of the fixed assets have been sold during the period then the realised capital gains are nil.

(d) *Realised cost savings*

The excess of the current cost over the historic cost of inputs used in producing the output sold.

	£
For stock	
Current cost of goods sold	275
Historic cost of goods sold	250
Realised cost saving	25
For fixed assets	
Current cost depreciation	300
Historic cost depreciation	200
Realised cost saving	100
Total realised cost saving	£125

The approach of distinguishing between current operating profits and holding gains has been accepted by the ASC and incorporated in CCA.

CHAPTER 3
Concepts in Accounting

3.1 INTRODUCTION

Chapter 1 argued that 'practice' in accounting could not develop properly to meet the ever increasing demands of a complex society without reference to a coherent underlying theory. However, it also noted that there are a variety of ways of constructing such a theory and that a variety of theories can be developed. Unfortunately there is no general agreement among academics or practitioners as to the best way of proceeding. In Chapter 2, the fundamental concepts of income, capital and value, which are at the heart of all accounting statements, were considered in some depth and it was seen that they are in no sense unambiguous. In fact the very definition of these basic concepts is still a matter of controversy. When the problems of measurement are added to the problems of definition it will be readily appreciated that the preparation of an adequate set of financial statements remains a particularly difficult problem.

If the study of accounting was of purely 'academic' concern the problems alluded to above would not matter very much. A mass of writers would produce a plethora of learned literature arguing for and against various possibilities. Scores of statistical surveys would be undertaken to produce a vast array of conflicting and inconclusive evidence supporting and refuting various beliefs. Text books in their dozens could be produced summarising the arguments and concluding 'on the one hand, yes, on the other hand, no, and in conclusion, maybe'! Unfortunately or perhaps fortunately, accounting is not a purely academic discipline. Accountants work in a real world which requires them to produce sets of accounts regularly. Therefore they cannot agree to differ on *all* the various issues that surround the preparation of financial statements. There must be some consensus if accounts are to be produced at all!

Over the years, practising accountants have evolved a number of rules of accounting practice, variously referred to as assumptions, postulates, conventions, principles and so on, the objective of which has primarily been to ensure that there will be some comparability between the accounts produced within an enterprise and those produced by other organisations. Some of these have become enshrined in law. Others have been given quasi-legal status in various statements of standard accounting practice. Others remain accounting folk-lore, part of the somewhat nebulous 'generally accepted accounting principles'. Together they form what can be referred to as the 'framework of accounting'. This framework cannot be argued to be complete. Occasionally it is internally inconsistent. There are times when it appears illogical, being apparently little more than a random collection of unconnected and unsupported conventions. However, this framework of accounting undoubtedly exists.* If the need for a generally acceptable theory can be supported by the argument 'if you don't know where you are going then there is only a random chance that you will get there' then the need to understand the existing framework can be supported by an argument such as 'it is hard to work out where to go if you don't know where you are!'

As was noted above, parts of the accounting framework are now incorporated in legislation and accounting standards. However, generally accepted accounting principles predate both standards and law. This chapter will consider the development of the accounting framework from generally accepted accounting principles through standards to law.

3.2 THE DEVELOPMENT OF A FRAMEWORK OF ACCOUNTING

The legal requirements for company accounts are laid out in the Companies Acts. These specify the major items to be disclosed but until the 1981 Companies Act gave no guidance on the methods to be used. Before the 1981 Act the only guidance contained in the Companies Acts with respect to the quality of financial information was found in Section 149(1) of the 1948 Act which requires that:

> every balance sheet of a company shall give a true and fair view of the state of affairs of the company as at the end of its financial year, and the profit and loss account of a company shall give a true and fair view of the profit or loss of the company for the financial year.[1]

The interpretation of 'truth' and 'fairness' has been left to the accounting profession and the detail has been worked out by the profession largely in

---

* This 'framework of accounting' is not the same thing as the 'conceptual framework' discussed in Chapter 1 on page 13. The former, a simple yet pragmatic framework of what is currently held to be good (or at least acceptable) practice, the latter, theoretical endeavour to provide a comprehensive framework with agreed definitions for such terms as 'income' and 'value' and agreed practice which will suit the needs of all user groups.

response to auditing requirements. The general rule as evolved by the profession is that accounts should accord with 'generally accepted accounting principles'. However, as has been shown earlier, those principles have been neither rigorously defined nor clearly related to any underlying body of accounting theory. In consequence there has been considerable argument and debate as to exactly what constitutes 'generally accepted accounting principles'.

In response to the need for a consensus on the nature of generally accepted accounting principles the Institute of Chartered Accountants in England and Wales has, since 1942, been publishing *Recommendations on Accounting Principles*.[2] However, since these were only recommendations and there were no sanctions to ensure compliance with them they could only go a small part of the way to restrict the extremely wide range of practices used by accountants in the preparation of financial statements. The need for a more clearly defined set of principles was self-evident.

The development of a framework of principles to underpin the preparation of financial accounts has perhaps received even greater attention in the USA. As a result of the great depression the US Government in 1934 set up a Securities and Exchange Commission (SEC). This agency has the authority to prescribe the principles to be applied by the American accounting profession in the preparation of financial statements. In fact this power has not been used but the very existence of the SEC may have spurred the American Institute of Certified Public Accountants (AICPA) into taking a more positive approach in the establishment of a coherent set of accounting principles. The AICPA established the Committee on Accounting Procedure (CAP) in 1938 which was replaced in 1959 by the Accounting Principles Board (APB). This in turn was superseded in 1973 by the Financial Accounting Standards Board (FASB). The recommendations of the FASB are published as 'Statements of Financial Accounting Standards' and provide the definitive statements of the basis on which financial accounts are prepared in the USA.

The increasingly multi-national nature of business has resulted in the move towards internationally accepted accounting principles to facilitate the comparison of corporate activity across national frontiers. Developments in this area include the establishment of the International Accounting Standards Committee (IASC).*

A relatively recent development in the UK has been the incorporation of a number of accounting principles into statute law. A consequence of the United Kingdom joining the European Economic Community (EEC), has been the need to bring about harmonisation of UK company law with that of other member states of the community. Of particular significance to

---

* All these developments are discussed fully in Chapter 8.

ıntants has been the incorporation of the second and fourth directives*
e EEC into the 1980 and 1981 Companies Acts. In that the later Act
ᴄᴏ...ains detailed requirements as to the form and content of financial
statements and furthermore contains specific requirements with respect to
the application of accounting principles, it marks a change of direction
compared with the more general accounting requirement of S149 of the
1948 Companies Act.

3.3   GENERALLY ACCEPTED ACCOUNTING PRINCIPLES

The terms, concepts, conventions, practices and principles are often used
synonymously. In fact SSAP 2 suggests that the words 'accounting practices' should be taken as a general term to mean these and similar words.
In this book, the terms 'accounting principles' and 'accounting practices'
will generally be the ones used. The distinction between these two words
will be that 'principles' will be used for the more theoretical assumptions,
whereas 'practices' will be used for the rules of accounting, i.e. standards
underlying the preparation of accounts.

Over 150 accounting principles, varying in acceptance from those having
major importance through to those which are only of academic interest
have been listed by various writers. For example, Professor L. Spacek lists
nearly 70,[3] while Professor R.J. Chambers has about 100,[4] and both include
terms not provided by the other in their lists.

One of the more helpful classifications of these accounting principles or
practices, although it is by no means comprehensive, is provided by
Professors Harold Bierman and Allan Drebin.[5] They classify them under
the headings of assumptions about the world, operating conventions and
quality considerations.

Assumptions about the World

In drawing up accounts certain key assumptions are made by accountants
about the state of the entities with which they are dealing and the economic
environment within which they operate, i.e. the state of the accountant's
world. The more important of these assumptions are as follows:

(a) Business Entity[6]
That the business can be separated from its owners and the environment in
which it operates is necessarily assumed in order to set a boundary to the

---

* The objective of the Second Directive is both to regulate the formation of public companies, which are specifically defined and have to have a suitable designation in their title,
and the maintenance of their minimally specified capital and alterations to this.
    The Fourth Directive concerns: the presentation and contents of annual financial state-
ments, which include the accounts and the report of management; the methods of valuation
used in these; and their audit and publication.

accounts: only those transactions directly affecting the entity are recorded in financial statements. However, it can sometimes be somewhat arbitrary, particularly for small businesses where the affairs of the owners and the business are often inextricably interwoven. Furthermore, it results in certain information which may be useful in the evaluation of the position of the entity being excluded from the accounts.

(b) Going Concern[7]

This concept can be thought of as following on from the entity concept. In drawing up financial statements it is assumed that the entity will continue more or less in its present form into the indefinite future. This is an important assumption as far as the valuation of assets is concerned, since the value to a firm of very specific assets such as plant or equipment, will be much higher on the going-concern basis than it would be if the organisation were to go into liquidation.*

(c) Stable Monetary Unit[8]

At the present time the majority of accounting statements are based on the assumption that the value of the monetary unit used in drawing them up is constant over time. The validity of such an assumption is obviously very questionable. However, its existence is apparent from the additive nature of accounting data. Within a set of accounts all the numbers are assumed to be capable of addition and subtraction. Yet even infant school arithmetic teaches that it is not possible to add unlike items and get a meaningful result—two elephants, five apples and one double-decker bus do not make a useful total of eight anything. However, the fact that values of property, plant and machinery, and stock, all of which may have been obtained at different times, plus debtors and cash, are added together by accountants in a balance sheet, implies the assumption that all their money terms are identical even though the transactions may have taken place at different times.

The assumption of the stability of the monetary unit overlooks the fact that its purchasing power constantly changes. As early as 1920, Professor Irving Fisher wrote 'Imagine the modern American businessman tolerating a yard defined as the girth of the President of the United States.'[9] Yet changes in money terms have been tolerated by the accountant who uses historic costs to draw up financial statements.

In recent years considerable effort has been devoted to removing this assumption in the preparation of financial statements. However, it would be fair to say that at the time of writing the difficulties of so doing have not been entirely resolved. Although SSAP 16 is now accepted the majority of

---

* This is frequently the case for undertakings in air or marine transportation where an aeroplane's or ship's value under this assumption is likely to be vastly different from its realisable value. The Companies Act 1981 states that 'The company shall be presumed to be carrying on business as a going concern', Sch. 1 Part 4, para 10, p. 140.

firms which fall within the scope of the standard publish current cost accounts as supplementary statements. Therefore the mainstream of accounting reporting is still firmly based on historic cost accounting.

(d) Accounting Periods[10]

It is assumed that the continuum of time can be sub-divided into a number of discrete time periods (accounting periods) and accounts drawn up for each of these periods. Ironically this apparently harmless assumption is at the heart of many of the most fundamental problems in accountancy. In the long run it does not matter whether stock is valued at full cost or marginal cost, it does not matter whether depreciation is charged on a straight-line basis or by using a declining balance method. Similarly in the long run it does not matter whether deferred taxation is provided for or not, and so on. However, all these things *do* matter in terms of short run profit measurement. To paraphrase Lord Keynes—in the long run we are all dead![11]

Operating Conventions

Having made assumptions about the state of his world, the accountant then draws up accounts to represent the relevant economic events using a set of conventions. The following are the most important of these.

(a) Historic Cost*[12]

At the present time the basis of valuation used in the preparation of published financial statements is historic cost. That is, all assets are shown in the accounts at the cost of acquiring them, adjusted for depreciation where applicable. Although SSAP 16 was published in March 1980 the majority of firms continue to prepare their main accounts on the historic cost convention. The use of historic cost stems from the original purpose of drawing up accounts, i.e. the stewardship function. A conventional balance sheet is a historic record of all the money that has ever been made available to the entity (the liabilities) and all of the items that have been acquired by the entity (the assets). If the assets are valued at historic cost and the balance of cash outstanding is included among the assets, the sum of the assets must equal the sum of the liabilities, i.e. the balance sheet must balance. As accounts developed into more comprehensive financial statements and have come to be used for more than merely stewardship purposes, historic cost as a basis has come under increasing criticism. The relevance of historic cost figures during periods of inflation has been increasingly questioned.

---

* Frequently the accounting conventions used to produce the accounting framework are closely linked. For example historic cost is closely linked with the idea of the stability of the monetary unit.

(b) Realisation[13]

An example helps in the understanding of the importance of the realisation principle. Suppose an entity produces a motor car in one accounting period, stores it through a second, sells it in the third and collects the cash in the fourth. If the cost of the car is £3000 and the selling price is £6000, the profit is obviously £3000. A problem arises because of the accounting period assumption—accounts need to be produced for each of the four periods, but how is the £3000 profit divided up between these four periods? Obviously a number of possibilities exist, but by convention the whole of the profit is recognised in the period in which the sale is made, i.e. the period in which the revenue is *realised.** In this example it is the third period when the business transaction, in the form of a contract for the sale of the motor car, is agreed.

(c) Matching[14]

This convention leads to the matching of expenses with the revenues that they generate. The matching process deals with such things as the allocation of capital costs between periods. The combination of the matching principle with that of realisation gives rise to the so-called accruals system of accounting. This simply means that profits will be recorded at the point of sale whether cash is received or not. For example, where sales are made on credit the profit is recognised at the point of sale and the cash due accrues (or is in arrears). Similarly, the matching principle leads to the association of an expense with the revenue that it generated, irrespective of the timing of the cash payment connected with that expense. Therefore the expense associated with the use of electricity or gas is recognised in the period in which it is incurred even though the actual payment of the bill may be delayed for some months. Here again the debt is said to accrue.

(d) Duality[15]

This is a convention associated with the system of double entry bookkeeping. It simply requires that the accountant enters both aspects of every transaction in the books of account because in business every action has an equal and opposite reaction. Thus, as well as entering every application of funds the bookkeeper must also record the appropriate source. Hence for every entry in a ledger an entry of equal magnitude must be made on the opposite side of the same or another ledger. Therefore, the sum of the entries on both sides of all ledgers, barring errors, must always be equal, i.e. 'in balance'.

(e) Quantifiability or Money Measurement[16]

This convention says that all items included in accounts must be *measurable*

---

* There is an exception to this rule in the case of large contracts in progress, where the construction period spans a number of accounting periods.

cardinally, i.e. must be able to have some money value placed upon them. This assumption means that it would be insufficient to include non-quantifiable items in traditional accounts merely using an ordinal ranking for them.

Quality Considerations

In the application of the operating conventions the accountant will strive to achieve certain qualitative characteristics in the financial statements prepared.

(a) Objectivity[17]

Entries made in ledger and accounts must be capable of verification by an independent party and thus are said to be objective. This is to ensure that financial statements are free from bias and so minimises the possibility of subjective judgements being made by accountants in the preparation of accounts. It is perhaps sad to report that many proposals for the reform of financial accounting fail the 'objectivity test' and thus fall by the wayside. In this context it is worth noting that even traditional historic cost accounts cannot be completely objective. For example, within the context of an historic cost accounting system, in order to determine the depreciation charge it is necessary to know the cost of the acquisition, the terminal value and the useful life. Of these three variables only one, the cost of acquisition, can be objectively determined. Estimates must be made concerning the other two variables, and different accountants are likely to make different estimates for them.

(b) Prudence[18]

This used to be more commonly referred to and certainly still is in the American literature, as conservatism. This principle states that where an accountant could deal with an item in more than one way, his choice between the alternatives should give precedence to that which provides the most conservative result. For example, in the valuation of stock, if the current price is lower than the cost of acquisition the stock should be recorded at its current price. However, if the stock has gained in value this gain should not be recorded until the asset is sold. Traditionally the requirement has been that accountants should 'anticipate no profits but provide for all possible losses'.

(c) Consistency[19]

This consideration requires that where a transaction or economic event is repeated in different time periods then the accounting representation should be the same in all time periods. Needless to say, the requirement is not absolute in that it does not preclude mistakes being rectified nor accounting treatments being altered where the change seems beneficial in terms of giving a better representation of reality. However, it does require that where the accounting treatment is changed, for example as in the case of a change from straight line to a declining balance system of depreciation, the effects of the change and the position under both the original and the revised accounting treatments should be clearly shown.

An associated idea is that of uniformity which requires that where a similar event takes place in two or more entities at the same time then it should be represented in the same way in the various accounts.

(d) Materiality[20]

The materiality principle simply states that the way an item is treated in the accounts should depend upon its materiality. Thus it is a concept of relevance. For example, a pair of scissors in an office should last over a number of accounting periods, but it would not be relevant to match the cost of its use over the periods concerned. Thus it will be classed as an expense of the period in which the scissors were purchased. Where amounts of expenditure involved are insignificant, i.e. not material, they are not capitalised and their costs are not spread over a number of periods. Materiality, as well as determining the way in which items may be classified as between revenue and capital, is also relevant in determining whether particular items or transactions should be separately disclosed in the accounts or not. This depends upon the influence the item will have on the interpretation of the accounts in question. A number of SSAPs include the word 'material'* in their provisions, for example, SSAP 4 *The Accounting Treatment of Government Grants*, states that 'the amount of the deferred credit should, if material, be shown separately in the balance sheet'.[21]

Later SSAPs clearly state that they do not apply in the case of immaterial items, for example SSAP 17 *Post Balance Sheet Events*, states this.[22] Also the Preface to International Accounting Standards clearly states that IASs are not intended to apply to immaterial items.

3.4 THE ROLE OF ACCOUNTING STANDARDS IN THE FRAMEWORK OF ACCOUNTING

Today it is impossible to discuss a framework of accounting without considering the role of accounting standards. Therefore, although the development of accounting standards will be dealt with fully in Chapter 8, their place in the accounting framework will be briefly discussed here.

---

* Paragraph 12 of the preface to IASs and IAS 1 *Disclosure of Accounting Policies* says that one of three considerations which should govern the selection and application of appropriate accounting policies is materiality. However, there is no blanket mention of materiality in SSAPs, either in the Explanatory Foreword to them or in SSAP 2 *Disclosure of Accounting Policies*.

As has been seen generally accepted accounting principles predate standards by a considerable period. Professor Basil Yamey notes that most of the principles referred to earlier were developed during the latter part of the nineteenth century.[23] A problem arose in that within these generally accepted principles it was, and indeed is, possible to depict the same economic transactions in a number of ways. Of course this has always been the case and the thoughtful accountant realises that it is unlikely that two different accountants working separately would produce identical sets of accounts from the same data. This is because they are likely to select different accounting policies when a number of possible bases are available. However, the lay public have a rather different view of accountancy. To the layman accounts have an aura of precision. The very fact that balance sheets balance confirm their belief in the accuracy of accounts, and when financial statements are published in printed form this heightens the belief in their infallibility. When the inherent flexibility of the accounting framework was brought to the attention of the public in one or two well publicised takeover battles during the 1960s* there was a considerable furore which led to a disquiet with the accounting profession. As a result of this concern there arose pressure for more standardisation in accounting. It was felt in many non-accounting circles that there was a need to tighten up the framework of accounting. As a result of this feeling the Accounting Standards Steering Committee was established by the Institute of Chartered Accountants in England and Wales during 1970. The development and work of the ASSC will be considered in greater detail in Chapter 8. In the context of this chapter the most important pronouncement has been SSAP 2[24] *The Disclosure of Accounting Policies*.

Disclosures of Accounting Policies

SSAP 2 made a number of statements with respect to the provision of an accounting framework. It is worth looking at these at this early stage to find out which accounting concepts it considered to be fundamental to the production of financial accounting reports.

First, it is interesting to note that SSAP 2 suggested that the words 'principles', 'practices', 'rules', 'conventions', 'methods' and 'procedures' could all be taken as synonymous for the word 'practices' which has been used by the Statement as a generic term to cover them all.

Second it listed the fundamental accounting concepts as 'going concern', 'accruals', 'consistency' and 'prudence', and also said that because they have such general acceptance and usage, that no explanation of them was called for in published accounts.

---

* See for example the reference to the GEC/AEI takeover discussed on page 3, Chapter 1 of this book.

Accounting Bases and Policies

SSAP 2 also discusses the distinction between accounting bases and policies. It defines *accounting bases* as the acceptable ways of expressing or applying the fundamental accounting concepts to financial transactions or items. It defines *accounting policies* as the specific accounting bases judged by management to be most appropriate to their circumstances and adopted by them for the purpose of preparing the enterprise's financial accounts so as to ensure a true and fair view of its performance and financial position. Thus the statement recognises that accounting bases may be numerous noting for example a number of different bases exist for such things as depreciation and charging the consumption of stock. However, the statement says that when there are a number of possible different accounting bases that could be used, then an organisation should select one from them and use this consistently. It does not restrict an enterprise completely to the use of a single base. In fact it provides for exceptions to this in appropriate situations. Nevertheless, it concludes:

> If accounts are prepared on the basis of assumptions which differ in material respects from any of the generally accepted fundamental concepts defined ... *the facts should be explained.* In the absence of a clear statement to the contrary, there is a presumption that the four fundamental concepts have been observed [our italics].[25]

It is interesting to note that SSAP 2 does not prescribe which accounting policy should be adopted. It does not even provide any guidance as to how the choice between alternative policies should be made. It simply requires that the policy adopted should be disclosed. In this sense it does not tighten up the accounting framework, it merely gives a formal recognition to some of the underlying principles.

3.5 STATUTE LAW AND THE ACCOUNTING FRAMEWORK

As noted earlier in this chapter prior to the 1980 Companies Act, the only guidance contained in the legislation as to how accounts should be prepared was the true and fair view requirements of Section 149 of the 1948 Act.* For many years the accounting profession has resisted legislation on any detailed methodology concerning the preparation of financial statements. As recently as March 1981 the Consultative Committee of Accounting Bodies (CCAB) argued:

> We believe it is important that accounting standards should continue to operate

---

* UK law has traditionally restricted itself to requirements on what should be disclosed—the so-called disclosure requirements. These are numerous, particularly in the Companies Acts 1948 and 1967.

without apparent conflict with statutory provisions. The risks of such conflict are heightened where detailed specification of accounting rules, including valuation rules, are incorporated in statute law.[26]

Such resistance was successful until the 1980 Companies Act and more significantly the 1981 Companies Act. Both of these Acts were due at least in part, to the need to harmonise British company law with that of other Member States of the EEC. The 1980 Act includes, among other things, detailed rules for determing the amount of profit available for distribution. The 1981 Act contains rules on the form and content of accounts as well as setting out rules for the valuation of a company's assets. SSAP 2 is to all intents and purposes given statutory force by the 1981 Act.* The overriding requirements of the 1981 Act is that accounts should continue to 'give a true and fair view'.[27] However it marks a watershed in that for the first time a Companies Act contains detailed instructions as to how accountants should set about doing this. It should be emphasised that it does not significantly tighten up the accounting framework in that there remains considerable discretion within its regulations. However it clearly represents a further step in the direction of standardisation and formalisation of 'generally accepted accounting principles' by giving legal force to some of them.

3.6   THE ACCEPTABILITY OF THE ACCOUNTING FRAMEWORK

The need for an accounting framework was explained in terms of the fundamental ambiguities inherent in the basic concepts of income and value used by accountants to report upon the progress and current status of an entity in financial terms. That the framework of accounting is incomplete is evidenced by the wide range of possible accounting treatments that are acceptable for specific economic events. The debate on takeovers and the arguments and controversies concerning these during the mid to late 1960s prompted the establishment of the ASC to formalise the principles upon which accounting statements were to be based. However, largely due to the incomplete nature of the underlying framework of accounting principles,

---

* Companies Act 1981, Schedule 1, Part II Section A says of Accounting Principles that 'The company shall be presumed to be carrying on business as a '*going concern*' (para. 10). 'Accounting policies shall be applied *consistently* from one financial year to the next' (para. 11). 'The amount of any item shall be determined on a *prudent* basis' (para. 12). 'All income and charges relating to the financial year to which accounts relate shall be taken into account without regard to the date of receipt of payment' (para. 13). This last one the principle of accrual [the italic is ours].

even the SSAPs and the EDs issued by the ASC frequently allow for a wide range of accounting treatments of specific issues.

For example, SSAP 12 on accounting for depreciation is quite categoric that the necesary and sufficient condition for charging depreciation is that the asset in question should have a finite life. However, it has nothing to say on whether the cost of the asset should be allocated over that life using the straight line or the accelerated depreciation methods, or on what should be done about major repair costs, or whether interest should be taken into account in determining depreciation charges. The same could be said of para. 18 of Schedule 1 of the 1981 Companies Act.

Similarly, SSAP 9 on stock valuation states that in the valuation of finished goods and work in progress accountants should include in the value those items of indirect cost incurred in bringing the inventory to its 'current condition and location'. However, it has nothing to say about the process by which indirect costs should be allocated to cost centres or departments and absorbed into the cost of production. See also paras. 26 and 27 of Schedule 1 of the 1981 Companies Act.

It may be argued that the incompleteness of the accounting framework is inevitable due to the complexity of the problems it is being used to resolve. However, an even greater difficulty may lie in its internal inconsistency. For example, one of the most important properties that a set of accounts should possess is that they should be objective and verifiable. From the viewpoint of the auditor, in order for him to be able to discharge successfully the stewardship function, subjective opinion and the possibility of personal bias should preferably be eliminated or at least be kept to a minimum. It is this need for objectivity that has ensured the continued survival of the historic cost basis of accounts in spite of its obvious shortcomings. Yet within the generally accepted framework of accounting it is impossible to maintain total objectivity.

For example, the matching principle requires expenses to be matched with the revenues they are incurred in generating. This in turn necessitates the distinction of capital as against revenue expenditures and the allocation of capital costs over the period of the useful life of assets through the process of depreciation. However, the calculation of depreciation charges necessitates an estimation of both the useful life and the terminal value of an asset and therefore cannot possibly be objective. As a further example of internal conflict, the going-concern assumption together with the historic cost principle enables even highly specialised assets to be valued at their cost of acquisition on the assumption that the business will continue in existence and the assets will be put to the use for which they were acquired. This is in spite of the fact that the cost of the assets may be considerably in excess of their realisable value. Therefore this practice is apparently in conflict with the principle of conservatism, or prudence.

It may be concluded that many of the difficulties faced by accountants stem from the fact that the framework of principles upon which accounts are based is neither complete nor consistent.* The inadequacies of the framework are, of course, in part due to the enormous complexity of the problems it is being used to resolve. Yet it must surely be concluded that some of the difficulties have come about from the piecemeal development of the principles of accounting and the failure to relate them to a coherent body of theory.

3.7 CONCLUSIONS

The basic ambiguity of the fundamental concepts of value and income may well mean that some variation in the accounting treatment of economic transactions is inevitable. The variety of demands that the various user groups makes of accounting information may even mean that it is desirable.† However it must be recognised that a variability in treatment would cause difficulties in the interpretation of financial statements and is a particular problem to those seeking to make comparisons between different organisations. It is probably true to say that the majority of accountants and users of accounts agree on the need for some standardisation. This has resulted in the establishment of the ASC in the UK and similar bodies in other countries and the publication of a number of accounting standards. It is however equally true that most accountants probably believe that the wide range of differing situations they face makes complete standardisation impossible and, if it were possible, probably undesirable.

The trend over recent years has been for generally accepted accounting principles to become recognised in a more formal way firstly through the SSAPs and more recently in the latest Companies Act. While there has undoubtedly been some tightening up of the accounting framework, notably through the SSAPs, considerable flexibility still remains. It is also true that the increased formality has not changed the essential nature of the accounting framework. Notwithstanding its current status (in part at least) as statute law it still lacks the support of a coherent underlying theory. Its inconsistencies and incompleteness remain with us and while they do, so will many of the problems of accountancy.

---

* If the profession were to wait for a complete and comprehensive conceptual framework which was acceptable to all, in our view they would be likely to wait for ever. The accounting framework that this chapter has discussed may be incomplete but it is being built upon and continually improved.

† This would be an argument for producing financial statements showing multiple measurements perhaps as multi-column reports using different conceptual frameworks for different needs rather than seeking a compromise that will satisfy nobody. This approach was suggested in *A Statement of Basic Accounting Theory*, American Accounting Association, 1966.

REFERENCES

1. *Companies Act 1948*, 11 and 12 Geo, 6. Chapter 38, Section 149(1) page 89.
2. *Recommendations on Accounting Principles*, The Institute of Chartered Accountants in England and Wales, 1975.
3. Spacek, L. *The Basic Postulates of Accounting*, Accounting Research Study No. 1, American Institute of Certified Public Accountants 1961.
4. Chambers, R.J. *Accounting, Evaluation and Economic Behaviour*, Prentice-Hall 1966.
5. Bierman, H. and Drebin, A.R. *Financial Accounting, an Introduction*, Collier-Macmillan 1972, page 10.
6. For a discussion on the *business entity* assumption see Husband, G.R. 'The entity concept in accounting', *The Accounting Review*, October 1954.
7. For a discussion on the *going concern* assumption see Fremgen, J.M. 'The going concern assumption: a critical appraisal', *The Accounting Review*, October 1968.
8. Buckmaster D. and Brooks L.D. 'Effects of price level changes in operating income', *CPA Journal*, May 1974.
9. Fisher, I. *Stabilising the Dollar*, Macmillan, 1920, page 83.
10. For a discussion on the *accounting periods* assumption see 'The accounting period', *British Institute of Management Information*, Note 22, 1964.
11. The Lord Keynes quote 'In the long run . . . we are all dead', can be found in *The Penguin Dictionary of Modern Quotations* by J.M. and M.J. Cohen, Penguin, 1980, p. 183.
12. For a discussion on the *historic cost* assumption see Kohler, E.L. 'Why not retain historic cost?', *The Journal of Accountancy*, October 193.
13. For a discussion on the *realisation* assumption see 'The report of the American Accounting Association Concepts and Standards Research Study Committee "The Realisation Concept",' *The Accounting Review*, April 1965.
14. For a discussion on the *matching* assumption see Hylton, D.P. 'On matching revenue with expense', *The Accounting Review*, October 1965.
15. For a discussion on the *duality* assumption see Sterling, R.R. 'An explication and analysis of the structure of accounting', *Abacus*, December 1972.
16. For a discussion on the *quantifiability* assumption see Bierman, H. 'Measurement and accountancy', *The Accounting Review*, July 1963.
17. For a discussion on the *objectivity* assumption see Arnett, H.E. 'What does "objectivity" mean to accountants', *The Journal of Accountancy*, May 1961.
18. For a discussion on the *prudence* assumption see Moore, M.L. 'Conservatism', *Texas CPA*, October 1972.
19. For a discussion on the *consistency* assumption see Burk, M. 'Reporting on consistency and accounting changes', *CPA Journal*, June 1973.
20. For a discussion on the *materiality* assumption see Chase, K.W. 'The limits of materiality', *CA Magazine (Canada)*, June 1979.
21. SSAP 4 *The Accounting Treatment of Government Grants*, ASC, April 1974, para. 9.
22. SSAP 17 *Post Balance Sheet Events*, Accounting Standards Committee, 1981, preamble.
23. See Yamey, B.S. 'The development of company accounting conventions', *The Three Banks Review*, 1960.

24. SSAP 2 *Disclosure of Accounting Policies*, Accounting Standards Committee, November 1971.
25. *Ibid*, para. 17.
26. *Memorandum on the Companies Bill 1981*, Consultative Committee of Accounting Bodies, 9 March 1981. Ref. TR429.
27. *Companies Act 1981*, HMSO 1981, Chapter 62, Part 1 149(2).

QUESTIONS AND DISCUSSION PROBLEMS

1. Many accounting concepts, conventions, principles, practices, etc. have developed. State ten of the more important of these, carefully defining them and provide examples which show how or when they might be invoked.
2. Frequently the major concepts underlying the accounting framework will come into conflict. Provide examples showing such conflicts and, with reasons, say which one of the concepts in your example has precedence and why.
3. Critically discuss whether historic cost accounting really is objective.
4. SSAP 2 states that there are four fundamental accounting concepts. IAS 1 says that there are three fundamental accounting assumptions. Compare the approaches taken to the 'disclosure of accounting policies' by these two statements, and give your opinion as to whether there are any fundamental differences between them.
5. With the help of examples from depreciation, stock and two other areas, define and distinguish between accounting bases and policies.
6. 'An accounting framework is necessary for the production of financial statements'. Explain what an 'accounting framework' is. Do you agree with the statement that such a framework is necessary? Provide reasons for the stance that you take.
7. Does/do Company Law and accounting standards have any contribution to make in the provision of an accounting framework?

CHAPTER 4
The Stock Valuation Debate

4.1   INTRODUCTION

The introduction to SSAP 9 *Stocks and Work-in-Progress*, quotes that:

No area of accounting has produced wider differences in practice than the computation of the amount at which stocks and work-in-progress are stated in financial accounts.[1]

In the preparation of financial statements the matching principle requires that all expenditures be classified either as assets or expenses. In essence, assets are those past expenditures which retain a revenue-generating potential for the future, whereas expenses are the assets consumed in generating the revenues of the preceding accounting period. In traditional accounts, profit is simply revenue less the cost of the assets used up in the generation of that revenue. Expenditures on stocks and work-in-progress still held at the end of an accounting period cannot be treated as an expense of the period. The stocks to which the expenditure relates are being held in the expectation of their generating revenues in future accounting periods. These stocks and work-in-progress are obviously assets and therefore it is incumbent on the accountant to place a value on them for their inclusion in the balance sheet.

As has already been seen in Chapter 2, the concept of value is an ambiguous one. Value may be thought of as historic cost, replacement cost, net realisable value or the discounted present value of the future benefits from ownership, which is often referred to as economic value. It should be noted that for assets such as stocks which are held with the intention of resale, the future benefits arising from their ownership equal their net realisable value.

Furthermore many attempts have been made to combine these various concepts into a single, all-embracing definition of value, for example, the idea of deprival value.* A particular problem is that stock valuation is one

---
* For a fuller discussion of the definition of value, refer back to Chapter 2 Section 2.3.

of the major areas of overlap between financial and management accounting and, as will be seen later the requirements of the two accounting systems may differ. Traditionally accountants have avoided the problems of definition referred to above by taking historic cost as their basic definition of value. For example the Committee on Accounting Procedure of the American Institute of Certified Public Accountants in Statement 5 stated 'A departure from the cost basis of pricing inventory is required when the utility of the goods is no longer as great as its cost',[2] and continued in Statement 6 that 'As used in the phrase *lower of cost or market* the term *market* means current replacement cost except that market should not exceed the net realisable value'.[3] These together provide one of the numerous confirmations of the acceptance of historic cost as the base value for the application of the 'lower of' rule. More recently the development of various systems of inflation accounting have placed upon the practising accountant the need to consider other possible value concepts. The particular valuation problems of stocks and work-in-progress with reference to SSAP 16* will be considered towards the end of this chapter. This chapter is not concerned with the general problems associated with the definition of value, nor at this stage, with the problems of current cost accounting. However, as will be seen, the selection of historic cost as the basis of valuation does not eliminate the problems inherent in placing a value on stocks and work-in-progress. Indeed, the quotation from SSAP 9 at the beginning of this chapter, was made in the context of an historic cost accounting system.†

In outline the problems are twofold. Firstly, when buying costs have changed over a period there may be left in stock homogeneous items which cost different amounts. Secondly, where an enterprise is engaged in manufacture the question arises as to exactly which costs should be included in the value of the stock and how much of these costs should be included. Where stock is bought in from outside the enterprise the cost is the cost of acquisition and its ascertainment is relatively straightforward. However, where an enterprise is engaged in manufacture the problem is more complex. Just how much, if any, of the production manager's secretary's salary is to be included in the cost of the closing stock of a product?

4.2   THE VALUATION OF STOCKS AS COSTS CHANGE

An example may clarify the nature of the problem associated with the valuation of residual stock where the goods concerned have been purchased at different prices.

---

* SSAP 16, *Current Cost Accounting*, issued March 1980.
† Note that the IAS called its statement on this subject, IAS 2 'Valuation and Presentation of Inventories in the Context of the *Historic Cost System*' (our italics).

Example A coal merchant, who has no opening stock, has four deliveries of coal made to the same delivery bay during a three month period. The quantities delivered and the invoiced costs are as follows:

1 January	1000 tonnes @ £80 per tonne
4 February	600 tonnes @ £84 per tonne
26 February	800 tonnes @ £101 per tonne
15 March	1200 tonnes @ £100 per tonne

During the same period he sells 2200 tonnes of the 3600 tonnes of coal delivered at £120 per tonne. Obviously he has 1400 tonnes left, but what was the cost of it? One piece of coal looks very like another so it is unlikely that the various deliveries could have been identified. Furthermore the coal merchant has obviously made a profit, but how much? The problem lies in the valuation of the closing stock.

In measuring profit, four separate pieces of information need to be determined. These are the sales, the purchases, and the opening and the closing stock. Of these three numbers the first two are matters of fact. In this example* that the figures for the sales are £264,000 and the purchases £331,200 cannot be disputed. It depends on the assumptions made about the flow of costs.

At this stage, three separate possibilities will be considered. These are the so-called FIFO, LIFO and weighted average methods of charging out stocks.

(a) FIFO

This is an abbreviation of first in, first out. The assumption underlying it is that the first stock to be bought is the first to be sold. The closing stock is therefore the most recently acquired. In the example being considered the value of the 1400 tonnes of stock which is left, the closing stock, would be:

		£
1200 tonnes at £100	=	120,000
200 tonnes at £101	=	20,200
		£140,200

The profit for the period using this method of charging out stocks consumed would be:

---

* As the business has just commenced it has no opening stock so this enters into the calculation as zero.

		£
Sales		264,000
Opening stock	Nil	
Purchases	331,200	
less:		
Closing stock	140,200	
Cost of sales		191,000
Profit		£73,000

(b) LIFO

This is the last in, first out method. Its underlying assumption is that the last stock to be bought is the first to be sold. The value of the closing stock is therefore that of the earliest stock acquired. In this example:

1000 tonnes at £80	=	80,000
400 tonnes at £84	=	33,600
		£113,600

The profit for the period using this method would be:

Sales		264,000
Opening stock	Nil	
Purchases	331,200	
less:		
Closing stock	113,600	
Cost of sales		217,600
Profit		£47,400

(c) Weighted Average

Here the underlying assumption in charging out the stock sold is that the value of the closing stock is the average price paid for it over the period. In this case:

$$\frac{\text{Purchases in £s}}{\text{Purchases in tonnes}} = \text{an average price of £92 per tonne.}$$

Therefore the value of the closing stock in this example is:

$$1400 \times 92 = \text{£128,800.}$$

The profit for the period using this method would be:

		£
Sales		264,000
Opening stock	Nil	
Purchases	331,200	
less:		
Closing stock	128,800	
Cost of sales		202,400
Profit		£61,600

These results are summarised as follows:

Method	FIFO	LIFO	Weighted average
Closing stock valuation	£140,200	£113,600	£128,800
Profit reported for period	£ 73,000	£ 47,400	£ 61,600

So which figures should the coal merchant select? The CAP of the AICPA states that 'the major objective in selecting a method should be to choose the one which under the circumstances, most clearly reflects periodic income'.[4] Such an approach should normally ensure that a 'true and fair' financial statement is produced.

The Misconception of the Relationship Between Cash Flows and Physical Flows*

Before considering the relative merits of the three approaches to stock valuation outlined above it is important to eliminate one widespread misconception at the outset. In terms of the physical movement of stock, most businesses strive for a pattern similar to that underlying the FIFO approach. That is, they try to sell their oldest stock first. This is particularly true of any business that deals in perishable goods such as the food retailer. This compatibility with the physical flow of stock is often used as a justification for the use of a FIFO approach in determining the flow of costs. However, thinking of the movement of the costs associated with stocks in relation to their physical movement can lead to misunderstandings in that it ignores the fundamental issues of the nature of profit and the reasons for measuring it.

---

* For another discussion on cost flow assumptions see pages 186 to 196 of Edwards, E.O., Bell, P.W., Johnson, L.T. and Jones, J.H., *Accounting for Economic Events*, Scholars Book, 1979.

As has been seen in earlier chapters, profit is an abstraction and the concept underlying it is ambiguous. There is controversy as to the basic nature of profit.[5] What is clear is that in evaluating various profit figures the question to be asked is not which of the alternative figures are true or false (all of the profit figures in the earlier example are true), but whether one measure is more or less useful than those obtained using alternative approaches. It is generally accepted that the purpose of measuring profit is to provide a measure of efficiency and a guide to consumption.* It is in this context that the various assumptions regarding the flow of costs have to be judged rather than their relationships with the physical flow of stock.

Consider a situation in which it is possible to keep specific records of the costs of various items in stock, for example where the goods sold are sufficiently large, such as machine tools. In such a case it would be possible to specifically identify the costs of the various items in stock. However, a machine tool manufacturer could have in stock three identical machines which had been made at different points in time and which had cost differing amounts to produce. Because the machines are large and expensive it has been possible to identify the cost of each of these identical machines. A customer now appears for one of the machines. The customer is likely to be indifferent as to which machine he buys as they are all identical. Furthermore the difference in cost of the three machines will not influence the price he is prepared to pay. The manufacturer will be in an identical position after the transaction whichever machine is sold to the customer. After the sale the manufacturer will have a sum of money equal to the purchase price and two identical machines in stock.

However, on the assumption that the machines cost differing amounts to produce, the manufacturer's profit figure will be affected by his choice of which machine to sell. Yet it is hard to see that the efficiency of the organisation or its ability to pay out profits can be affected by that particular decision. Therein is the essence of the stock valuation problem.

4.3   A CRITICAL COMPARISON OF THE FIFO, LIFO AND WEIGHTED AVERAGE METHODS

It is often claimed that valuing closing stock on the LIFO basis will ensure that the cost of goods sold will be based on something approaching the current cost of stock. In that the LIFO method will tend to eliminate any inflationary element from profits it is argued that it provides a more meaningful measure of efficiency. Furthermore, since businesses must replace their stock if they are to survive, profit based on a LIFO stock valuation gives a better indication of how much of the firm's profits may safely be paid out. There are a number of difficulties associated with this line of

---

* See Hick's concept discussed in Chapter 2, page 20.

argument. Firstly, the cost of goods sold based on LIFO valuation of the closing stock will only approximate to current cost when the stock turnover ratio is reasonably high. Where stock turnover rates are low then even the LIFO cost of sales could be considerably out-of-date.* Secondly, the price paid for obtaining the LIFO up-to-date cost of sales figure is a progressively out-of-date valuation for closing stock in the balance sheet. In that the closing stock forms part of the current assets and because considerable significance is often attached to such things as the current ratios as indicators of the firm's liquidity position, the advantages of using LIFO in the measurement of profit may be more than off-set by the disadvantages for the valuation of the firm's assets as far as the majority of the users of the accounts are concerned. Thirdly, the use of LIFO can produce periodic peaks in the profit measured as stock levels are run down and old costs are brought out of the value of closing stock to be matched against new (possibly higher) revenues. Recalling what was discussed earlier, that the physical stock need not be old, it is the costs at which it is valued which are outdated. LIFO is an assumption about the flow of costs which can be made independently of the physical flow of the stocks.

It is generally thought that the advantages of LIFO are outweighed by its disadvantages and because of this it is not frequently used in the UK. Furthermore the use of LIFO is not permitted in the UK for the purposes of measuring taxable profit.† In the USA where LIFO is permitted for tax purposes its use has become more widespread. Needless to say this is because the use of LIFO in an inflationary period during which stock levels are constant or increasing, ensures lower profits than FIFO and hence correspondingly lower tax assessments.

The principal advantage claimed for the use of a weighted average approach in the valuation of stock is that it ensures that the cost of sales is measured in £s that are compatible with the revenues. The point is that if sales take place more or less evenly over an accounting period, then they will automatically be stated at the average price level for that period. Profit is then determined by subtracting cost of sales from the revenues. As one of the fundamental principles of measurement is that it is meaningless to subtract unlike items one from the other, then it follows that for the profit figure to have any meaning, the cost of sales and the revenues must be expressed in like terms. As the revenues are automatically stated at the average price level for the period then so too must the cost of sales. This can be achieved by valuing the closing stock on the basis of the weighted average approach.

By far the most widely used system in the UK is FIFO. Its principal advantages are that it is easy to use with or without a perpetual inventory

---

* The use of the NIFO approach, i.e. next in first out, is said to be better in such situations.
† See Minister of National Revenue v Anaconda American Brass Ltd, Privy Council 1956 A.C. 85.

system, and furthermore it provides the most recent prices for the valuation of the closing stock.

4.4 THE DEFINITION OF THE VALUATION OF STOCKS

Notwithstanding the problems associated with the valuation of residual stocks when these were purchased at different prices, a further problem is encountered in the evaluation of stocks concerned when joint production costs are involved. Consider a simple example of a furniture manufacturer who makes a variety of types of furniture from wood. In determining the cost of his closing stock certain categories of cost must obviously be included. In order to manufacture the furniture, as well as wood, he needs glue, screws, varnish, handles, hinges, etc. The wood also has to be cut to shape, assembled and finished. The materials have to be paid for as do the wages of employees who cut the wood and assemble and finish the furniture. These costs, which are called direct costs,* are obviously part of the cost of the product and must clearly be included in the cost of the finished stock. They present no conceptual problems although there may be substantial practical difficulties in measuring and recording them. However, in order to make the furniture, other costs are necessarily incurred.

Premises to operate from are required which may be rented† and various other occupancy costs will be incurred. It will also be necessary to employ foremen, cleaners, fork-lift truck drivers and so on. The machinery used to cut and assemble the wood is likely to lose value and so will depreciate. It may be necessary to employ a factory manager who will probably need a secretary. These costs, which are called indirect costs‡ or overheads, are all necessary if production is to take place, although they are not directly associated with the manufacture of the product. Furthermore, to enable the business as a whole to operate other costs related to the general administration and accounting and marketing functions of advertising and selling will be incurred. The problems relating to these overhead costs§ are twofold. Firstly, which if any of them, should be included in the cost of the product for stock valuation purposes? Secondly, if it is accepted that some overheads should be included in product cost, on what basis should they be incorporated in this ?

---

* Direct costs are defined as 'The *total* of all the *costs* which are a direct part of the cost of a *product*' in Houghton, D. and Wallace, R.G., *Students' Accounting Vocabulary*, Gower 1980.
† Even if owned they have an opportunity cost associated with them.
‡ Indirect costs are defined as '*expenses* in the *manufacturing accounts* or costing accounts which do NOT belong to one particular *product* which the business is making' in Houghton, D. and Wallace, R.G., *Students' Accounting Vocabulary*, Gower 1980.
§ William L. Ferrara says 'Income can be measured properly only when every attempt is made to segregate and allocate overhead costs to units of output so that costs of products may be matched or associated with the revenues derived from the sale of merchandise', 'Overhead costs and income measurement', *The Accounting Review*, January 1961, page 70.

Absorption and Variable Costing

In answer to the first question posed above there are two opposing views. Broadly these may be referred to as absorption costing and variable costing.* The essential difference between the two schools of thought can be illustrated with the simple diagram shown in Exhibit 4(a).

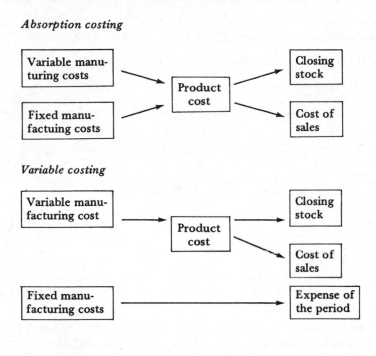

Absorption costing

Variable costing

Exhibit 4(a)

Using absorption costing the overheads are included in the cost of the product and thence in the closing stock value and the cost of sales. With variable costing, the fixed overheads are treated in their entirety as an expense of the period and are not included in the product cost and therefore are not included in the value of the closing stock.

Example   A single product business has the following results for its first accounting period:

Variable costs	=	£4 per unit
Overheads (all fixed)	=	£40,000
Production	=	8000 units
Sales	=	6000 units at £12 each

---

* Which are sometimes referred to as product and period costing, respectively.

On page 63 it was stated that in order to calculate the profit for a period three variables must be known. Two of these, the costs and the revenues, are fixed by business transactions. The third, the value of the closing stock, is a matter of opinion. Obviously the closing physical stock is 2000 units (8000 have been made and 6000 sold).*

Using variable costing the value of the 2000 units which remain unsold would be:

$$2000 \times \text{variable cost per unit} = 2000 \times £4 = £8000$$

Using absorption costing the value of the closing stock would be:

$$2000 \times \text{total cost per unit}† = 2000 \times £9 = £18,000$$

The implication of these differing stock valuations for the measurement of profit is as follows:

Variable costing				£	£
Sales 6000 × £12	=				72,000
Variable cost of production	=	8000 × 4	=	32,000	
Less closing stock		2000 × 4	=	8000	
Variable cost of sales					24,000
Contribution					48,000
Fixed overheads					40,000
		Profit			£8000

Absorption costing					
Sales 6000 × £12					72,000
Variable cost of production	=	8000 × 4	=	32,000	
Overheads				40,000	
				72,000	
Less closing stock		2000 × 9		18,000	
Total cost of sales					54,000
		Profit			£18,000

---

* In this example as the business has just commenced, its opening stock will be zero, and does not need to be brought into the calculations.

†Total cost per unit = variable cost per unit + overheads per unit

$$= £4 + \frac{£40,000}{8000}$$

$$= £4 + £5$$

$$= £9$$

The difference of £10,000 between the profit figures obtained using the two different methods is due to the inclusion of £10,000 of this period's fixed overheads in the value of the closing stock using absorption costing. This results in the £10,000 being carried forward to future periods as an asset, whereas using variable costing the whole of the fixed overhead is written off as an expense of the period.

4.5 A CRITICAL COMPARISON OF ABSORPTION AND DIRECT COSTING

Obviously the differences in stock valuation and hence profit measurement resulting from the use of the approaches of absorption and direct costing in the above section, are caused by differences in the way in which indirect costs are treated. The problems are particularly acute with respect to the treatment of fixed manufacturing overheads. Using absorption costing the fixed overheads are included in the cost of the 'product cost' and therefore in the value of closing stock, whereas direct costing treats the fixed overheads as a 'period cost' so they are expenses in their entirety against revenues of the period and do not form part of the value of the closing stock. This is why the techniques are sometimes referred to as product and period costing.

Both systems have their advocates and the arguments as to their relative merits are largely unresolved.* Those who support the absorption costing approach argue that manufacturing overheads represent the costs of facilities without which production could not take place. They say that failure to include these costs in the value of stock, results in undervaluation of closing stock with the consequent implications for profit measurement. This view is encapsulated by William Ferrara who says that, 'If costs are absolutely necessary for production, they cannot be considered other than true costs of production and thus allocatable to units produced'.[6] He goes on to say that if the system of accounting used does not allow for unit cost figures to fluctuate on the basis of the volume produced and indivisible costs then it will be inaccurate. Elsewhere Ferrara concludes that 'the process of income measurement inherently involves a long-run conceptual framework which demands the inclusion of at least some fixed production costs in inventories'.[7] Whereas those who favour direct or variable costing argue that fixed costs are costs of being in business for a particular period of time rather than costs of the goods produced during that period. In an article which discussed joint-cost allocations, Arthur Thomas concluded 'Joint-cost allocations are arbitrary and serve no positive information or decision purpose . . . We really shouldn't make joint-cost allocations at all'.[8] The issue is essentially

---

* The controversy still exists. However the ASC has made definite proposals for the area as will be seen later.

one concerning the matching of costs or expenses with revenues. Using absorption costing, fixed costs are treated as a cost of the product and are matched with revenues obtained from the sales of the product in whichever time period these take place. With variable or direct costing fixed costs are treated as a cost of the period and are matched with revenues of the period irrespective of how much of the production of the period was sold. In making a judgement as to which seems more appropriate it is worth noting that in developing economies the pattern is for more costs to become relatively fixed.* The ultimate example is perhaps the oil refinery where virtually all costs except raw materials are fixed. The consequence of this is that all stocks, whether raw materials, work-in-progress or finished goods would be valued at the same cost.

However, there are three important criticisms of absorption costing as a method of stock valuation. The first is that it is inevitably arbitrary as will be seen in the following sections. The second is that absorption cost information may be misleading if used by management for the purpose of making short run pricing and output decisions. The third is that it permits the manipulation of profit by altering stock levels. An example best illustrates the third point.

Example   A single product firm has variable costs of £5 per unit and fixed costs of £40,000 in its first year of operation. Its sales are 8000 units at £15 each. Calculate the profit for the year if it produces: (a) 8000; (b) 10,000; (c) 16,000 units.

The profit reported will depend upon the method of costing used.

Absorption costing

Production	8000	10,000	16,000
	£	£	£
Selling price per unit	15	15	15
Variable cost per unit	5	5	5
Fixed costs per unit (Note 1)	5	4	2.5
Total cost per unit	10	9	7.5
Profit per unit	5	6	7.5
Sales volume	8000 units	8000 units	8000 units
Total profit	£40,000	£48,000	£60,000
Closing stock	Nil	£18,000	£60,000
Note 1: Calculated by dividing fixed costs by output			

---

* For example the trend of replacing piece rate schemes with guaranteed weekly wages for direct labour which in effect puts them on par with salaried employees.

Direct costing

Production	8000	10,000	16,000
	£	£	£
Selling price per unit	15	15	15
Variable cost per unit	5	5	5
Profit per unit	10	10	10
Sales volume	8000 units	8000 units	8000 units
Total contribution	£80,000	£80,000	£80,000
Fixed costs	£40,000	£40,000	£40,000
Total profit	£40,000	£40,000	£40,000
Closing stock	Nil	£10,000	£40,000

Clearly, using absorption costing it is possible to increase profits by producing for stock, and things look even better when this is done because the value of the unsold stock carries forward some of the period's fixed costs which enhance its value. Obviously the figures in the example are exaggerated to illustrate the principle, but the principle is nonetheless valid.

As was noted in the introduction to this chapter the requirements of financial accountants and management accountants may differ. James Fremgen wrote some 20 years ago: 'Direct costing has undoubtedly attained the status of an accepted technique of internal reporting to management ... In the area of external reports to stockholders, creditors and other interested outside parties, however, the controversy is in full bloom' and this still applies today. James Fremgen goes on to say that direct costing's utility to management is easy to ascertain, but its usefulness in external reporting is more difficult to define, and he continues 'in practice, the criterion of utility as applied to external reports has come to be interpreted as general acceptance'.[9]

In spite of the obvious and well documented problems associated with absorption costing* it remains the most widely used method in practice, as Exhibit 4(b) which is extracted from the survey of published accounts, 1980 published by the Institute of Chartered Accountants in England and Wales, shows.

David Solomons says that there can be no definite answer to the question of which technique provides the right profit figure, continuing 'The traditional view that profit is the result of a matching process implies that neither of them is clearly wrong, while the alternative view, that profit is the result of a valuation process suggests that neither of them is right'. Professor Solomons concludes 'Generally in normal circumstances, absorption costing

---

* See for example Horngren, C.T. and Sorter, G.H., 'Direct costing for external reporting', *The Accounting Review*, January 1961.

Basis of	Number of Companies			
Valuation	1980–81	1979–80	1978–79	1977–78
Production, works or manufacturing overhead included	146	171	160	155
'Appropriate' overheads included	69	59	67	66
Administrative overheads included in addition to manufacturing overheads	7	5	7	11
All overheads specifically excluded	9	7	5	1
	231	242	239	233
No information given	67	56	59	66
No stocks shown	2	2	2	1
	300	300	300	300

Source: Survey of Published Accounts (over recent years), ICAEW

Exhibit 4(b) Treatment of overheads in cost of stock and work-in-progress

gives a better answer'.[10] However, perhaps P.F. Bourke summarises conclusions that can be drawn from all aspects of this absorption versus direct costing debate when he concludes 'No single concept of cost is valid under all circumstances. We need different cost constructions and income concepts for different purposes. Costs take on a useful meaning only in relation to the specific objectives for which they are accumulated.'[11]

4.6   ABSORPTION COSTING—SOME PRACTICAL DIFFICULTIES

The following sections will consider particular problems associated with the operation of a system of absorption costing.

Errors in Estimates of Fixed Cost and Output

The use of a system of absorption costing involves calculating the total cost of each item of stock. Stated simply, total cost is variable cost plus fixed cost per unit. Fixed cost per unit is found by dividing total fixed costs by total output. Unfortunately neither of the variables involved will be known until the end of the relevant accounting period. Obviously it will be necessary to know costs earlier and therefore it becomes necessary to estimate both fixed cost and output at the beginning of the accounting period to make possible the calculation of a 'predetermined' overhead recovery rate. This rate will then be used to charge overheads to production over the relevant period. Unfortunately, the one thing that can be said with confidence about the estimates is that they will be wrong. The inevitable result is that the amount of overhead charged to production is unlikely to be the same as that which is actually found to have been incurred *ex post*.[12] It is then necessary to decide what is to be done with the balance of over or under applied overhead. Two possibilities exist. Firstly, the over or under applied amount can be written off to the profit and loss account by adjusting the cost of sales. However, as it could be argued that as the over or under applied overhead relates to the goods produced rather than those sold, the balance could be shared out or pro-rated between the work-in-progress, finished goods and cost of sales accounts. In practice most businesses would take the former option, possibly on the grounds of materiality. However, the choice should really be made on the basis of the cause of the over or under applied balance. Essentially if the balance is caused by fundamental errors in the estimates the appropriate response would be to pro-rate. If it is the result of events which are particular to the period in question it should be written off.

The Measurement of Output

As has been seen, in the operation of a system of absorption costing it is necessary to calculate the total cost of the product which entails the determination of fixed cost per unit. This in turn involves dividing total fixed costs by output. In the examples dealt with so far this has simply involved dividing estimated fixed cost by the estimated number of units produced. However, in practice it is not so simple for a number of reasons. A major one is that most organisations do not produce 'units'! Typically most firms produce a variety of products and at any point in time the stocks of what they produce will be at a variety of stages of completion. The measurement of output is a difficult problem. Consider how the question 'how much was produced yesterday?' might be answered for each of the following types of business:

(a) The service department of a large car dealership.
(b) A medium-sized light engineering company producing a variety of components for the car industry.
(c) An oil refinery.

The quest for a single homogeneous measure of output for each of these businesses is a difficult one. However, a homogeneous measure is what is required as a basis for recovering overheads if a system of absorption costing is to be used (fixed cost per unit?). In fact, paradoxically, most organisations are forced to measure output in terms of inputs consumed. Typically, for overhead recovery purposes, output will be measured as direct labour hours worked, direct labour costs incurred or materials processed. Once again an example may clarify the point.

Example A particular business estimates its levels of activity for the next twelve weeks as follows:

Direct labour 48,000 hours (100 employees/working a 40 hour week)
Direct labour cost £96,000 (*average* rate £2 per hour)
Materials processed £64,000
Fixed overheads £144,000

Towards the end of the first four-week period it is necessary to estimate the cost of a batch of 100 special components. Labour required to produce these is highly skilled and paid at £3 per hour. The estimating department has produced the following costs per unit:

Labour 3 hrs at £3	£9
Material	£5
Direct costs	£14

The firm uses absorption costing, and could recover direct overheads as a rate per labour hour, or either a percentage of direct labour cost or direct material cost. The recovery results obtained using each of these three recovery methods would be as follows:

Rate per labour hour

£144,000 ÷ 48,000 hrs = £3 per hour

The total cost per component becomes:

£14 + (3 × £3)   = £23

Percentage of direct labour cost

£144,000 ÷ £96,000   = 150% of labour cost

The total cost per component becomes:

£14 + (150% × 9)   = £27.50

Percentage of direct material cost

£144,000 ÷ £64,000   = 225%

The total cost per component becomes:

£14 + (225% × 5)   = £25.25

But which of these costs is the 'true' cost? Obviously the answer is that they are all equally true! The choice of the measure of output, and hence the basis for overhead recovery, must be made in the light of the nature of the business in which the particular firm is engaged. The problem is that no matter how carefully the choice is made it must inevitably be arbitrary.

Joint Costs

A further problem associated with absorption costing is that whereas certain categories of overheads can reasonably be identified with certain products or processes, others such as factory rates or rent are joint costs. In order to incorporate these joint costs into the cost of the product they must first be allocated to productive cost centres. As with the choice of output measure the basis of allocation of joint costs must inevitably be arbitrary.

4.7 THE VALUATION OF STOCKS IN PRACTICE

This section will consider the valuation of stocks in practice by examining the requirements of accounting standards and company law for this area.

SSAP 9 The Valuation of Stocks and Work-in-progress[13]

The basic requirement of SSAP 9 is that 'The amount at which stocks and work-in-progress . . ., is stated in periodic financial statements should be . . . the lower of costs and net realisable value'. However, as has already been observed this statement, of itself, does not answer all of the problems arising in the valuation of stocks. Further guidance is provided in the introduction to the Standard, the section on the definition of terms and the appendices to the Standard.

Firstly, the standard makes it clear that the comparison between cost and net realisable value should be on an item by item basis or if this is not practical then on the basis of groups of similar items. This is the 'unacceptable off-setting' rule which is to avoid the setting off of foreseeable losses on certain categories of stock against unrealised gains on others. The Companies Act 1981 states 'In determining the aggregate amount of any item the amount of each individual asset or liability that fails to be taken into account shall be determined separately'.[14]

Cost is defined as 'that expenditure which has been incurred in the normal course of business in bringing the product or service to its current condition or location'. In this context cost includes the costs of purchase and costs of conversion. The costs of conversion are defined to include direct costs, production overhead (including those accuring wholly or partly on a time basis, i.e. fixed overheads) and 'other overheads,* if any, attributable in

---

* Ron Paterson points out that 'Since the introduction of SSAP 9, certain companies have consistently declined to include overheads since they believe that it is imprudent to do so'. Paterson, R., 'Stock valuation since SSAP 9', *Accountancy*, 1979.

the particular circumstances of the business to bringing the product or service to its present location and condition'. Therefore any material costs associated with moving stock to a location which enhances its value have to be included.

Thus there is a clear presumption in favour of absorption costing. As has been seen the mechanics of charging overheads, particularly fixed overheads, to production presents difficulties. These problems are considered in greater detail in Appendix I to SSAP 9.*

The particular points made in Appendix I on the allocation of overheads are as follows. Firstly, in considering which costs should be included it is clear that abnormal conversion costs, such as abnormal spoilage, idle time, etc. should be excluded. Obviously this is because these are considered costs of the accounting period and as such they must be written off. Furthermore it is noted that as the costs of general management are not directly related to current production these must be excluded from the valuation of stock. Secondly, in determing the basis of overhead absorption the measure of output should be 'based on the normal level of activity taking one year with another'. There is no guidance as to which measure of output should be used although it is clear that the costs of under utilisation of capacity must be written off in the year in which they are incurred. Finally in considering the relative merits of methods of charging out stock† the criterion to be applied is that the method chosen must provide the fairest possible approximation to actual cost. It should be noted that the LIFO method is unlikely to do this.

One further point is worth making in the context of the requirements of SSAP 9 and this concerns the use of standard costs to value inventory. Many businesses operate standard costing systems and there are obviously considerable advantages in using the standards to value stocks for financial accounting purposes. This would appear to be acceptable with the proviso that the standard costs are reviewed frequently to ensure that they bear a reasonable relationship to actual costs obtained during the period.

Long Term Contracts and Work-in-progress

One of the basic conventions in the preparation of financial statements is the realisation principle. That is that profits are recognised at the point of sale as against during production or on the collection of cash. For firms engaged in industries, such as construction, where contracts are frequently spread over more than one accounting period this can create difficulties. A

---

* This Appendix is for general guidance and does not form part of the SSAP.
† SSAP 9 does not detail methods, although IAS 2, *Valuation and Presentation of Inventories in the Context of the Historic Cost System*, refers to a number of these such as LIFO, FIFO, and the weighted average and also mentions other techniques such as base stock, standard costs and the retail method.

rigid application of the realisation principle for such businesses would distort the profit and loss account in that it would tend to show profits on contracts completed in the previous accounting period rather than the profit on the work done.

To avoid these difficulties SSAP 9 does provide for some recognition of profit on long term contracts and work-in-progress before their completion. However, the prudence concept requires that fairly stringent guidelines are established for this.

Baldly the Standard says:

> The amount at which long term contract work-in-progress is stated in periodic financial statements should be cost plus any attributable profit less any foreseeable losses and progress payments received and receivable. If, however, anticipated losses on individual contracts exceed cost incurred to date less progress payments received and receivable such excesses should be shown separately as provisions.

In determining the amount of attributable profit the standard is adamant that the guiding principle must be prudence. Specifically there must be no attributable profit until the outcome of the project can reasonably be foreseen.

The Valuation of Stock in Inflation Adjusted Accounts

A detailed consideration of the requirements of SSAP 16 *Current Cost Accounting*[15] will be found in Chapter 7. However, it may be appropriate to consider briefly the requirements with respect to the valuation of stock at this juncture. Most readers will be aware that SSAP 16 requires that many businesses should produce accounts in current cost form in which the basis of valuation of assets and for the calculation of expenses is 'value to the business'. In the context of stocks, value to the business is defined as the lower of replacement cost and net realisable value. Under this the charge for stock compared with that obtained using SSAP 9 is simply the substitution of replacement cost for historic cost.

Replacement cost is the cost of replacing stock in the normal course of business either on the date that it was consumed or the balance sheet date. Strictly the cost should be for goods delivered on the valuation date not the order price at the time. To facilitate the calculation of replacement cost the guidance notes to SSAP 16 divide stocks into two broad categories, one where it is not intended to trace the movement of individual items, the other where it is intended to do so.

In the first case (which is most likely to be found in practice) it is recommended that replacement cost is calculated using either relevant indices or standard costs which have been updated by the allocation of the relevant price variances. Following the recommendations of the Sandilands Committee the Central Statistical Office now publishes Price Index Numbers for Current Cost Accounting (PINCCA),[16] to enable these calculations to be made. In the second case it is suggested that the business values its stock by using costs actually being incurred by the business at the valuation date or, for purchased items, the suppliers current price list or by applying appropriate price indices to the cost of individual items of stock.

Stock Valuation and Company Law[17]

The 1981 Companies Act marks a change of direction in UK Company Law. Before the 1981 Act, legislation with respect to published accounts had restricted itself to requirements on the quantity of information to be disclosed. The only qualitative requirement was that accounts should give a 'true and fair' view.* The 1981 Act contains a number of requirements concerning the nature of the information to be disclosed. It identifies two sets of accounting rules: the 'historic cost accounting rules' and the 'alternative accounting rules'. To comply with the requirements of the Act, companies may produce accounts on either basis.

The historic cost rules in effect incorporate the requirements of SSAP 9 in the legislation with two notable exceptions. Following SSAP 9 it states that 'If the net realisable value of any current asset is lower than its purchase price or production cost the amount to be included in respect of that asset shall be the net realisable value' and 'The production cost of an asset shall be determined by adding to the purchase price of the raw materials and consumables used the amount of the costs incurred by the company which are directly attributable the production of that asset', continuing that 'In addition, there may be included in the production cost of an asset a reasonable proportion of the costs incurred by the company which are only indirectly attributable to the production of that asset, but only to the extent that they relate to the period of production'. All of which, in effect, legislates for the requirements of SSAP 9.

Two exceptions to SSAP 9 are to be found in the 1981 Companies Act. Firstly it specifically permits the use of LIFO as well as FIFO and the weighted average method as a method of stock valuation if it appears 'appropriate to the circumstances of the company'. Secondly, even within the context of historic cost accounts, it permits stock to be valued at replacement cost with the proviso that the difference between historic cost and replacement cost should be disclosed by way of a note. Under the alternative accounting rules stock should be valued at current cost and unlike fixed assets, there is no need to include historic cost information for stock by way of a note.

---

* The Companies Act 1981 states 'Every balance sheet of a company so prepared shall give a true and fair view of the state of affairs of the company as at the end of its financial year and every profit and loss account of a company so prepared shall give a true and fair view of the profit and loss of the company for the financial year.' *Companies Act 1981*, Chapter 62, Part 1, page 1.

4.8 CONCLUSIONS

The area of the valuation of stock and work-in-progress is one in which various accounting concepts, such as conservatism and realisation, often exert contradictory influences. Possibly because of this accounting practice is very diverse in this area and many of the methods of valuation originate from the pragmatic considerations of management accountants and decision takers. Recently moves to achieve a greater uniformity of practice have been enshrined in SSAP 9 and the 1981 Companies Act. However, the debate is not ended. Consideration of which members of the 'IFO family or averages is more appropriate for stock valuation purposes will continue. Further debate is also likely on the relative merit of absorption or variable costing for stock valuation in financial statements.

REFERENCES

1. SSAP 9 *Stocks and Work-in-Progress*, Accounting Standards Committee, May 1975.
2. Restatement and Revision of Accounting Research Bulletins, *Accounting Research Bulletin, No. 43*, Committee on Accounting Procedure of the American Institute of Accountants, 1953, Statement 5.
3. *Ibid*, Statement 6.
4. *Ibid*, Statement 4.
5. For example see Edey, H.C., 'The nature of profit', *Accounting and Business Research*, No. 1, Winter 1970.
6. Ferrara, W., 'Overhead costs and income measurement', *The Accounting Review*, January 1961, page 66.
7. Ferrara, W., 'Are direct costs relevant costs?', *The Accounting Review*, August 1961, page 61.
8. Thomas, A.L., 'On joint cost allocations' cost and management, *Journal of the Society of Industrial Accountants of Canada*, September/October 1974, page 21.
9. Fremgen, J.M., 'The direct costing controversy—an identification of issues', *The Accounting Review*, 1964, page 44.
10. Solomons, D., *Divisional Performance: Measurement and Control*, Richard D. Irwin, 1965, page 104.
11. Bourke, P.F., 'What does it cost?', *The Australian Accountant*, April 1969, page 82.
12. For example, see Harvey, M. and Thompson, T., 'The cost-plus pricing fallacy', *Accountancy*, August 1980.
13. SSAP 9 *Stocks and Work-in-Progress*, Accounting Standards Committee, May 1975.
14. *Companies Act 1981*, HMSO 1981, Schedule 1 Part 2, Section 4, paragraph 14.
15. SSAP 16 *Current Cost Accounting*, Accounting Standards Committee, March 1980.
16. *Price Index Numbers for Current Cost Accounting*, Central Statistical Office, published quarterly.
17. The relevant Act is the Companies Act 1981.

QUESTIONS AND DISCUSSION PROBLEMS

1. Why is the valuation of stock taught in both financial and management accounting?

2. IAS 2, *Valuation and Presentation of Inventories in the Context of the Historical Cost System*, says 'Several different formulas with widely different effects are in current use for the purpose of assigning costs, including the following:

   (a) First-in, first-out (FIFO)
   (b) Weighted average cost
   (c) Last-in, first-out (LIFO)
   (d) Base Stock
   (e) Specific identification
   (f) Next-in, first-out (NIFO)
   (g) Latest purchase price' (para 13)

   and 'Techniques such as the standard cost method of valuing products or the retail method of valuing merchandise may be used for convenience if they approximate consistently the results that would be obtained (using the lower of historic cost and net realisable value)' (para 27). Explain six of these nine methods used to value stock. Briefly compare the effect on profits and stock values for each of the methods dealt with.

3. The selection of either LIFO or FIFO as the accounting policy from the accounting bases available for stock valuation purposes will have an effect on reported profit and the balance sheet values of stock for the same period and entity. Use a numerical example to illustrate these differences and explain the reason for them in terms that a layman would be able to understand.

4. What do you understand by the term 'period or product' costing and how does this relate to the absorption vs variable costing debate?

5. In relation to SSAP 9 *Stocks and work-in-progress*, explain: the cost of conversion; the composition of stocks and work-in-progress; unacceptable off-setting; and matching.

6. Explain the essential difference between the 'historic cost accounting rules' and the 'alternative accounting rules' allowed by the 1981 Companies Act with respect to stock valuation and discuss how the alternative rules might be applied in practice.

7. The accounting policies used by the four PLCs to value their stock appear on pp. 186–191. Compare and critically discuss the methods disclosed. Do you feel that the disclosures made would be adequate in helping you to appraise this aspect of each firm's balance sheet? If not, why not?

CHAPTER 5

The Depreciation Problem

5.1 INTRODUCTION

The problems associated with depreciation arise from the definition of profit adopted by accountants and the postulates, conventions and principles used in measuring it. Accounting profit is defined as revenues minus expenses. Revenues are increases in the assets of the business which result from sale of either stock in trade or the services that the business is in existence to provide. The expenses matched with the revenues in the determination of accounting profit are those reductions in the value of assets incurred in generating the revenues.

Many of the accounting problems associated with the measurement of profit stem from the need to make periodic reports on the progress of the business. Because of the necessity to define accounting periods, the allocation of profit over the life of the enterprise to these discrete time periods becomes a source of considerable difficulty.

Depreciation is necessitated by the fact that certain categories of expenditure called capital expenditures, result in the creation of assets that are classified as fixed in financial statements. Such assets are capable of generating revenues over a number of periods. In consequence it becomes necessary to spread the cost of fixed assets over the accounting periods during which part of their value is used up. It is this process of spreading costs over a number of accounting periods that is called depreciation.

In studying the problems of depreciation it is as well to remember that the definition of profit from which it arises is not the only possible definition. A system of cash flow accounting in which profit is thought of simply as net cash flow has perhaps an even greater antiquity than the system now used. Furthermore, the case for using such a system of cash flow accounting does not lie exclusively in its antiquity. Some writers on accounting matters, notably Professor Gerald Lawson,[1] have made cogent and extremely persuasive arguments for the adoption of cash flow accounting as an alternative to the accruals system. Not least among the advantages of such a proposal is that it would resolve the problems of depreciation. Furthermore, in considering the appropriateness of various depreciation proposals it is important to remember the purposes of profit measurement. Paraphrasing Professor Harold Edey, a successful firm is one that is able to maintain and increase its dividend payments to shareholders.[2] To do this the successful firm needs to ensure that on balance its long run cash flows are positive. Profit is simply a surrogate measure of this ability and its success as a surrogate depends upon the relationship between the firm's ability to maintain positive net cash flows and the profit figure reported.

5.2   CONCEPTS OF DEPRECIATION

Over the years a number of different approaches have been taken in considering the nature of depreciation. Louis Goldberg says that the word 'depreciation' is used in several senses in accounting and business literature. These include: a fall in price; physical deterioration; a fall in value; or an allocation of cost.[3] This indicates the variety of approaches that have been, and can be, taken in the analysis of the area.

Over the years, the development of theory in the area has centred on three major points, namely the role of depreciation

(a) as a valuation technique;
(b) in helping to retain cash in the business for the replacement of assets;
(c) in enabling the matching of that part of an asset consumed to the generation of the revenues for a period.

However, the first two of these provide popular misconceptions of the idea of depreciation.

Depreciation as a Valuation Technique

This misconception can be traced back to Roman times when a Roman writer, Vitruvius, recorded rules for valuation based upon the deduction of one eightieth* of cost for each year that a party-wall stood to obtain its remaining value.[4] Such a view of depreciation as a valuation technique held great force to the early 1970s until when it was still widely, but mistakenly, believed that the written down or book value of an asset (i.e. its historic cost less accumulated depreciation) provided a measure of the asset's current value.† Inflation has made it clear that this is unlikely to be the case.

---

* The 'straight line' method of depreciation was being advocated.
† For example Erich Helfert says 'The formal adjustment of value is called "depreciation" in the case of assets subject to physical wear and tear (i.e. fixed assets). Thus on the balance sheet of companies we find fixed asset values that consist of three elements: the original cost of the asset, the depreciation, depletion or amortisation accumulated against

It is truly said that depreciation is a 'process of allocation not valuation',* for depreciation is a process of allocating the historic cost of an asset over its useful life.[5] Notwithstanding the difficulties of deciding on the process of allocation to be used, the result of that process can only approximate to current value when the underlying valuation method used is a good measure for the value of the asset to the business, and the judgements made in the model about the asset's useful life and any likely residual value ultimately turn out to approximate to the truth. Therefore since the historic cost, on which conventional accounts are based, only coincidentally reflects value to the business then the written down value can also only coincidentally reflect current value.

Depreciation Provides for the Replacement of Assets

Although this concept of depreciation is rarely found in professional or academic accounting publications it is still to be occasionally found in general business and other non-accounting publications,†Professor William Baxter says that 'You will sooner or later meet the view that the aim of depreciation policy is to save up the money needed to replace the asset after its death'.[6] He continues that 'A corollary to this view is that, if we are to abandon historical cost and to turn to inflation accounting, the right depreciation charge for any year must be a function of replacement price'.[7] This belief presumably stems from the simple examples used to illustrate bookkeeping for depreciation.

Example   A firm dealing entirely in cash acquires a single fixed asset for £2500, the initial cash having been provided by the owner. The machine is estimated to have a life of five years and a zero terminal value at the end of that period. Revenues are expected to be £3000 per annum and costs of operating the asset (other than depreciation) are expected to be £1500 per annum.

---

it over time, and the net of the two amounts, the so-called "book value".' However he goes on to say 'The last represents the net recorded value of an asset owned by a company, and often bears only a cursory resemblance to what might be the true or fair economic value of the asset'. Helfert, E. *Valuation: Concepts and Practices*, Wadsworth 1966, pp. 29, 30.

* For example Benjamin Newman and Martin Mellman say '*Depreciation-allocation versus valuation*. Fixed assets should be depreciated over their economically useful lives. As a process of allocation and not of valuation, depreciation designed to achieve proper matching of cost and revenue rather than a balance sheet valuation suggestive of resale or realisable values. The focus is on fair income determination'. Newman, B., Mellman, M. *Accounting Theory*, ACPA Review, Wiley 1967, p. 90.

† For example Alan Fiber writing on retailing says 'depreciation on equipment should be charged against gross profit. The shop is a going concern and equipment has to be replaced periodically if it is to continue. Finance must be available for this at appropriate times, which means setting aside a proportion of the replacement cost so that it is spread evenly over the life of the equipment'. Fiber, A., *The Complete Guide to Retail Management*, Penguin 1972, p. 67.

The balance sheet at the start of the life of the business will be as follows:

Balance sheet as at t_0

Assets employed	
Fixed asset	£2500
Financed by	
Owner's equity	£2500

Profit and loss account for year ending t_1

		£
Sales		3000
Less Operating costs	1500	
Depreciation	500	2000
		£1000

If all profits are paid out as dividends the balance sheet at the end of the first year will appear as:

Balance sheet as at t_1

	£	£
Assets employed		
Fixed assets at cost	2500	
Less accumulated depreciation	500	2000
Cash		500
		£2500
Financed by		
Owner's equity		£2500

It is clear that by repeating the above process five times the balance sheet at the end of the fifth year will be as follows:

Balance sheet as at t_5

	£	£
Assets employed		
Fixed assets at cost	2500	
Less accumulated depreciation	2500	0
Cash		2500
		£2500
Financed by		
Owner's equity		£2500

The process of depreciation has converted the fixed asset back into cash over its useful life. However, the impression that by charging depreciation the replacement of the asset has been provided for is false. This is so for two reasons. Firstly, over the life of the asset assuming unchanged technology, the replacement cost of the asset is likely to rise if price levels increase. Since the depreciation provisions are based on the historic cost of the asset the amount provided by depreciation is unlikely to be sufficient to replace the asset. Secondly, and perhaps more importantly, the example above is oversimplified in that it has been assumed that all the transactions were for cash. In the event this is unlikely to be the case, for during the life of the asset the cash balance is likely to become invested in other fixed assets, stock, debtors and so on. Thus it becomes extremely unlikely that the depreciation provisions will be matched by cash at the bank or even in the form of liquid assets. Ensuring that there is sufficient cash available to replace assets as and when it becomes necessary is a problem of cash management rather than depreciation.* This is because replacement decisions are an investment decision which is separate from any decision about depreciation policy. Thus what depreciation is really doing is to ensure that funds equal to the depreciation of an asset in a period are not distributed and are retained in the business to maintain its asset strength. However this process says nothing about the form in which these funds are to be retained.

Depreciation as a Matching Concept

The Accounting Standards Committee defines depreciation in SSAP 12: *Accounting for Depreciation*, in the context of the historic cost accounting convention† as:

> the measure of the wearing out, consumption or other loss of value of a fixed asset whether arising from use, effluxion of time or obsolescence through technology and market changes.[8]

This clearly confirms the technique, at least for practical purposes as one of matching costs with revenues. Elsewhere, SSAP 12 emphasises that this matching must be carried out in a systematic and fair way. Professor Baxter suggests that depreciating assets could be looked upon as stores purchased in bulk.[9] He suggests that because machines are classed as fixed assets and stocks as current assets this may cause them to be looked upon as requiring different concepts to deal with them, whereas the fact is that although they are classified differently they both require the use of the matching concept. It may help an understanding of this concept of depreciation if a fixed asset

---

* Which is the point Alan Fiber has overlooked in his advice to retailers cited in the footnote on page 85.
† The ASC 'confirms' that their definition is equally applicable to times of stable or changing prices by repeating it in paragraph 4 of the Guidance Notes to SSAP 16, issued March 1981.

is looked at as a store of service potential. However, in practice there may be problems associated with trying to use this matching concept. What if there is no revenue? Or what if all the cost of an asset which still has some service potential has already been matched with revenues of some previous period? The remainder of this chapter will concentrate on the problems associated with depreciation as a technique for matching costs against the revenues they are incurred in generating.

5.3　DEPRECIATION IN CONVENTIONAL ACCOUNTS

In order to calculate annual depreciation charges for matching purposes in the preparation of historic cost accounts, three pieces of information are necessary. These are, the initial cost of the asset, its estimated life and its terminal value at the end of that life. It is worth noting that of these three components only one, initial cost, can be objectively determined. The other two depend upon subjective estimates. Hence even HCA depreciation cannot claim to be truly objective. In measuring the cost of an asset it is usual to include all items of cost necessary to get the asset installed and working properly. Therefore, delivery and installation charges would normally be included in the depreciable amount,* this being defined as that amount which is to be depreciated.

Difficulties in Estimating the Life of an Asset

The estimation of an asset's life presents rather more substantial difficulties. As Professor Baxter notes in his major work on depreciation[10] the concept of life is borrowed from the biological sciences. For a living organism the extent of its life is determined by an internal change within the organism that we call death. This change is, of course, not applicable to inanimate business assets. The duration of useful life for a business asset is determined by its economic viability. A machine's physical life, i.e. the period until it literally falls to pieces, can be extended almost indefinitely by expenditure on maintenance, repairs and the replacement of parts as they wear out. However, a point must inevitably be reached at which this operation ceases to make economic sense. The cost in terms of lost production time, due to inactivity while repairs are being carried out together with the cost of the repairs themselves, means that at some point it becomes cheaper to replace the machine. Similarly, a business asset's life may be brought to an untimely

---

* ED 18 *Current Cost Accounting* which was subsequently replaced by ED 24, defined 'depreciable amount' as fixed asset which should be subject to depreciation. Neither SSAP 12 nor SSAP 16 provide a definition of depreciable amount. However, IAS 4 *Depreciation Accounting* provides precise definition of the term, saying that the *depreciable amount* of a depreciable asset is its historic cost or other amount substituted for historic cost in the financial statement, less the estimated residual value.'

end by either the development of superior equipment which renders it obsolete or the end of the product life cycle of the item the machine was acquired to produce.

Therefore when an asset's useful life is discussed in terms of the calculation of depreciation charges what is meant is its *economic life*. This in turn will depend upon the cost associated with maintaining the asset as an operating physical entity, the technological developments and the market conditions for the final product. Of these the physical, engineering life of the asset can usually be fairly accurately estimated, whereas the estimation of the other two presents great difficulty. A second consideration is whether the life of the asset is constrained by *time* or by *use*.

The lives of some assets are solely a function of time—an extreme example would be a lease on a piece of real estate. If a lease is granted for ten years, its life as an asset is ten years whether or not any use whatsoever is made of the property concerned. At the other end of the spectrum the life of some assets depends entirely on the use to which they are put. The coal contained within a coal mine is a good example—the life of the asset, the coal mine, depends entirely on the rate at which the coal is mined, which is influenced by the costs of operation and the price of coal.

Needless to say, most business assets fall between these two extremes. Consider, for example, a decision as to the optimal life of a motor car. The decision to replace a motor car will presumably depend jointly on its running costs and its resale value. Typically, running costs (notably repairs and maintenance) depend upon mileage or use made of the vehicle. For example, new brakes may be required every 20,000 miles and a new clutch every 30,000 and so on. However, the value of second hand motor cars is determined largely by their age. Hence in deciding on the optimal replacement policy for a motor car the decision maker is confronted by a combination of time-life and use-life and must possibly make an arbitrary decision as to which will be used in determining the appropriate depreciation charges.*

Treatment of Repair Costs

In the calculation of depreciation charges a further difficulty arises in the treatment of repair and maintenance expenditure. Should this be treated as an expense in the year in which the expenditure is made or should it be included as part of the capital cost of the asset, because of the element of repair costs which goes to maintain the value of the asset? An example may clarify the point.

---

* It is interesting to note that *Glass's Guide to Used Car Values*, which the motor trade uses as a guide to second hand car prices, bases the prices shown for second hand cars mainly on age (time) but also takes some cognisance of mileage (use) by quoting prices for popular models based on both average and higher mileage. Thus it tries to combine both aspects in determining the price of second hand cars within the trade.

Example Suppose an organisation procures a new lorry for £24,000. Its past experience with vehicles of the same type suggests that they should be retained for five years, after which time the vehicle ceases to be sufficiently reliable for the purposes required. Furthermore, it is expected that at the end of its five-year use the lorry will have a resale value of £6000. Also, normal servicing costs are anticipated to be £1200 per year with additional major overhauls costing £3000 during the second and fourth years. However, after the event, in addition to these expected costs there has been an unforeseen serious breakdown during the third year which costs £2700 to rectify. In calculating the depreciation charge how should the firm deal with the repair costs? Clearly, the yearly recurring service charges present no difficulty. Whether these are added up and averaged out over the asset's life, or charged for directly as they are incurred, the total annual expense of operating the vehicle will be the same. However, dealing with the other three items is more difficult.

The relevant cash flows* associated with the operation of the lorry are as follows:

Year (all figures in £s)	0	1	2	3	4	5
Cost	24,000					
Resale receipts						(6000)
Normal annual servicing costs		1200	1200	1200	1200	1200
Expected overhauls			3000		3000	
Unexpected repairs				2700		

If the business decides to pursue a policy of charging all maintenance expense in the year during which it is incurred its annual depreciation will be (£24,000 − 6000) ÷ 5 or £3600 per annum. The amount charged as an expense against revenue in each year will be £3600, £6600, £6300, £6600 and £3600 respectively. Assuming operating revenues and other operating expenses are constant over the five-year period, the annual profit figure will be affected accordingly. Although this approach is the most common practice found in business it hardly seems satisfactory. Bearing in mind the joint purposes of profit measurement as a measure of efficiency and as a guide to the distribution or consumption of funds it would appear that the business has been operated more successfully in years 1 and 5 than in years

---

* As the normal servicing costs are revenue expenditure and clearly regular they can (and in this case will) be omitted from the depreciation analysis, although if, as in practice, they fluctuate they could be included.

2, 3 or 4 and furthermore that year 3 was a better year than either of 2 or 4. Obviously this can hardly be the case.

Alternatively, if the business decides at the outset of the vehicles' life to capitalise estimated overhaul expenditure the annual charge will be (£24,000 + 3000 + 3000 − 6000) ÷ 5 or £4800 per year. The resultant charges against revenues will be £4800, £4800, £7500, £4800 and £4800 respectively, and profit will be affected accordingly. In terms of usefulness of the profit figure, this approach is clearly preferable. Even a cursory glance at the profit figures would appear to indicate that years 1, 2, 4 and 5 were similar although something unfortunate appears to have happened in year 3.

A final and perhaps extreme alternative would be to capitalise all overhaul and repair cost whether anticipated or not. In this case the depreciation charges would be (£24,000 + 3000 + 3000 − 6000) ÷ 5 or £4800 for years 1 and 2 but when the unexpected breakdown occurred depreciation would be reappraised to [4800 + (2700 ÷ 3)] or £5700 during years 3, 4 and 5. However, the resulting profit figures would appear to be less helpful than those under the second alternative.

5.4 CALCULATION OF CONVENTIONAL DEPRECIATION CHARGES

Having decided on the amount of the cost to be spread and the life of the asset over which this cost has to be allocated, the next problem is to determine the basis of allocation. The reader is no doubt familiar with simple depreciation techniques which fall into the two categories of straight line and accelerated depreciation. As a reminder, these will be briefly discussed.

Straight Line Depreciation (D_s)

This involves a constant annual charge and is arrived at by subtracting the terminal or scrap value (S) from the historic cost of the asset (C) and dividing the resultant figure by its estimated life (N), i.e. notationally

$$D_s = \frac{(C - S)}{N}$$

Example Information on asset: cost £10,000; terminal value £1000; useful life 5 years.

$$\text{Annual depreciation charge} = \frac{10,000 - 1000}{5} = £1800 \text{ per annum.}$$

The schedule of depreciation charges and net book value over the period, leaving a residual of £1000 is as follows:

Year	1	2	3	4	5
Net book value at start of period	10,000	8200	6400	4600	2800
Depreciation for period	1800	1800	1800	1800	1800

The profile of the remaining book value of the asset and its annual depreciation charge is shown graphically in Exhibit 5(a).

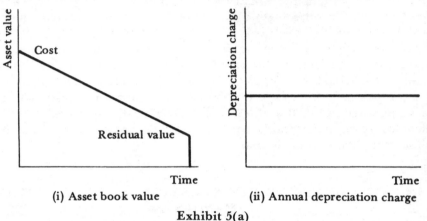

(i) Asset book value   (ii) Annual depreciation charge

Exhibit 5(a)

Straight line depreciation: book value and depreciation charge profiles

Accelerated Depreciation

This involves charging higher amounts for depreciation in the earlier years of the asset's life. Perhaps this is for one of two reasons:

   (a) To compensate for the rising repair costs in later years, thereby making the combined charge of these two against revenues over the life of the asset more constant. This is because one component of this charge (repairs) increases as the other (depreciation) decreases.

   (b) To more nearly approximate differential loss of value in earlier compared to later years.

Two such techniques for accelerated depreciation will be described.

Reducing Balance Method or Fixed Percentage of Declining Balance (D_p)

Using this technique a fixed percentage of the written down value of the asset at the start of a period is subtracted from the value of the asset and charged as an expense in the profit and loss account. Using the data from the example above and a rate of 37 per cent for the fixed percentage to be applied in the computation of the depreciation charges, the schedule of depreciation charges and net book values over the period, leaving a residual of approximately £1000, is as follows:

Year	1	2	3	4	5
Net book value at start of period	10,000	6300	3969	2500	1575
Depreciation for period (37%)	3700	2331	1469	925	582

The percentage to apply (D_p) which exactly depreciates the asset by the end of its estimated life is:

$$D_p = \left(1 - \sqrt[N]{\frac{S}{C}}\right) \times 100\%$$

The profile of the remaining book value of the asset and its annual depreciation charge is shown graphically in Exhibit 5(b).

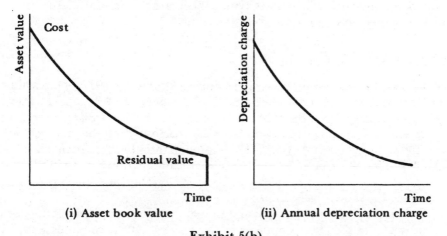

(i) Asset book value   **(ii) Annual depreciation charge**

Exhibit 5(b)
Reducing balance depreciation: book value and depreciation charge profiles

Sum of the Year's Digits Method

This method derives from North America, and although little used in the UK* is creating greater interest because of the growth and spread of US based multinational enterprises.

Using this approach the digits of each year of the expected life of the asset

---

* The sum of the years digits may have become more important recently in that it is one of the acceptable methods in ED 29 *Accounting for leases and hire purchase contracts* (Accounting Standards Committee, October 1981).

are summed and divided into the asset's historic cost minus its terminal value. Using the data from previous examples, the sum of the year's digits is $5 + 4 + 3 + 2 + 1 = 15$ and the depreciation factor becomes £9000 ÷ 15 or £600. The annual charge is then simply found by multiplying the digits for the remaining life expectancy of the asset by the depreciation factor. Thus the depreciation for the first year becomes 600 × 5 (the digit for the asset's remaining life expectancy) which is £3000, year two 600 × 4 = £2400, and so on. The schedule of depreciation charges and net book values is as follows:

Year	1	2	3	4	5
Net book value at start of period	10,000	7000	4600	2800	1600
Depreciation for period	3000	2400	1800	1200	600

The profiles for depreciation charges provided in the exhibits are particularly interesting as they highlight the effect of the method used on both book value of assets in the balance sheet and the annual charges made to an organisation's profit and loss account.

Methods Used in Practice

SSAP 12 on depreciation was issued during December 1977. This will be considered in more detail in Section 5.8 of this chapter. Appropriate information extracted from the ICAEW's *Survey of Published Accounts* for recent years shows a strong trend towards the disclosure of the depreciation method used even before SSAP 12 became mandatory for financial statements prepared for periods beginning on or after 1 January 1978. This is no doubt because of the influence of SSAP 2 *Disclosure on Accounting Policies*. This trend is shown in Exhibit 5(c).

The most recent information shows that straight line depreciation was used by 265 of the 300 companies in the survey. Of the remaining 35, 21 used the reducing balance or a combination of methods and 14 gave no explicit statement of the method used.

5.5   FURTHER CONSIDERATION OF SIMPLE DEPRECIATION TECHNIQUES

It has been suggested that a helpful way of thinking of depreciation is to imagine it as the periodic payments that a firm would have to make for the use of an asset if it rented it.* If a firm made regular rental payments for the

---

* Earlier in this chapter it was seen that Professor Baxter suggested a different approach of looking at a depreciating asset as stores purchased in bulk.

Basis adopted for most assets	Number of companies			
	1981/2	1975/6	1974/5	1968/9
Straight line	265	226	222	65
Declining balance		3	6	3
Mixture of both techniques	21	33	29	16
	286	262	257	84
Method not disclosed	14	38	43	216
	300	300	300	300

Source: Survey of Published Accounts (over recent years) ICAEW

Exhibit 5(c)
Listed company practice with respect to depreciation

assets that it used there would be no depreciation difficulty as the hire expense would be readily ascertainable as annual payments to set against revenues. The problem comes because an asset is purchased rather than hired and the requisite payments are not made in regular monthly or yearly payments and even in the case of hire purchase payments these do not extend over the life of the asset.

In order to arrive at a profit measure it is conventional to try, even if only crudely, to smooth the lumpy payments made for an asset and repairs to it over its life. The cash flows associated with an asset over its life are the initial cost, the terminal value and periodic repair and maintenance costs. Where the post-acquisition cash flows are constant, i.e. repair costs etc. which are fairly equal amounts in each period, they do not need to be smoothed. They can be disregarded in the calculation of depreciation and charged direct to the revenue in the years in which the payments are made [Exhibit 5(d)(i)]. In such cases where it is simply a constant annual depreciation charge that is needed a straight line approach to depreciation would be appropriate.

However, if post-acquisition cash flows deteriorate, i.e. repair costs, etc. increase as time passes, which is generally the situation in the real world, then things become rather different. If a straight line approach is used in these circumstances the total annual charge for the use of the machine would increase [Exhibit 5(d)(ii)]. In order to avoid this and achieve the even charges against revenues, which ideally should be sought for, there are two options open. Firstly, one of the accelerated depreciation techniques could be used so that the falling depreciation charges would complement the rising repair costs to give an approximation of the constant annual charge desired. Exhibit 5(e) shows the result of this. Secondly, all extraordinary or irregular post-acquisition cash flows could be capitalised and included in the calculation of the straight line depreciation provision. On

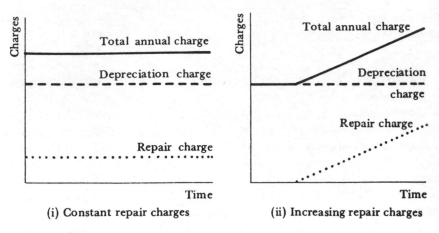

(i) Constant repair charges   (ii) Increasing repair charges

Exhibit 5(d)
Straight line depreciation plus repairs: total charge profile

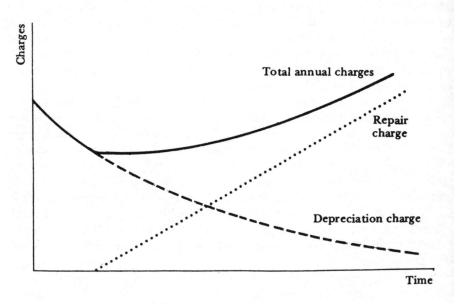

Exhibit 5(e)
Total charges for reducing balance depreciation and repairs

balance this latter approach would seem easier and more likely to achieve the desired result of an even stream of charges against revenue.

As can be seen from Exhibit 5(c) the most common depreciation method used in practice is the straight line method. Furthermore most firms write off repair costs in the year in which they are incurred. A justification of this approach could be that where it is applied to a group of assets, such as a fleet of vehicles, the cancelling out effect is such that it approximates closely to the theoretically superior methods used above.

5.6 DEPRECIATION ALLOWING FOR COST OF CAPITAL

A shortcoming of the depreciation techniques discussed so far is that they take no cognisance of the time value of money,* that is they make no allowance for interest on capital employed which can cause comparison problems. For example, if depreciation methods that recognise the cost of capital are used in situations where assets could be financed in different ways this helps to make the profits of these alternatives more comparable, and in turn an analysis of the options becomes easier.[11]

Example A firm with a single asset acquired at a cost of £10,000 deals entirely for cash. Its profit (excluding depreciation) is £4000 per year. The firm is able to invest all its cash balances to earn interest at a rate of 10 per cent. The asset is expected to have a life of four years. The firm pays out the whole of its net profit (after depreciation) as a dividend.

If the firm charges depreciation on a straight line basis and invests all its cash balances in secondary assets to earn interest at 10 per cent the cash flow pattern over the asset's life will be as follows:

Year (all figures in £'s)	1	2	3	4
Written down value of asset	10,000	7,500	5,000	2,500
Depreciation	2,500	2,500	2,500	2,500
Secondary assets (see note)	Nil	2,500	5,000	7,500
Operating profit	4,000	4,000	4,000	4,000
Interest on secondary assets	Nil	250	500	750
Total profit	4,000	4,250	4,500	4,750
Less depreciation	2,500	2,500	2,500	2,500
Dividends (all paid out)	£1,500	£1,750	£2,000	£2,250

Note: Purchased with funds retained in the business through depreciation

The apparent increase in total profit shown above is entirely due to interest on the secondary assets.† This provides a false picture and moves away from the desired pattern of even annual charges against revenues.

---

* For an explanation of this idea refer to Appendix A in Chapter 2.

† Professor Baxter introduces this term. Basically he says that as depreciation leads to lower profit figures, which cause smaller distributions and the accumulation of new assets, it is convenient to refer to the original asset as the *primary* asset, and the new asset obtained using depreciation retained funds, the *secondary* asset. See Baxter, W.T. *Depreciation*, Sweet & Maxwell 1971, pp. 83 and 124.

There are several techniques available which enable interest in depreciation calculations to be taken into account to overcome the problem outlined above. Two of the more important are the sinking fund and the annuity methods which will be explained in relation to the above example.

Sinking Fund Method

Using this method the sum that must be invested annually to accumulate with interest at 10 per cent to £10,000 at the end of four years is calculated. Using discount tables* this is found to be £2155 which accumulates as follows:

Year (all figures in £'s)	1	2	3	4
Investment	2,155	4,310	6,681	9,289
Interest	Nil	216	453	713
Total	£2,155	£4,526	£7,134	£10,002†

†Difference due to rounding

The bookkeeping procedure here is to debit the profit and loss account with the necessary investment of £2155 per year as depreciation and to credit the asset account. At the same time cash is invested in the requisite secondary assets to earn the 10 per cent, cash being credited and the investment account debited. The interest earned by the secondary asset is credited to the asset account and debited to the investment account. It does not appear in the profit and loss account at all. Continuing the example, the profit and dividend performance would be shown as follows:

Year (all figures in £'s)	1	2	3	4
Written down value of asset	10,000	7,845	5,474	2,866
Less depreciation	2,155	2,155	2,155	2,155
	7,845	5,690	3,319	711
Less interest on Investment Fund	—	216	453	713
	£7,845	£5,474	£2,866	£(2)‡
Operating profit	4,000	4,000	4,000	4,000
Less depreciation	2,155	2,155	2,155	2,155
Dividend	£1,845	£1,845	£1,845	£1,845

‡Difference due to rounding

---

* An explanation of the mechanics of discounting for those not familiar with it will be found in Wright, M.G. *Discounted Cash Flow*, McGraw-Hill 1967, Chapter 2 'Present Value' and Chapter 5 'DCF Problems and Solutions'.

A criticism often levied at this method is that it understates the depreciation charged in arriving at operating profit because this has been reduced to take account of the interest on the secondary assets. It is argued that this interest should properly be thought of as a return to the financial management of the business. To overcome this criticism, interest could be shown as a revenue item resulting through financing decisions rather than as a reduction in operating expenses.

Annuity Method

It has been suggested that the annuity method is to be preferred to deal with the effect of the cost of capital in depreciation situations because it makes this treatment of interest more explicit by showing the interest payments in the profit and loss account.

Using the annuity method, the annual annuity equivalent of the sum invested is worked out, i.e. the regular payments over the life of the asset that discount back to the same present value as the original cost of the asset. It is this amount that is then charged as depreciation in arriving at operating profit. The interest element in the depreciation charge is debited to the asset and credited to profit and loss account. Similarly, interest on the secondary assets is credited to the profit and loss account and debited to the appropriate secondary asset account. Using this approach the relevant asset values and income schedule from the previous example become:

Year (all figures in £'s)	1	2	3	4
Written down value of asset	10,000	7,845	5,475	2,867
Interest element in depreciation charge	1,000	785	547	287
	11,000	8,630	6,022	3,154
Less depreciation	3,155	3,155	3,155	3,155
	£7,845	£5,475	£2,867	£(1)*
Operating profit	4,000	4,000	4,000	4,000
Interest in depreciation charge	1,000	785	547	287
Interest from secondary assets *	—	216	453	713
	5,000	5,001	5,000	5,000
Depreciation	3,155	3,155	3,155	3,155
Dividend	£1,845	£1,846*	£1,845	£1,845

*Difference due to rounding

Clearly, the resultant profit and dividend figures are the same under both methods; however, the explicit treatment of interest in the annuity approach makes it preferred to the sinking fund method.[12]

5.7 DEPRECIATION AND CHANGING PRICE LEVELS

Rising price levels present problems in every aspect of financial and managerial accounting and depreciation is no exception. It seems anomalous that depreciation provisions should be made when the value of an asset is likely to be appreciating. However, the anomaly if it exists, is superficial and stems from the misconception regarding depreciation as a valuation concept. This point has been discussed previously. Since depreciation is the spreading of the cost of an asset over its useful life a necessary and sufficient condition for depreciation to be charged is that the asset has a finite life.

Where an asset has appreciated in value the appropriate amendments to the gross asset value (by adjustments to its original cost) and the accumulated depreciation so far must be made and shown in the balance sheet. Thereafter these adjusted figures, i.e. the current value, will be spread over the asset's remaining useful life. This procedure is similar in principle whether current purchasing power or current cost accounting are used to adjust the accounts for inflation. However, the calculations involved will obviously vary for the different methods. An example shows this.

Example A business acquired a 20-year lease on some property five years ago at a cost of £20,000. Its gross current replacement cost (i.e. the cost of a full 20-year lease for a similar property today) is £40,000. Its net current replacement cost (i.e. that part of the lease's gross current replacement cost yet unexpired) is £30,000. Since the asset was acquired the retail prices index has increased by 50 per cent. The calculation of the appropriate depreciation provisions, using different accounting systems, is as follows:

(a) *Historic Cost Accounting (HCA)*

Balance sheet as at t_5

	£
Asset at cost	20,000
Less Accumulated depreciation	5,000
Written down value	£15,000

Profit and Loss account for period ending t_5

Anticipated depreciation expense	£1,000

(b) *Current Purchasing Power Accounting (CPP)*

Balance sheet as at t_s

	Unadjusted (HCA) £		Adjusted (CPP) £
Cost	20,000		30,000
Less Accumulated depreciation	5,000	$\times \dfrac{150}{100}$	7,500
Written down value	£15,000		£22,500

Profit and Loss account for period ending t_s

Anticipated depreciation expense	£1500

The increase in written down value is automatically dealt with in the balance sheet by revaluing the owner's equity and calculating the gains and losses on monetary items.

(c) *Current Cost Accounting (CCA)*

Balance sheet as at t_s

	Unadjusted (HCA) £	Adjusted (CCA)	£
Cost	20,000	Gross current replacement cost	40,000
Depreciation	5,000	Depreciation	10,000
		Net current replacement	
Written down value	£15,000	cost	£30,000

Profit and Loss account for period ending t_s

Anticipated depreciation expense	£2,000

The alteration in asset value is brought about by calculating what is termed 'backlog' depreciation* which is subtracted from the revaluation

---

* ED 18 *Current Cost Accounting* defined backlog depreciation as 'the additional amount required to raise the sum of the accumulated depreciation at the beginning of any accounting year and the charge for depreciation for that year to the amount required to equal the difference between the gross and the net current replacement cost of an asset at the end of the year'.

surplus. The treatment of the resultant figure, i.e. the gross revaluation surplus less the backlog depreciation differs under (P)SSAP 7 and SSAP 16. (P)SSAP 7 showed it as a credit in the appropriation section of the profit and loss account. In SSAP 16 it is credited to a special reserve in the balance sheet called the current cost reserve (CCR). Backlog depreciation is found by comparing the accumulated depreciation provisions made so far with the depreciation necessary to reduce the gross current replacement cost to net current replacement cost. In this example the accumulated depreciation to date has been £5000 whereas the difference between gross current replacement cost and net current replacement cost is £10,000. Hence backlog depreciation is £5000. The revaluation surplus is found by comparing historic cost with the gross current replacement cost, i.e. in this case it is £40,000 − £20,000 = £20,000. The net transfer to the credit of the appropriation account or the CCR is therefore £15,000. Henceforth annual depreciation expense will be based on the amount necessary to spread the net current replacement cost of the asset over its remaining useful life. In this example the depreciation charge, assuming no further inflation, will be £2,000 per year. However, if inflation continued during the next period this would necessitate the calculation of a further sum for the backlog depreciation referred to as 'prior years' backlog depreciation as well as the 'current' backlog depreciation.

5.8 DEPRECIATION AND THE ACCOUNTING STANDARDS COMMITTEE AND INTERNATIONAL STANDARDS

The views of the ASC on depreciation are to be found in SSAP 12 *Accounting for Depreciation* issued in December 1977.* Many of the principles contained in SSAP 12 are equally applicable to historic cost, current purchasing power and current cost accounting.

The SSAP 12 definition of depreciation will be found on page 87 and enshrined the matching concept. In the calculation of the appropriate depreciation charge it requires the consideration of three factors:

(a) the asset's cost (or valuation if it has been revalued);
(b) the nature of the asset and its useful life;
(c) the asset's estimated residual value,

the objective being to allocate or spread the differences between the first and third of these factors over the period of the second. The ASC has no recommendation to make as to the process of allocation that is to be used; it is silent as to the respective merits of straight line and accelerated depreciation techniques. It has nothing to say as to the desirability of allowing for

---

* Since SSAP 12 was issued it has been felt to be inapplicable to investment properties and the ASC has made amendments to it in respect of these in SSAP 19.

the cost of capital in depreciation calculations. In fact, SSAP 12 is extremely brief. However, it is quite clear on four points.

(a) Where an asset is revalued, or the estimate of its remaining useful life is altered, it is the new value which is to be spread over the remaining useful life of an asset.

(b) Where the cost or value of the asset is unlikely to be recoverable out of the revenues generated from it, the value of the asset should be written down by an appropriate amount immediately.

(c) Where assets are revalued, or estimated life is altered, or the depreciation technique changed, the consequences of the revaluation and the change should be disclosed in the notes.

(d) It is not appropriate to omit any charges in the depreciation of a fixed asset simply because its market value is greater than its net book value. If account is taken of such increases in value it will be necessary to increase the charge for depreciation accordingly.

SSAP 12 has many similarities with IAS 4 *Depreciation Accounting*,[13] the International Accounting Standard on the subject, which defines depreciation as 'the allocation of the depreciable amount of an asset over its estimated useful life', and continues, 'depreciation for the accounting period is charged to income either directly or indirectly'. It will be seen that the last paragraph of SSAP 12 states that 'compliance with the requirements of Statement of Standard Accounting Practice No. 12 *Accounting for Depreciation* will automatically ensure compliance with International Accounting Standard No. 4 *Depreciation Accounting*'.

The ASC has also issued two other SSAPs which have implications for the depreciation problem. SSAP 12 requires that fixed assets should be subject to a depreciation charge which reflects any loss in value due to use, obsolescence or the passing of time. SSAP 19, *Accounting for Investment Properties*,[14] requires a rather different treatment for fixed assets which are held not for the purpose of use during operations but as investments. For such assets the important information is that with respect to their current value and any changes in that value. However, where properties are held on a short lease, depreciation must be charged to prevent an overstatement of profit resulting from crediting the profit and loss account with the rental income while amortising the lease against the investment revaluation reserve.

The category of fixed assets referred to above are called 'investment properties' in the standard which defines them as developed and completed land and buildings held for investment purposes for which arms length negotiations have taken place to ascertain their rental value. This definition excludes properties owned and occupied by the company or group. SSAP 19 states that investment properties should not be subject to depreciation charges as per SSAP 12 unless they are leased and the lease has an unexpired term of less than 20 years. For such short term leases the requirements of SSAP 12 apply.

In SSAP 16, *Current Cost Accounting*, depreciation is covered in relation to changing price levels. Basically this reiterates the need for depreciation, saying that even when fixed assets in the HCAs have been completely written off, if they still have some service potential associated with them, any loss in this associated with the generation of the revenues of a period needs to be brought into the CCAs. However, the main depreciation related requirement of SSAP 16 is for a depreciation adjustment, which in effect 'makes up' any deficiency in depreciation in the HCAs to its current cost level for CCA purposes, which is discussed in Chapter 7.

5.9 CONCLUSIONS

It has been seen that over the years the accounting theoretician has considered many concepts of depreciation, the most important of these concern its implications for valuation and replacement of assets, and the matching concept. Although there can be persuasive arguments regarding the significance of depreciation to the valuation and eventual replacement of assets, especially where the depreciation charge is made in current cost terms, the fallacies inherent in this approach have been highlighted. This leaves the matching concept which has relatively recently been enshrined into accounting standards and company law.

There is still a problem concerning the place of the cost of capital in accounting for depreciating assets which, although subject to intensive academic debate, still has not been touched by the profession.

REFERENCES

1. For example see Lawson, G.H., Cash flow accounting, *The Accountant*, 28 October and 4 November 1971.
2. Edey, H.C., 'The nature of profit', *Accounting and Business Research*, No. 1, Winter 1970.
3. Goldberg, L., 'Concepts of depreciation', *Accounting Review*, July 1955.
4. See Hatfield, H.R., 'What they say about depreciation', *Accounting Review*, March 1936, pp. 18–26.
5. SSAP 12 *Accounting for Depreciation*, Accounting Standards Committee, December 1977, para. 15.
6. Baxter, W.T., *Depreciation: Depreciating Assets—An Introduction*, Gee & Co., 1981, page 11.
7. *Ibid*, page 12.
8. SSAP 12, *op. cit.*
9. Baxter, *op. cit.* page 4.
10. Baxter, W.T., *Depreciation*, Sweet & Maxwell, 1971. For a detailed discussion

on the estimation of the optimal life of an asset see Chapter 2, 'Choice of optimal life'.

11. *Ibid.* Chapter 8 'Cost of capital and depreciation' fully discusses the arguments for recognising the cost of capital in depreciation.

12. For a fuller explanation of these approaches see Lee, G.A., *Modern Financial Accounting*, Nelson 1981 or Baxter, *op. cit.*

13. IAS 4, *Depreciation Accounting*, International Accounting Standards Committee, October 1976.

14. SSAP 19, *Accounting for Investment Properties*, Accounting Standards Committee, November 1981.

QUESTIONS AND DISCUSSION PROBLEMS

1. In discussions about depreciation, three words—'valuation', 'replacement' and 'allocation'—are frequently introduced. Carefully consider the place and appropriateness of these words in a definition of depreciation.

2. The International Accounting Standard on depreciation states that one of the estimates that has to be made to enable depreciation computations to be carried out is that of the useful life of an asset. Discuss the difficulties in estimating the useful life of an asset and carefully distinguish between the two major influences on this life.

3. When matching the use of an asset with the revenues generated by it over a number of periods, both depreciation and repair costs may cause the reported profit figures for these periods to show large fluctuations.

   (a) Why may this be?
   (b) Should, and could, anything be done to try to iron out such fluctuations in reported income caused by these two factors?

4. 'Depreciation provides for the replacement of assets'. With reasons, state whether you agree or disagree with this statement.

5. 'In fact, cost of capital's role (in depreciation) is not so much to create new methods as to add an extra dimension to each of the old ones' (from *Depreciation* by W.T. Baxter). Briefly state the major methods used in depreciation which do not take cognisance of the cost of capital. Carefully explain how the superimposition of the cost of capital onto these methods can provide them with an additional dimension.

6. Discuss the relationship of depreciation in historic cost and current cost terms, from the standpoints of both accounting theory and accounting standards.

7. On pp. 186 – 191 the accounting policies used by four PLCs in relation to *depreciation* appear. Compare and critically discuss the methods disclosed. Do you feel that the disclosures made would be adequate in helping you to appraise this aspect of each firm's balance sheet? If not, why not?

CHAPTER 6

Income and Value During Periods of Changing Price Levels

6.1 INTRODUCTION

During the 1970s the difficulties and problems for accounting that result from changing price levels prompted the most active debate and created more interest than any other area of accounting theory. After much consideration and a certain amount of recrimination, 1980 saw the publication of a definitive standard on accounting during periods of changing prices— SSAP 16 *Current Cost Accounting*.* This is primarily concerned with large companies.

Readers will find that a knowledge of the history and background to the debate on price level accounting will help them understand the nature of, and the justification for, existing requirements. Even more importantly this understanding should enable them to cope more effectively with subsequent developments in this area—for such developments appear inevitable.

6.2 HISTORICAL BACKGROUND

Today accountants and executives in businesses have become more concerned about the way in which inflation has affected the utility of company accounting records prepared on a historic cost basis both from the point of view of internal and external users.

Within the firm the sensible decision path taken in times of changing price levels will be based upon accounting information which adjusts HCAs (whether explicitly or implicitly) before the decision is made. Thus when historic information is used for financial management or management accounting purposes it should have been either formally or informally adjusted for any changes in price levels. However, this book is concerned primarily with external financial reporting, and therefore will only examine those aspects of the changing price level problem associated with published

---

* Standards Committee, March 1980. Concurrently *Guidance Notes on SSAP 16: Current Cost Accounting* were issued with SSAP 16.

financial statements. Thus the question being considered is 'should published accounts be adjusted to take into consideration price level changes and if so, how should the adjustment be made?' This still remains either unanswered or unsolved in the majority of countries.

The attention given to this problem is not new. It goes back many years. Perhaps it was Sweeney[1] who formally introduced the idea in his *Stabilised Accounting* in 1936.* However with the increasing rate of inflation since World War II academic accountants have turned their attention more and more towards this area. Finally, practising accountants have paid increasing attention to the need to formally adjust published accounts for the effects of inflation.

The annual accounts of the Iowa-Illinois Gas and Electricity Company in 1958 charged depreciation based upon increased price levels. In their *Accountants Certificate* (the US equivalent of the UK *Auditor's Report*) Arthur Andersen and Company included the statement:

> We approve of the practice adopted by the Company, since it results, in our opinion, in a fairer statement of income for the year than that resulting from the application of generally accepted accounting principles.[2]

In the UK, the ASSC† issued its important exposure draft ED 8 *Accounting for Changes in the Purchasing Power of Money*, on 17 January 1973. It was followed by (P)SSAP 7[3] which was issued during May 1974 with the same title. However, it should be noted that this was a provisional SSAP which recommended that supplementary statements showing an organisation's HCAs adjusted to Current Purchasing Power (CPP) should be attached by companies to their published financial reports. (P)SSAP 7 was then superseded by *Inflation Accounting: Report of the Inflation Accounting Committee*[4] published on 4 September 1975, generally referred to as the Sandilands Report after the Chairman of the Committee. As a result of the recommendations in this Report the Government sponsored the Inflation Accounting Steering Group (IASG) which was to introduce Sandilands' recommendations for Current Cost Accounting (CCA). The IASG was set up under the chairmanship of Douglas Morpeth during January 1976. The IASG's recommendations were published as ED 18, *Current Cost Accounting*[5] on 30 November 1976. As a result of the pressure from the profession the ASC set up a sub-committee under the chairmanship of William Hyde during July 1977 to reconsider ED 18. On 4 November 1977 on this sub-committee's recommendations the ASC published *Inflation Accounting—an Interim Recommendation*,[6] which was popularly referred to as the Hyde Guidelines. A new exposure draft on CCA, ED 24, was issued by the ASC on 30 April 1979 and, without too much controversy, this became SSAP 16 in March 1980.

---

* Ecnomic aspects of this problem had been discussed for many years previously notably by Irving Fisher in his *The Purchasing Power of Money*, Macmillan 1911 and *Stabilising the Dollar*, Macmillan 1920.

† Later to become the ASC.

6.3 THE PROBLEM IN PERSPECTIVE: INFLATION AND CONVENTIONAL ACCOUNTS

Conventionally financial accounts are based on historic cost; that is, assets are valued in the balance sheet at their cost of acquisition. Expenses are also charged against revenues in the determination of profit based upon historic cost of the assets used up in generating the revenues. This system was originally developed during decades of relatively stable price levels and continued to be used exclusively before the consequences of inflation on the preparation of financial accounts were recognised. The principal advantage claimed for HCA* is that it enables the preparation of accounts on an objective basis. However, as seen in Chapter 3, p. 52 there are difficulties associated with objectivity. In the context of accounts objectivity seems to mean that several different accountants faced with the same set of economic transactions would produce identical sets of accounts. In order to achieve this, accountants have evolved a set of principles or practices of accounting. The ASC's fundamental accounting concepts for the UK as outlined in SSAP 2 (which were discussed in Chapter 3) are: going concern, accruals, consistency and prudence. In Chapter 3 many other possible principles or practices were also listed.

Nevertheless, even with so impressive a list to work with, accountants have been unable to achieve the total objectivity they require. Particularly significant and important discrepancies in published accounts, highlighted by the bout of takeovers in the late 1960s,[7] resulted in the establishment of the ASSC. The principle function of the ASSC was by way of its EDs and SSAPs, to reduce the range of accounting treatments possible in presenting a 'true and fair view' of the economic events that lead up to a company's published financial statements. (These developments are dealt with more fully in Chapter 8.) Yet even after the publication of numerous EDs and SSAPs the accounting profession is still a long way from achieving complete objectivity. For example, SSAP 9, *Stocks and Work in Progress*, recognises that

> problems arise on the allocation of overheads which must usually involve the exercise of personal judgement in the selection of an appropriate convention.[8]

This chapter is not concerned with the general problems of objectivity in accounting but with the specific problems of the effect of changing price levels upon financial accounts. The purpose of the foregoing discussion is simply to suggest that in considering techniques for allowing for inflation the accounting profession should not be eager to let objectivity be the overriding consideration when formulating ground rules for the preparation of

---

* Until the development of CPP accounting and CCA, HCA was simply referred to as 'accounting', it is only recently that the traditional form of accounting has been distinguished by calling it HCA.

financial statements, since even the existing system of HCA frequently proves inadequate for preparing completely objective financial reports.

The Limitations of Accounts when Prepared on a Historic Cost Basis

In order to evaluate the merits of anything, first of all some consideration needs to be given to its purpose or objective. However, it is obvious that this question of the purpose which financial statements are intended to serve has proved to be a vexed one for the profession in general and the ASC in particular. It was not until July 1975 that anything like an authoritative statement from the UK accounting profession was prepared on the objectives of financial reports with the publication of *The Corporate Report*.[9] This document suggests* that accounts should seek to satisfy the information needs of users. It identified the users in a variety of user groups which it defines as: the equity investor group; the loan creditor group; the employee group; the analyst-adviser group; the business contact group; the government and public. The report enumerates a number of uses to which the accounts may be put by the various user groups and these uses may be summarised by saying that the accounts should aid these groups in making decisions concerning the performance, efficiency, stability, vulnerability and future prospects of the enterprise. In the foreword to the Corporate Report, Mr Ronald Leach, then Chairman of ASSC, makes it quite clear that the Report does not 'necessarily reflect the views of the ASSC nor of any individual accounting body'.[10] However, it is an important document and its conclusions are undoubtedly significant.

In Chapter 8 suggested groupings of users and their requirements of published accounting reports will be discussed more fully. There it will be concluded that financial statements are intended to aid the various user groups making decisions of one kind or another. Traditionally the two most important statements in a set of accounts are the balance sheet and the profit and loss account. The balance sheet is intended to provide an indication of the value of the assets and liabilities of a business at a *point in time* and the profit and loss account is intended to measure the progress made by the business over a *period of time*. (A fuller discussion of the nature of income and value was provided in Chapter 2.) Inflation produces two specific problems, related to each other, which affect these statements. Firstly as the value of money falls the historic cost of assets becomes increasingly inappropriate as a measure of their value. Secondly, because profit is the result of charges based on historic cost to revenues, profit becomes overstated.

To understand the second point it is helpful to consider more fully the purposes of income measurement. Probably, its two most important func-

---

* It should be noted in fact that *The Corporate Report* was only a discussion paper published for comment.

tions are as a measure of efficiency, for example by comparing the profitability of two or more businesses or departments within a business and as a
guide to the possible limits of consumption. In the latter case a business
needs to know its profit for a period in order to determine how much its
owners may spend or consume* without placing the business's future income
prospects in jeopardy.

Example   Consider two similar businesses, say car hire firms. Firm A
was established on 1 January 19X6 and Firm B on 1 January 19X7. Both
businesses bought the same models and years of motor cars on the days
that they commenced business and both currently have exactly the same
operating revenues and expenses. Furthermore, let it be supposed that the
motor cars will have an overall economic life of four years and at the end of
that period they will have no terminal or scrap value. The cost of Firm A's
new car was £6000 on 1 January 19X6. However, because of inflation
Firm B paid £6600 on 1 January 19X7 for a similar second-hand model,
i.e. the same model which by that time was one year old. If both companies
have operating revenues of £12,000 per year and operating costs excluding
depreciation of £4000 per year their profit and loss accounts based on HCA
will be as follows:

| | Firm A | | Firm B | |
	£	£	£	£
Revenues		12,000		12,000
less				
Operating costs	4,000		4,000	
Depreciation	1,500	5,500	2,200	6,200
Net profit		£6,500		£5,800

Note: Depreciation is calculated as historic cost less terminal value
    divided by remaining life

Now consider the two profit figures in the light of the purposes they are
intended to serve. Firm A appears to have made a greater profit than Firm
B. However it is hard to conclude that A, running an identical car with the
same revenues and operating costs, is more efficient than B. Furthermore,
how helpful are the profit figures as a guide to consumption for the two
businesses? If Firm A consumes the whole of the £6500 it will, through the
depreciation process, retain funds within the business totalling £6000 over
the four-year life. Assuming all A's transactions are for cash and it does not
acquire any other assets, at the end of the four-year period it will have cash

---

* In the case of a company a knowledge of profits is one of the requirements in enabling the
  directors determine the dividend they recommend.

at the bank equal to its depreciation provision, i.e. will have recovered the sum that it started with. Similarly, Firm B will recover £6600 over a three-year period. However, if inflation continues it is likely that a replacement motor car will cost considerably in excess of £6000 or £6600. If neither A nor B have access to any additional funds they will be forced out of business because they will be unable to replace their revenue generating asset. Therefore it is clear that profits based on historic costs are inadequate either as measures of efficiency or guides to consumption in periods of inflation (see also pp. 85 – 87).

Problems Associated with Monetary Items

ED 18* defines monetary items as:

> assets, liabilities or capital, the amounts of which are fixed by contract or statute in terms of numbers of pounds regardless of changes in the value of money.[11]

Such items create particular problems in times of changing price levels, whether inflation or deflation. £10 deposited in a current account during a period in which prices rise is still shown as £10 at the end of that period. Yet clearly the £10 at the end of the period will procure fewer goods and/or services than it could have at the beginning of the period. The purchasing power of the deposit is said to have been reduced. Clearly, this results in an economic loss to the owner of the deposit (and therefore somebody else must have gained the amount lost).

Similarly, if £10 is borrowed at the start of a period in which prices are rising then the goods and/or services which could be bought with the £10 will be greater than the goods and services that would have to be foregone at the end of the period in order to repay the loan. Hence the borrower has enjoyed an economic gain or benefit. The significance of the gain or loss in both these cases is dependent upon the rates of change in the price level. Generally speaking, this gain or loss on monetary items can be calculated by comparing the fixed value (in pounds) of the monetary item concerned with the value it would have after a period of inflation or deflation if, instead of being held in a monetary form, it had appreciated along with the general increase in price levels.

Example† The following are extracts from the balance sheet of a firm at the beginning and end of a period in which the index of retail prices moves smoothly as shown:

---

* There is no specific definition of 'monetary items' in SSAP 16's section on Definition of Terms.
† To be able to work through this example, and others in this section based on indexation, there is a need to be able to carry out simple index adjustments. Appendix A at the end of this chapter explains index adjustment computations for those not familiar with them.

	Beginning £	End £
8% Debentures	1000	1000
Creditors	80	100
Cash	140	80
Debtors	200	300
Index of retail prices	100	140

It is also to be assumed that all transactions have been evenly spread throughout the period, therefore any increases or decreases in the value of assets or liabilities may be treated as being effected in full at the mid-point of the year when the index stands at 120.

The firm's gains and losses on monetary items may be computed as follows:

(a) *Debentures*   Had the firm's indebtedness appreciated in harmony with the index of retail prices at the end of the period it would have owed:

$$£1000 \times \frac{140}{100} = \underline{\underline{£1400}}$$

In fact its contractual liability remains at £1000. Therefore the firm has made a *gain* on this monetary item of £400.

(b) *Creditors*   These have increased from £80 to £100. This is best analysed as a debt of £80 that the firm has owed throughout the period plus a further £20 borrowed at the mid-point of the period. If the £80 owed throughout the year had appreciated in line with the retail price index it would owe:

$$80 \times \frac{140}{100} = \underline{\underline{£112}}$$

The £20 borrowed at the mid-point would now be worth:

$$20 \times \frac{140}{120} = \underline{\underline{£23}} \text{ to nearest } £$$

The appreciation the firm's creditors would have required to maintain their purchasing power would have been £112 + £23 = £135; but the firm's debt remains at £100 so it has a *gain* on this monetary item of £35.

(c) *Cash*   The firm's cash holdings have fallen from £140 to £80. Since transactions accrue evenly throughout the year this can again be thought of as £80 held throughout the period plus £60 held from the start until the mid-point of the period. Had the firm invested the £80 in assets which appreciated in line with the retail price index these would now be worth:

$$80 \times \frac{140}{100} = \underline{\underline{£112}}$$

If the £60 held from the start of the year to the period's mid-point had also been in assets which appreciated in line with the retail price index, it would have increased to:

$$60 \times \frac{120}{100} = \underline{\underline{£72}}$$

Thus in order to maintain its purchasing power the firm would have to receive £72 during the period and hold £112 at the end of the period, a total of £184. In fact the firm received £60 during the year and holds £80 at the end of the period, a total of £140. Therefore its loss on cash holdings is $\underline{\underline{£44}}$.

(d) *Debtors* These have increased from £200 to £300. Following the reasoning for creditors and cash, debtors may be treated as £200 lent throughout the period plus a further £100 lent at the period's mid-point. Had the £200 been invested in appreciating assets it would now be worth:

$$200 \times \frac{140}{100} = \underline{\underline{£280}}$$

The £100 lent at the mid-point when the index stood at 120 would now be worth:

$$100 \times \frac{140}{120} = \underline{\underline{£117}} \text{ to the nearest £}$$

The total in this case being £397, but in fact the firm is owed £300 therefore it faces a *loss* on this monetary item of $\underline{\underline{£97}}$.

(e) *Summary* The various gains and losses made by the firm on its monetary items can now be summarised as follows:

		£	
Gains	—	Debenture	400
		Creditors	35
			435
Less Losses	—	Cash	44
		Debtors	97
			141
Total (Net *gain* on monetary items)			£294

Gains and losses on monetary items can have a considerable effect on reported profits. For an indication of the magnitude of these effects see Exhibit 6f, a table prepared by Phillips and Drew on page 131.

6.4 CAUSES OF PRICE LEVEL CHANGES

The question arises as to whether price level changes are exclusively the result of inflation or deflation. Careful consideration will reveal that price level changes are made up of three major components. These are: scarcity, i.e. supply and demand factors; changes in technology; and a pure inflationary effect.* From the combination of the effects of these three factors will come the total price level change in which it is virtually impossible to isolate completely any effects of the other factors from the inflationary or deflationary component. Because any, or all, of these factors may be working on price levels even in times of general price stability there will still be changes in relative prices. For example, during a period in which the general price index remained stable, there may have been increases in the price of labour which have been offset by cost reductions resulting from improved technology.

Thus it becomes important that any system developed to adjust accounts for changes in price levels must be able to cope with the possibility of prices in different factor and product groupings changing at different rates.†

6.5 PARTIAL METHODS FOR MITIGATING THE EFFECT OF CHANGES IN PRICE LEVELS ON ACCOUNTS

There are a number of developments that have been used to try to deal with the effects that changing price levels have on accounts. These include: revaluing fixed assets (by writing them up); valuing assets at their replacement cost (called Replacement Cost Accounting (RCA)); and valuing assets at their current value. In the past a number of European enterprises have tried some form of partial adjustments to their accounts based on the above approaches; however, partial adjustments provide an incomplete solution to the problem.

Examples of Partial Adjustments

(a) The fixed asset replacement reserve
The establishment of a fixed asset replacement reserve was recommended

---

* This could be negative, i.e. deflation.
† One major criticism of (P)SSAP 7 was that in its recommendation that the general index of retail prices should be used to adjust accounts, such an all-embracing index did not take cognisance of the fact that relative price level changes would have different effects on different entities, which may or may not have been satisfactorily compensated for by the use of such a single all-embracing general type of index. Even in (P)SSAP 7's objectives for financial statements to show whether shareholders' purchasing power was maintained through its selection of the general index of retail prices it did not recognise that small, large and institutional investors may have different requirements in this respect.

by the Institute of Chartered Accountants in England and Wales some years ago to help firms overcome the problem of having insufficient funds to replace assets when their renewal was due.* For example, Unilever Ltd provided for replacement reserves to the extent of £5.6 million during 1972.

(b) Depreciation based upon current replacement costs
Guest, Keen and Nettlefolds Ltd allowed for depreciation based on the current replacement cost of their assets in 1972 using the appropriate price index to enable them to make the computation. They showed depreciation in their accounts of:

	£ millions
Based on historic cost	19.27
Based on replacement cost (additional)	4.28
	£23.55

(c) LIFO for stock valuation
One approach to the problem of stock valuation taken in the USA was to use the last-in first-out (LIFO) method. However, it offers only a partial solution as the 'last-in' price of stock may not equal current stock costs, especially when the stock turnover rate is slow. Perhaps using Next-in First-Out (NIFO) could provide an even better approach as stock would be valued or charged out based on its replacement cost.

6.6 THE DEVELOPMENT OF COMPREHENSIVE METHODS TO DEAL WITH THE EFFECT OF CHANGES IN PRICE LEVELS ON FINANCIAL STATEMENTS

This chapter is principally concerned with the more comprehensive proposals for adjusting accounts for inflation. Basically these fall into two categories: those which allow for general price increases and those which make specific allowance for changes in relative prices. In order to understand this basic distinction, it is helpful to revert back to the idea of profit as defined by Hicks. This is that profit is capital appreciation plus consumption.† Such a fundamental definition is rarely in dispute nor is its related concept of capital maintenance. Any controversy generally concerns the nature of the capital to be maintained.

---

* The Institute of Chartered Accountants in England and Wales *Recommendations on Accounting Principles No. 9: Depreciation of Fixed Assets*, issued on 12 January 1945 stated in Paragraph 15: 'Amounts set aside out of profits for obsolescence which cannot be foreseen or for a possible increase in the cost of replacement are matters of financial prudence'.
† For a full discussion of this see pages 20–22.

Disagreement on the Nature of Capital

There are three possible concepts concerning the maintenance of capital. HCAs measure profit based on the maintenance of *money capital*. Those who advocate allowing for general price increases only seek to measure profit while maintaining *purchasing power* intact. Finally those who wish to make specific allowance for changes in relative prices seek to maintain intact the *physical capital* that a business owns. In fact even in ED 18 the ASC had formalised their recognition of this definition problem by saying:

> Part of the problem is a lack of consensus on what is the substance of the business (is it the physical assets, or all the assets, or the long-term capital, or the owners' capital, etc.?) and whether it should be maintained in money or real terms. [12]

The distinction between these three possible forms of capital maintenance can best be described using an example.

Example Consider a situation in which an organisation purchases a tonne of a commodity at the commencement of the year for a price of £300. During the course of the year the general index of retail prices moves from 100 to 120, and at the end of the year the cost of a tonne of the commodity is £400. Now suppose that the commodity is sold at the end of the period for £500. If the organisation seeks to maintain its money capital intact the profit computation will be £500 − £300 = £200. If it wishes to maintain its purchasing power intact then profit becomes £500 − (£300 × 120/100) = £140. Finally, if it wishes to maintain its stock of physical assets intact then its profit figure will be £500 − £400 = £100. Thus the three concepts of capital maintenance have provided three distinct concepts of profit. Traditionally, accounts have been based upon historic cost and profits have been measured keeping money capital intact. Increasing rates of inflation have produced pressure to adjust accounts for inflation and in fact both alternatives discussed above have been suggested. ED 8 and (P)SSAP 7 advocated allowing for changes based on general price indexing accounts using the general index of consumer prices. The Sandilands Report, ED 18, ED 24 and SSAP 16 are based on the maintenance of physical capital by revaluing assets and calculating expenses on the basis of their 'value to the business'.

6.7   CURRENT PURCHASING POWER ACCOUNTING—ED 8 AND (P)SSAP 7

(P)SSAP 7 recommended that all accounts should include a supplementary statement annexed to the traditional HCAs which showed the financial statements adjusted for changes in the general price level. The proposal was that items in the accounts, with the exception of monetary items, should be restated in their CPP equivalent by indexing the figures using the general index of retail prices (RPI). Appendix A to this chapter deals with some of the problems in the compilation, selection and use of indices. Furthermore (P)SSAP 7 required that in profit calculations for the year allowance must be made for gains and losses on monetary items.

Examples of Current Purchasing Power Accounting: Currys Ltd and Marks and Spencer Ltd*

Exhibits 6(a) and 6(b) provide examples of company accounts prepared in accordance with (P)SSAP 7's provision for CPP for Currys Ltd (for the year ended 30.1.75) and Marks and Spencer Ltd (for the year ended 31.3.75), respectively, both of which were prepared in 1975.

6.8 REPORT OF THE INFLATION ACCOUNTING COMMITTEE

The uncertainty about the most appropriate way to allow for inflation in accounts is evidenced by the fact that a few days before the end of the exposure period for ED 8 (which ended on 31 July 1973) the Secretary for Trade and Industry announced that the Government was to set up an independent Committee of Enquiry to consider whether, and if so how, company financial statements should be adjusted to allow for changes in costs and prices. The Chairman of this Committee was to be Francis Sandilands. In consequence the ASSC decided that the standard which resulted from ED 8 should only be provisional, i.e. (P)SSAP 7. The Committee's work culminated on 4 September 1975 in the production of the *Report of the Inflation Accounting Committee* which as has already been seen, is popularly referred to as 'Sandilands'. The recommendations in this report were slightly modified by the IASG in its first attempt to produce a standard based on CCA as seen in ED 18. Nevertheless the essential prin ciples of Sandilands have been left intact and in particular the fundamental method of CCA remained the basis of all subsequent proposals.

Accounting for price level changes is an interesting example of how one branch of accounting theory has developed towards a practical application. Therefore it will be useful to look at the terms of reference, methodology, conclusions and recommendations of the Sandilands Report in greater detail.

Sandilands' Terms of Reference

The terms of reference given to the Inflation Accounting Committee were:

> To consider whether, and if so how, company accounts should allow for changes (including relative changes) in costs and prices, having regard to established

---

* Quoted limited companies are now called Public Limited Companies (PLCs)

Currys

Consolidated Profit and Loss Account
Year Ended 30th January 1975

Notes See pages 8 to 14							Historical basis		Current Purchasing Power basis (CPP) (1975 pounds)	
							1975 52 weeks £'000	1974 53 weeks £'000	1975 52 weeks £'000	1974 53 weeks £'000
2	Group Turnover ...	...	...	...	...	...	100,578	86,443	109,597	109,381
3	Group Trading Profit ...	...	...	...	...		6,730	7,767	5,316	8,605
	Surplus on Sale of Properties	...	...	...	...		128	92	78	(32)
	Group Profit before Taxation	...	...	...	...		6,858	7,859	5,394	8,573
7	Taxation ...	...	...	...	...	...	3,762	3,878	3,762	4,650
	Group Profit Available after Taxation	...	...	...			3,096	3,981	1,632	3,923
	Appropriated as follows:									
8	Inflation Reserve	...	...	...	...	... 1,465		710	—	—
9	Dividends	...	...	...	...	... 812		748	813	898
							2,277	1,458		
	Group Profit Unappropriated for year	...	...	...		819	2,523	819	3,025
10	Earnings per Share	...	...	...	...	...	13.9p	16.7p	7.6p	16.3p

Financial Position—Historical and CPP Compared

						Historical basis		Current Purchasing Power basis (CPP)	
Net Current Assets	...	...	...	...	...	14,556	11,362	15,018	13,913
Fixed Assets less Depreciation	...	...	...	...	...	14,909	12,497	25,042	22,823
						29,465	23,859	40,060	36,736
Less: Preference Shares ...	...	...	...	... 660	660	660	792		
Deferred Taxation	...	...	...	... 6,766	3,444	6,766	4,129		
					7,426	4,104	7,426	4,921	
Total Equity Interest	...	...	...	...	...	22,039	19,755	32,634	31,815
Ratios									
Return on Equity Interest	...	...	...	...	14.6%	19.8%	5.4%	12.0%	
Net Assets per Share	...	...	...	...	...	94.6p	84.1p	140.1p	135.8p

NOTE re CPP columns

The figures in the Current Purchasing Power basis columns were arrived at by converting the corresponding figures in the Historical basis columns by reference to the changes in price indices between the dates of the original transactions and January, 1975. As indicated the CPP figures for both 1975 and 1974 are measured in pounds of purchasing power at January, 1975. The Retail Price Index at January, 1975 was 119.9 and at January, 1974 was 100.0 and the rate of inflation for the year was 19.9% (12.0%).

Exhibit 6(a) CPP accounts for

8. Inflation Reserve

The Directors recommend a further transfer to Inflation Reserve of £1,465,000 (£710,000) bringing the total Reserve up to £3,525,000 (£2,060,000). As last year this transfer has been based on the difference between profit on a Historical basis and on a CPP basis and can be analysed as follows:—

	1975 £'000	1974 £'000
Group Profit after Taxation and Dividends (Historical basis)	2,284	3,233
Adjustments to convert to Current Purchasing Power basis:—		
Stocks	2,442	843
Additional charge based on restating the cost of Stocks at the beginning and end of the year in CPP pounds, thus taking the inflationary element out of the profit on the sale of Stocks.		
Depreciation	472	267
Additional Depreciation based on cost of Fixed Assets measured in CPP pounds.		
Monetary Items	(1,368)	(396)
Net gain in purchasing power resulting from the effects of inflation on the Group's net monetary liabilities.		
Sales; Purchases and all other Costs	(131)	(123)
These are increased by the change in the index between the average date at which they occurred and the end of the year. This adjustment increases profit as sales exceed the costs included in this heading.		
Surplus on Sale of Properties	50	119
Reduction of Surplus measured by relating sales proceeds to costs in CPP pounds.		
Transfer to Inflation Reserve	1,465	710
Group Profit Unappropriated (Current Purchasing Power pounds at end of 1975 and 1974 respectively)	819	2,523
Adjustment required to update 1974 profit from 1974 pounds to 1975 pounds	—	502
Group Profit Unappropriated (CPP basis at January, 1975)	819	3,025

Note:—

The Preference Share Capital of £660,386 at the beginning of the year is equivalent in purchasing power to £791,803 at the end of the year (because inflation has been 19.9% during the year). As the Company's liability to the Preference Shareholders is fixed in money terms this liability has declined during the year in real terms from £791,803 to £660,386. This reduction of £131,417 in the Company's obligation in CPP terms is included in the net gain on Monetary Items of £1,368,000 shown above.

Currys Ltd based on (P)SSAP 7

MARKS AND

SUMMARY OF RESULTS AND FINANCIAL POSITION
Adjusted for the Effects of Inflation (Note A)

	Historical pounds (pages 16 and 17)		Current pounds as at 31st March, 1975	
	1975	1974	1975	1974
	£'000	£'000	£'000	£'000
RESULTS FOR THE YEAR ENDED 31st MARCH, 1975				
Turnover	721,876	571,650	787,204	736,460
Operating Profit (Note B)	81,857	76,825	82,706	92,402
Taxation	42,500	39,900	42,500	48,279
Profit after taxation	39,357	36,925	40,206	44,123
Extraordinary item	49	2,383	52	2,260
Monetary gain attributable to Debenture Stock and Preference Shares	—	—	9,733	7,290
	39,406	39,308	49,991	53,673
Dividends	21,052	19,008	21,202	23,002
Undistributed surplus	18,354	20,300	28,789	30,671
Earnings per share	12·2p	11·4p	12·4p	13·6p
FINANCIAL POSITION AT 31st MARCH, 1975				
Fixed assets (Note C)	414,312	241,720	422,777	405,988
Investment in subsidiary and associated companies	6,540	2,210	6,540	2,674
Net current liabilities	(7,528)	(8,113)	(7,528)	(10,287)
	413,324	235,817	421,789	398,375
Less:				
Deferred taxation	21,150	18,400	25,014	22,264
Debenture stock	45,000	45,000	45,000	54,450
Preference shares	1,350	1,350	1,350	1,633
	67,500	64,750	71,364	78,347
Ordinary shareholders' interests (Note D)	345,824	171,067	350,425	320,028

Exhibit 6(b) CPP accounts for Marks

SPENCER LIMITED

NOTES

A. BASIS OF ADJUSTMENT

As a result of inflation the company's accounts on pages 16 to 23 are stated in a mixture of pounds of different purchasing power ("Historical pounds"). The summary on page 24 shows the effect of converting the results and the financial position in Historical pounds into pounds of current purchasing power as at 31st March, 1975 ("Current pounds").

The figures in Historical pounds have been converted into Current pounds by using factors derived from the index of retail prices, which in January 1974 was 100 and at 31st March, 1975 was estimated to have been 123.9, compared with 102.6 at 31st March, 1974.

B. OPERATING PROFIT

The difference between the operating profit in Historical pounds and the operating profit in Current pounds is made up as follows:—

	1975 £'000	1974 £'000
OPERATING PROFIT IN HISTORICAL POUNDS	81,857	76,825
ADJUSTMENTS TO CONVERT TO CURRENT POUNDS:		
Increase in the cost of opening stock	(6,609)	(3,853)
Increase in the charge for depreciation	(2,857)	(1,716)
Sales, purchases and expenses	7,839	7,523
	80,230	78,779
Gain/(Loss) on monetary items (excluding Debenture Stock and Preference Shares) ...	2,476	(2,414)
	82,706	76,365
Adjustment to update last year's profit to Current pounds	—	16,037
OPERATING PROFIT IN CURRENT POUNDS	82,706	92,402

C. FIXED ASSETS

A valuation of properties was made as at 31st March, 1974, which, following professional advice, has been revised to take account of the overall decline in property values in the year to 31st March, 1975. This revised value has been included in the statement of the financial position of the company in Current pounds at 31st March, 1975, and at 31st March, 1974, but has only been incorporated in the accounts in Historical pounds as at 31st March, 1975. Subsequent net additions of properties during the year have been converted into Current pounds using the factors described in Note A.

D. ORDINARY SHAREHOLDERS' INTERESTS

	Historical pounds £'000	Current pounds £'000
At 1st April, 1974	171,067	320,028
Amount capitalised or retained in respect of shares issued in lieu of cash dividend	1,608	1,608
Surplus arising on valuation of the company's properties	154,795	—
Undistributed surplus for the year	18,354	28,789
At 31st March, 1975	345,824	350,425

and Spencer Limited based on (P)SSAP 7

accounting conventions based on historic costs, the proposal for current general purchasing power accounting put forward by the Accounting Standards Steering Committee and other possible accounting methods of allowing for price changes, and to make recommendations. In considering the question the following matters, *inter alia*, should be taken into account.

(i)   The effects upon investment and other management decisions, and upon the efficiency of companies generally.

(ii)   The effect on the efficient allocation of resources through the capital market.

(iii)   The need to restrain inflation in the United Kingdom.

(iv)   The requirements of investors, creditors, employees, Government and the public for information.

(v)   Any implications for taxation of the profits and capital gains of companies, the assumption being that the share of the total direct tax burden by the company sector remains unchanged.

(vi)   The repercussions on the accounts of other corporate bodies.

(vii) Procedures in other countries, particularly EEC.[13]

The Methodology of Sandilands

In compiling their report the Committee used the following method of study and ways to obtain information:

(i)   Advertising to the public for their views;

(ii)   Writing to 60 organisations and individuals, including people from finance, accounting, academic fields, and financial journalists;

(iii) Sending out 242 questionnaires to UK companies, which included a sample of quoted companies, a sample of smaller unquoted companies, and the major nationalised industries. Two major questions were asked: (1) 'What are you doing in your accounting practices to cope with inflation?' and (2) 'What are your views about what should be done to cope with the "inflation and reporting" problem generally?'

(iv)   Holding 23 sessions during which witnesses presented oral evidence on their views.

(v)   Members of the Committee visited the USA and Holland to examine what was happening in those countries to deal with the problem of inflation and accounts.

It should be noted that associated with (i), (ii) and (iv) above, the Committee did not publish the names of respondents as it wanted to provide informality and confidentiality, and so synthesised all views under a cloak of anonymity in the report.

The Principal Conclusions of the Report

Three principal conclusions were drawn by the report as follows:

(i) The Committee considered that it was ·essential that published financial statements should allow for changes in costs and prices.

(ii) The Report concluded that existing accounting conventions are not adequate to allow for change in costs and prices in accounts and at that moment* the existing methods of preparing these cause companies' affairs to be presented in a misleading way.

(iii) To allow for changes in costs and prices some form of *value accounting* would be required rather than some general index approach.

Recommendations of the Report: The Development of 'Value Accounting' as Current Cost Accounting

The Sandilands Committee's Report recommended that:

(i)   CCA be developed in a fully comprehensive form to allow for the effect of inflation on accounts.† (Note: the Committee did not think that it would be useful to combine CCA with any of the beneficial CPP attributes, such as those concerning gains or losses on owing or holding money.)‡

(ii)   A steering committee be set up to supervise the practical implications of CCA and to deal with the detailed work required for its introduction.

(iii) Whenever possible, companies should adopt the essential features of CCA immediately.

(iv)   When the standard for CCA is issued it should initially be made mandatory for listed companies, large unlisted companies and the nationalised industries, and progressively extended to apply to all other companies if this proved to be feasible.

(v)   There should be a revision of the basis used for taxation of profits and incomes, and that in this revision there should be an examination of tax assessments on accounts drawn up in accordance with CCA.

(vi)   CCA accounts should replace existing accounts drawn up using historic cost conventions.

---

* The report was published on 4 September 1975.

† The Committee point out that this approach would be *evolutionary* rather than *revolutionary*, because it is a systematic development of the modifications already being carried out to historic cost accounting through revaluation processes. Revaluations were already being carried out by most organisations for such assets as land and buildings to help bring at least some of the balance sheet asset values into line with current values.

‡ A debate centred and still centres around this issue and the subsequent interim proposals for inflation accounting and SSAP 16 both recommend that some form of gearing adjustments be made to accounts to show the effects of inflation upon monetary items.

(vii)   A source and application of funds statement should be included with published accounts.*

(viii) The CPP method should not be used except in the restatement of past dividends paid in ten year summaries of these payments.†

(ix)   Operating and other types of gains (e.g. holding gains) should be separated out.

(x)   A statement showing the adequacy of cash resources available for the next year should be provided.

(xi)   The 100 per cent first year allowances and stock appreciation tax relief should be continued until the basis for taxation has been comprehensively reviewed.

(xii)   CCA should be used in: price control; non-competitive Government contracts; Monopoly Commission examinations of profits.

(xiii) Additional statistical data should be provided by the Government to help companies make CCA adjustments to their accounts.

The Basic Principle of Current Cost Accounting—Value to the Business

The basic principle of CCA is to provide more realistic costs and values in published financial statements. In arriving at current costs and values, the majority of items in accounts are to be considered on the basis of their 'value to the business'. The 'value to the business' of an asset is to be equated with the amount of the loss suffered by the company concerned if the asset is lost or destroyed.[14] It is based on Professor Baxter's‡ concept of deprival value[15] which is discussed in Chapter 2, pp. 25 – 27.

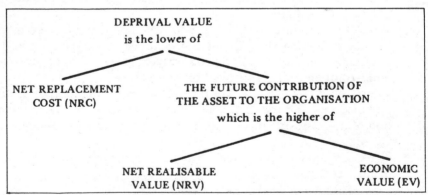

Exhibit 6(c) Decision tree to ascertain Deprival Values

---

* This was overtaken by the issue of SSAP 10: *Statements of Source and Application of Funds* by the ASSC during July 1975.

† The ASC issued *Corresponding Amounts and Ten Year Summaries in Current Cost Accounting: A Discussion Paper* in 1982 which implicitly preferred the use of a general index to adjust past figures.

‡ Deprival value was based on the concept of value to the owner developed by Professor J.C. Bonbright in his classic work first published in 1937 *Valuation of Property*, The Michie Company 1965.

To find the amount that an entity would lose if it were deprived of any of its assets, the decision tree shown in Exhibit 6(c) can be used. Note that the economic value of an asset is its value in use. The 'economic value' of an asset can be defined as 'the present value of the expected future earnings of the asset in discounted terms'.[16] A decision table to show the value of an asset to an organisation can be drawn up as shown in Exhibit 6(d).

Relationship between value concepts	Deprival value or value to the business
NRV > EV > NRC	NRC
NRV > NRC > EV	NRC
EV > NRC > NRV	NRC
EV > NRV > NRC	NRC
NRC > EV > NRV	EV
NRC > NRV > EV	NRV

Exhibit 6(d) Decision table to show value to the business

The table in Exhibit 6(d)* shows that any asset's value can be represented in only six ways, after the three bases for valuation have been ranked. From this table it can be seen that in most cases the value to the business is likely to be an asset's net replacement cost. Initially most of the literature suggested that it would only be on very rare occasions that the economic value of an asset would be its value to the business. For example, this situation would occur when, for a specific asset which has a very low NRV, the NRC is high, making it unlikely that the asset would eventually be replaced. Keeping the asset to generate future cash flows may be more beneficial to the firm than selling it, when perhaps only its scrap value would be realised. More recently it has been suggested that the need to determine economic value may rise more often than the table suggests. For example, in depressed economic conditions† many companies might find it hard to justify replacing their assets should they be deprived of them. Under such conditions realisable values are also likely to be very low so that the best policy may be to 'soldier on' with the existing assets. Therefore in these circumstances the value to the business of its assets would be their economic value. This situation is especially likely to be applicable to industries whose assets are large and highly specialised. Given the difficulties in calculating the economic value, which involves forecasting the future benefits likely to be derived from the use of the assets and, theoretically at least, the determination of a discount rate, deriving this could present difficulties.

---

* See also page 27.
† Such as appertained in the UK during the late 1970s and early 1980s.

An Example of Sandilands' Current Cost Accounting: Record Ridgway Ltd

Soon after the Sandilands Report had been published, a Sheffield firm Record Ridgway Ltd produced its accounts in CCA form. The relevant parts of these are shown in Exhibit 6(e).

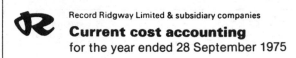

Record Ridgway Limited & subsidiary companies

Current cost accounting

for the year ended 28 September 1975

If company accounts are to measure the financial position and results of a Company, the implication of inflation must be considered. Existing accounting conventions fail to measure the effects of inflation and may even provide misleading information to management, employees and shareholders. The Directors believe that Current Cost Accounting, as proposed in the Report of the Inflation Accounting Committee, indicates more clearly the effects of inflation on company affairs than the existing accounting conventions. Accordingly, a Group profit and loss account and balance sheet, adjusted for the effects of inflation using Current Cost Accounting principles are set out on the following pages of this Report and Accounts.

Group financial statistics adjusted for the effects of inflation

Operating ratios :		Current Cost Accounting 1975	Historical Cost Accounting 1975
Profit before taxation to turnover	%	4·76	11·38
Profit before taxation to capital employed	%	6·72	18·62
Profit before taxation to shareholders' funds	%	8·64	22·76
Turnover to capital employed	*times*	1·41	1·64
Turnover to stocks and work-in-progress	*times*	3·11	3·17
Earnings per share	*pence*	3·22	8·54

Exhibit 6(e)
CCAs for Record Ridgway Limited based on Sandilands

**Group profit and loss account for the year to 28th September 1975
adjusted for the effects of inflation**

	Current Cost Accounting 1975 £	Historical Cost Accounting 1975 £	Notes
Turnover	11,992,956	11,992,956	
Profit before taxation	1,247,133	1,364,724	1
Cost of sales adjustment	676,422	—	2
Adjusted profit before taxation	570,711	1,364,724	
Taxation	276,034	627,773	
Profit after taxation	294,677	736,951	
Profit attributable to minorities	22,972	22,972	
Preference dividends	3,943	3,943	
Profit attributable to ordinary shareholders	267,762	710,036	
Ordinary dividends	229,790	229,790	
Profit retained for the year	£37,972	£480,246	
Earnings per share	3·22p	8·54p	

Summary of gains for the year to 28th September 1975

	1975 £	
Current cost profit after taxation	267,762	
Movement on reserves net of taxation:		
Fixed asset valuation reserve	692,230	5
Stock revaluation reserve	36,456	6
Stock adjustment reserve	324,683	7
Total gain for the year after taxation	£1,321,131	

Exhibit 6(e) continued

Group balance sheet at 28th September 1975 adjusted for the effects of inflation

	Current Cost Accounting 1975 £	Historical Cost Accounting 1975 £	Notes
Net assets			
Current assets			
Stocks and work-in-progress	3,858,050	3,782,094	3
Debtors	2,764,678	2,764,678	
Bank and cash balances	124,901	124,901	
	6,747,629	6,671,673	
Less			
Current liabilities			
Creditors	1,701,439	1,701,439	
Bank overdrafts	1,186,240	1,186,240	
Short term loan	11,473	11,473	
Taxation	125,609	338,266	
Dividends	229,790	229,790	
	3,254,551	3,467,208	
Capital employed			
Net current assets	3,493,078	3,204,465	
Fixed assets	4,997,176	4,125,837	4
Investments	650	650	
	£8,490,904	£7,330,952	
Share capital	2,079,546	2,079,546	
Reserves	3,474,039	3,916,313	
Fixed asset revaluation reserve	692,230	—	5
Stock revaluation reserve	36,456	—	6
Stock adjustment reserve	324,683	—	7
Shareholders' funds	6,606,954	5,995,859	
Minority interests	113,549	113,549	
Deferred taxation	1,770,401	1,221,544	
	£8,490,904	£7,330,952	

Exhibit 6(e) continued

Notes on Group profit and loss account and balance sheet adjusted for the effects of inflation

Note 1 **Profit before taxation**
The Group profit before taxation has been adjusted to reflect the increased depreciation charge calculated on Current Cost Accounting principles. The depreciation charge is required to be based on the replacement cost of plant, fixtures and vehicles at 28th September 1975.

The additional depreciation charged to profit is £117,591.

Note 2 **Cost of sales adjustment**
Current Cost Accounting requires that the charge for 'cost of sales' in the profit and loss account should reflect the 'value to the business' of stock consumed during the year. The directors consider that the 'value to the business' of stock consumed is reflected in the current cost of that stock at the time it is used up during the year. The cost of sales adjustment is calculated using indices determined from the internal records of the Company which represent cost increases for stocks.

The indices used are based on the stock and work-in-progress valuations of the largest United Kingdom operating company in the Group and are considered to reflect accurately the cost changes throughout the Group.

Calculation of the cost of sales adjustment:

1. Stock at 29th September 1974 is multiplied by the average price of stock for the year to 28th September 1975 and divided by the price of stock on hand at 29th September 1974:

2. Stock at 28th September 1975 is multiplied by the average price of stock for the year to 28th September 1975 and divided by the price of stock on hand at 28th September 1975:

3. The difference between the opening and closing stock values on the inflation adjusted basis is subtracted from the difference on the unadjusted basis:

	Adjusted £	Unadjusted £
Stock at 29th September 1974	3,861,974	3,248,858
Less:		
Stock at 28th September 1975	3,718,788	3,782,094
	£143,186	£(533,236)

The cost of sales adjustment is £676,422.

Note 3 **Stocks and work-in-progress**
Stocks and work-in-progress are shown in the balance sheet at their 'value to the business' at 28th September 1975. The directors consider that the 'value to the business' is the replacement cost at 28th September 1975 after deducting obsoléte and slow moving stock provisions.

	Current Cost Accounting 1975 £	Historical Cost Accounting 1975 £
Raw material stocks	554,848	543,052
Work-in-progress	1,460,968	1,439,288
Finished stocks	1,600,813	1,563,559
Sundry stocks	241,421	236,195
Total value to the business	£3,858,050	£3,782,094

Note 4 **Fixed assets**
Current Cost Accounting requires that assets should be shown in the balance sheet at their 'value to the business'. The Groups freehold and leasehold land and buildings held by United Kingdom subsidiaries were valued at 28th September 1975. The method of valuation was the existing use basis, these valuations have been adopted in the balance sheet as at 28th September 1975, prepared on historical accounting principles

Exhibit 6(e) continued

Notes on the Group profit and loss account and balance sheet adjusted for the effects of inflation (continued)

and shown on page 15 of the Report and Accounts. It is, therefore, necessary to revalue only the freehold and leasehold land and buildings held by overseas subsidiaries for Current Cost Accounting purposes.

Plant, fixtures and vehicles are shown in the balance sheet adjusted for the effects of inflation at their net replacement value as at 28th September 1975. The replacement cost is determined from indices relating to machine tools published by The Economist Intelligence Unit Limited. The depreciation charge is calculated by reference to the replacement cost and is deducted from the replacement cost to provide the net replacement value.

It is not necessary to revalue loose tools and patterns as it is considered that their value as stated in the balance sheet prepared on historical accounting principles represents the value to the business.

	Freehold land and buildings	Leasehold land and buildings long	short	Plant fixtures and vehicles	Total
	£	£	£	£	£
The Group:					
Cost or valuation at 28th September 1975	2,864,849	376,100	34,600	2,005,279	5,280,828
Surplus on revaluation of overseas land and buildings	178,560	—	—	—	178,560
Surplus on replacement cost of plant fixtures and vehicles	—	—	—	2,801,598	2,801,598
At 28th September 1975	£3,043,409	£376,100	£34,600	£4,806,877	£8,260,986
Depreciation for the year	1,198	2,223	519	252,890	256,830
Accumulated depreciation	(1,198)	(2,223)	(519)	3,110,394	3,106,454
At 28th September 1975	—	—	—	£3,363,284	£3,363,284
Value to the business at 28th September 1975	£3,043,409	£376,100	£34,600	£1,443,593	£4,897,702
Add loose tools and patterns					99,474
Value to the business at 28th September 1975					£4,997,176

Note 5 **Fixed assets valuation reserve**

The fixed asset revaluation reserve represents the excess of the fixed assets shown at the 'value to the business' in the balance sheet adjusted for the effects of inflation over the fixed assets at net book value shown in the balance sheet prepared on historical accounting principles and shown on page 15 of this Report and Accounts.

Note 6 **Stock revaluation reserve**

The stock revaluation reserve represents the excess of stocks and work-in-progress shown at the 'value to the business' in the balance sheet adjusted for the effects of inflation over the stocks and work-in-progress shown in the balance sheet prepared on historical accounting principles and shown on page 15 of this Report and Accounts.

Note 7 **Stock adjustment reserve**

The cost of sales adjustment is transferred from the profit and loss account to the stock adjustment reserve.

Exhibit 6(e) continued

The Possible Effect of CCA on Companies' Reported Profits

In the Record Ridgway example of CCA it is interesting to note the effect that the adjustments have had on the organisation's financial statistics, with the profitability ratios being reduced to some 30 to 40 per cent of the level shown using HCA conventions. Note the similar effect of CPP on Currys accounts as provided in Exhibit 6(a), although in this case it is noticeable that the net assets per share ratio for Currys increased considerably. A table prepared by Phillips and Drew during 1975, and presented below as Exhibit 6(f), shows the possible effects of CPP and CCA on companies' reported profits by industry groupings.

The Sandilands CCA method makes no adjustments for monetary items. However subsequently ED 18, ED 24 and in particular SSAP 16 make provisions to deal with the problem of these through the use of separate statements for gains and losses on monetary items.

Sector	% Change CPP method	% Change CC method
Building materials	+ 7	− 56
Contracting and construction	− 7	− 52
Electricals	− 27	− 60
General engineering	− 12	− 88
Misc. capital	− 3	− 104
Electronics and radio	− 14	− 51
Motors and distributors	− 45	− 151
Food retailing	+ 16	− 93
Breweries	+ 47	− 40
Entertaining and catering	+ 114	− 47
Food manufacturing	− 13	− 75
Packaging and paper	− 7	− 74
Stores	− 2	− 31
Textiles	− 25	− 54
Tobacco	+ 2	− 68
Chemicals	− 18	− 67
Shipping	+ 35	− 56
Misc. (unclassified)	+ 23	− 77
Office equipment	+ 21	− 46
Banks	− 26	− 8
Oils	− 14	− 129
Total industrial and commercial	− 1	− 65

Notes
(i)   These adjustments are basically for the 1974 results of the industrial and commercial groupings shown.
(ii)   The CC method follows Sandilands thus does not include adjustments for monetary items.
(iii)   Source: Phillips and Drew, Research, 4 Sept, 1975.

Exhibit 6(f) The effect of inflation accounting on published pretax profits

6.9 CONCLUSIONS

In this chapter the accounting problems resulting from inflation have been discussed and various approaches to resolving the difficulties have been considered. The alternative methods of CPP and CCA both have their advocates. However at the time of writing, the CCA system has achieved dominance. Chapter 7 will look at the evaluation of the basic idea of CCA into a practical standard. It is worth remembering that while CPP appears to have been rejected in favour of CCA it is by no means a dead letter. In the USA Statement of Financial Accounting Standard (SFAS) 33, which is their current standard on accounting for price level changes, requires a three column format showing accounts based on HCA, CCA and CPP. Furthermore a discussion document* issued in the UK subsequent to SSAP 16 recommend an application of CPP principles to enable the production of comparable figures for CCA adjusted accounts on an intertemporal basis. The suggestion was that this year's CCAs, last year's CCAs, and last year's CCAs adjusted to current price levels through the application of a general index adjustment, all be made available.

REFERENCES

1. Sweeney, H.W. *Stabilised Accounting*, Harper 1936, republished by Holt Rinehart and Winston, 1964.
2. *1958 Annual Report*, Iowa-Illinois Gas and Electricity Company.
3. (P)SSAP 7 *Accounting for Changes in the Purchasing Power of Money*, Accounting Standards Steering Committee, May 1974, and withdrawn afterwards.
4. *Inflation Accounting: Report of the Inflation Accounting Committee*, Cmnd 6225, HMSO, September 1975 (Sandilands).
5. ED 18 *Current Cost Accounting*, Accounting Standards Committee, 30 November 1976, which was supported by *Guidance Manual on Current Cost Accounting*, Tolley and ICA 1976.
6. *Inflation Accounting—an Interim Recommendation*, Accounting Standards Committee, 4 November 1977 (Hyde Guidelines).
7. See for example Stamp, E. and Marley, C., *Accounting Principles and the City Code*, Butterworth 1970.
8. SSAP 9 *Stocks and Work-in-Progress*, Accounting Standards Committee, May 1975, Appendix 1, para. 3.
9. *The Corporate Report*, Accounting Standards Steering Committee, July 1975.
10. *Ibid*, page 7.
11. ED 18 *op. cit.*, para. 122.
12. *Ibid*, para. 9.
13. Sandilands, *op. cit.*, p. iv.

---

* *Corresponding amounts and ten year summaries in current cost accounting: a discussion paper*, Accounting Standards Committee, 1982.

14. *Ibid*, para. 529.
15. See for example Edey H., 'Deprival value and financial accounting' in Edey, H. and Yamey, B.S. (eds), *Debits, Credits, Finance and Profits*, Sweet and Maxwell 1974.
16. Sandilands, *op. cit.*, para. 582.

FURTHER READING

Journal of Business Finance and Accounting, Vol. 3 No. 1, Spring 1976. This is a special issue entirely devoted to the subject of accounting during periods of changing price levels.

QUESTIONS AND DISCUSSION PROBLEMS

1. 'Accounts prepared on a historic cost basis are objective.' Critically discuss.
2. There are limitations to accounts prepared on a historic cost basis. Discuss these and the effect that they are likely to have upon user groups' interpretation of financial statements.
3. What major partial methods have been used in the past to try and make some allowance for the effect of price level changes on financial statements?
4. It seems a simple matter to apply an index to adjust figures in accounts, yet there are difficulties associated with the use of indexes. (i) State the major assumptions underlying indexes. (ii) Explain possible dangers associated with the analysis of financial statements that have been adjusted using indexes, with special regard to situations when the assumptions underlying their preparation were not realistic.
5. There has been a long controversy over the particular problems that monetary items cause in the appraisal of accounts during periods of price level changes. Critically discuss whether you think that monetary items require special attention when accounts adjusted for price level changes are prepared.

Appendix A

ADJUSTMENT OF STATED MONEY VALUES BY INDEXING

By a simple computation, items with the money label of one period can be stated in terms of their money value in another period using indexes. The procedure is to multiple the money value of the item to be converted by

$$\frac{\text{Index number to which it is to go}}{\text{Index number from which it came}}$$

Example   The index at year 1 is 100, and the index at year 4 is 150. What is the value of an asset which cost £1000 in year 1, in year 4 terms?

$$£1000 \times \frac{150}{100} = £1500$$

When it is necessary to adjust average revenue, or expenditure amounts accruing over a period the item to be converted is multiplied by:

$$\frac{\text{average index number for period}}{\text{index number at the commencement of the period}}$$

Example   Stock of value £1000 was purchased when the index number was 100, it was sold evenly over a period during which the index rose from 100 to 150. What is the average current cost of the stock?

$$£1000 \times \frac{(100 + 150)/2}{100} = £1250$$

Compiling the Index

In the compilation of an index it is first necessary to define the band of goods covered, and in the case of groups of assets in CCA these should be as homogeneous as possible. This will provide a more 'specific' index, compared with the 'general' index compiled on the basis of a basket of goods such as the RPI. However, the principles of compiling indexes are the same, and one important one is that of weighting the items according to the frequency of their appearance in the group.

Problems in Using Indexes

There are many problems associated with index adjustments to accounts prepared on a historic cost basis which arise from the implicit assumptions made about the figures being converted. The person using indexes needs to be aware of these problems as they might affect any interpretation that can be made about the adjusted, or 'stabilised' figures.

(a) The assumption that revenues and expenses accrue evenly
When adjusting profit and loss account items, indexation assumes that any sales and purchases are made evenly throughout the year. In a seasonal business this may not be so. Revenues especially may be bunched at a specific period. Exhibit 6(i) shows the seasonal revenue pattern for a firework manufacturer and a firm operating in the holiday industry, both as far as their UK sales are concerned. In such cases it may be that such seasonal patterns of sales will result in index adjustments being more difficult to make if they are to be useful.

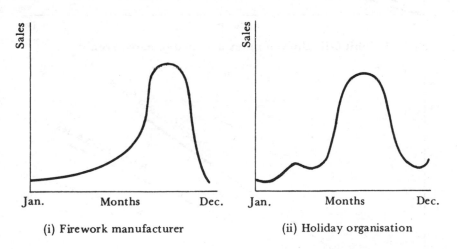

| (i) Firework manufacturer | (ii) Holiday organisation |

Exhibit 6(i) Example of UK seasonal sales patterns

(b) Does the index move evenly?
It is assumed that the retail price index moves evenly throughout the year. This may not be so, and there may be jumps, which will affect the adjust-

ments. For example, when the price of oil was increased dramatically during December 1973 this could have had an effect on the price index for petrol and caused it to jump. Thus the index may move as shown in Exhibit 6(ii), whereas in its use it will have been assumed to have moved evenly as shown by the dotted line.

(c) Special or general index

There has been much discussion as to whether, in using indexes to adjust accounts for inflation, it is sufficient to make allowances for a general decline in the purchasing power of money (by using a general index such as

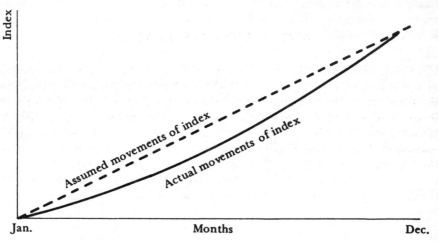

Exhibit 6(ii) Uneven index assumed to move evenly

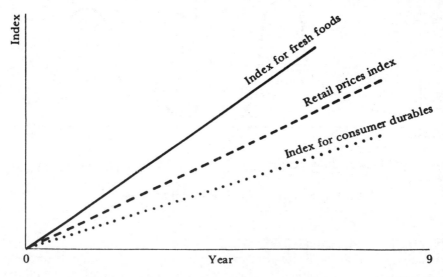

Exhibit 6(iii) Relative price level changes

the RPI) or whether it is necessary to adjust for relative price changes (by using special or specific indexes). The problem basically is that the general index is a weighted average of some basket of goods, made up from changes in the indexes of all these goods. However, different items which go to make up this basket may have great variations in their own indexes. For example, over the past decade the price of fresh foods has tended to rise faster than changes in the general index, whereas because of increased productivity and technological changes in methods used to produce consumer durables, their prices have on average moved less than the general index. Exhibit 6(iii) provides a conceptual representation of this problem.

WHICH GENERAL INDEX?

If, as decided by (P)SSAP 7, a general price index is to be used the question arises as to which general index? ED 8 decided that what was then called the Consumer Price Index (CPI)* was preferable to the RPI because the former had wider coverage. However, this is only calculated annually so it is also suggested that the appropriate monthly index of the RPI be used if necessary. In fact, whichever of the two indexes is used the variation in the final adjusted or stabilised figures is usually insignificant.

---

* Now known as the Consumers' Expenditure Deflator (CED).

CHAPTER 7

The Application of Current Cost Accounting

7.1 INTRODUCTION

As was seen in Chapter 6, while the accounting problems associated with inflation have been widely recognised there has been, and indeed still is, considerable disagreement as to the theoretical merits of the various methods of allowing for inflation in published accounts. After a lengthy debate CCA emerged, for the time being at least, as the dominant method. The aim of this chapter is to look at the development of the basic ideas of CCA, which were enshrined in the Sandilands Report, into the practical accounting standard, SSAP 16 *Current Cost Accounting*.

The Sandilands Report suggested that some form of steering group was required to push ahead with the development of their proposals for CCA and in January 1976 the Inflation Accounting Steering Group was set up by the ASSC under the chairmanship of Douglas Morpeth.

In outline the IASG's terms of reference were to develop a system of CCA from the Sandilands proposals, which would replace the existing HCA system. It was not to give further consideration to alternative methods, although obviously, where beneficial, it could 'bend' the Sandilands ideas. Thus its work was clearly defined and the ED eventually drawn up for the ASC* by the IASG was clearly based upon these terms of reference.

7.2 ED 18 CURRENT COST ACCOUNTING

The Morpeth Committee issued its system of CCA as ED 18 on 30 November 1976. It suggested that this would eventually entirely replace the old HCA method of preparing financial accounts. This was quite a difference from the CPP proposals in (P)SSAP 7 where HCA and CPP figures were to be provided side-by-side. The IASG provides a fairly long introduction to its draft, which in part seemed to be a marketing effort attempting to sell the idea of inflation accounting, especially CCA, to any remaining

---

* Which the ASSC became on 1 February 1976.

138

disbelievers —at a time when the majority of accountants appeared to be unbelievers as was seen by the grass roots reaction against this exposure draft. Nevertheless, the profession generally had by this time come to accept that some form of price level adjustment accounting was about to be imposed upon them, but wanted it to be as simple and uncomplicated as possible.

In the introduction to ED 18 it is interesting to note the emphasis placed by the IASG on its idea of the use of CCA in management accounts. It suggested, to help management accountants and decision-makers, that CCA must be an on-going form of accounting throughout the year, and not simply an adjustment to year-end accounts at one point in time. Continuing in this vein, ED 18 said that eventually CCA guidelines for management accountants were also to be produced.* A particular problem noted by the IASG was the 'possibility' of industry calculating the expired use value of fixed assets, i.e. depreciation and the cost of sales on the basis of historic costs. The ED expressed the hope that the use of CCA would avoid such errors on the part of management. However, the danger of such an approach fuelling inflation was also considered, but it was suggested that the effect of both market forces and the work of the Price Commission† would mitigate against such a possible effect.

Although (P)SSAP 7 had made provision to record any gains or losses associated with monetary items, Sandilands suggested that on balance no such adjustment was necessary. However, ED 18 proposed two statements to provide information about this: a statement of change in shareholders' net equity interest after allowing for the change in the value of money and a statement which showed the analysis for the gains/(losses) on monetary assets and liabilities after allowing for the change in the value of money.[1] This was probably the most innovative aspect of ED 18 in relation to the development of CCA. These two statements were to supplement the two traditional and other financial statements in the supply of supportive information to readers of published accounts.

An Example of ED 18 Current Cost Accounting: Redman Heenan International Ltd

Immediately after ED 18 was issued a number of firms produced accounts in the form that it had recommended. An example of the relevant parts of these CCAs for Redman Heenan International Ltd for the year ended 30.9.76 is provided in Exhibit 7(a).

---

* This point seemed to have got lost, no doubt because of the criticism that ED 18 ran into, by the time SSAP 16 was produced.
† The Price Commission was established under the Counter Inflation Act 1973 and disbanded in 1980.

Current Cost Accounts for the year ended 30th September 1976

PROFIT AND LOSS ACCOUNT

	Notes	£'000
Operating profit	2	1,443
Interest		(193)
		1,250
Taxation	3	(141)
Profit after taxation		1,109
Extraordinary item		(61)
Current cost profit		1,048

APPROPRIATION ACCOUNT

	Notes	£'000
Current cost profit		1,048
Net surplus arising from revaluation of assets	4	778
Total surplus		1,826
Appropriation to revaluation reserve	5	(778)
Net surplus available for distribution		1,048
Dividends		254
Added to general reserve	5	794

BALANCE SHEETS

	Notes	Current Cost Accounts 1976 £'000	1975 £'000	Historical Accounts 1976 £'000	1975 £'000
Employment of capital					
Land and buildings		3,780	3,776	3,767	3,763
Plant, machinery and equipment		2,605	2,417	1,451	1,255
Fixed Assets		6,385	6,193	5,218	5,018
Net Current Assets		2,560	1,180	2,392	1,005
		8,945	7,373	7,610	6,023
Capital employed					
Ordinary share capital		1,489	1,489	1,489	1,489
Share premium		2,535	2,535	2,535	2,535
Revaluation reserve	5	2,128	1,350	—	—
General reserve	5	2,037	1,243	2,830	1,243
Ordinary Shareholders' Funds		8,189	6,617	6,854	5,267
Preference shares and loans		756	756	756	756
		8,945	7,373	7,610	6,023
Net Assets per Ordinary share		55·0p	44·4p	46·0p	35·4p

Exhibit 7(a) CCAs for

STATEMENT OF CHANGE IN THE VALUE OF ORDINARY SHAREHOLDERS' FUNDS			£'000

STATEMENT OF CHANGE IN THE VALUE OF ORDINARY SHAREHOLDERS' FUNDS   £'000

Value of Ordinary shareholders' funds at 1st October 1975   6,617
Increase required to compensate for the fall in value of money during the year
(see footnote)   947

                                                                                                                  7,564
Value of Ordinary shareholders' funds at 30th September 1976   8,189

Gain in value, after Ordinary dividends   625
Ordinary dividends   242

Total gain during the year
after allowing for the fall in value of money   867

MADE UP AS FOLLOWS:
Net surplus available for distribution   1,048
Less : Preference dividends   12

                                                                                                                  1,036
Addition to compensate for the fall in value of money in respect of
revenue items   142

Loss on non-monetary assets	Stock £'000	Fixed Assets £'000	
Current cost holding gain	560	218	
Less : amount needed to compensate for fall in value of money	687	892	
	(127)	(674)	(801)
Gain on net monetary liabilities			
Long-term liabilities		108	
Other		382	
			490
			867

Footnote: The fall in the value of money during the year has been calculated by reference to the Retail Price Index which stood at 160·6 on 30th September 1976 compared with 140·5 on 30th September 1975.

NOTES ON THE ACCOUNTS
1. Basis
The current cost accounts presented in summarised form have been prepared on the basis of the principles recommended by the Accounting Standards Committee as set out in Exposure Draft No. 18.

Redman Heenan International Limited based on ED 18

2. Operating profit	£'000	£'000
Trading profit under historical cost convention		2,236
Cost of sales adjustment	(568)	
Additional depreciation	(327)	
Leasing charges	102	
		(793)
Operating profit under current cost convention		1,443

Cost of sales adjustment—calculated by reference to appropriate industry indices issued by the Central Statistical Office, has been made to charge the profit and loss account with the current cost of stocks at the time the sales were made. No adjustment has been made in respect of contract work in progress.

Additional depreciation—arises as a result of applying the existing rates of depreciation used by the group (see page 9, note 1 c) to the estimated value to the business at 30th September 1976 of fixed assets. No depreciation has been provided on buildings.

Leasing charges—represents adjustment in respect of leased plant now included at its current replacement cost in fixed assets and for which depreciation has now been charged.

3. Taxation

No adjustment has been made to the historical charge for taxation which comprises advance corporation tax on the dividends for the year and foreign tax.

4. Net surplus arising from revaluation of assets	1976 £'000	1975 £'000
This comprises:		
Land and buildings	—	13
Plant, machinery and equipment—revaluation at 30th September	320	1,162
—leasing charges adjustment	(102)	—
Fixed assets	218	1,175
Stocks—revaluation at 30th September	(8)	175
—cost of sales adjustment	568	—
	778	1,350

Assets have been restated at their value to the business. The following bases have been used:

Land and buildings—at open market value for existing use as estimated by the directors.

Plant, machinery and equipment—at gross current replacement cost calculated by reference to appropriate industry indices issued by the Central Statistical Office, less aggregate depreciation on the basis stated in note 2, above.

Stocks—at the lower of current replacement cost, calculated by reference to appropriate industry indices issued by the Central Statistical Office and net realisable value. Contract work in progress has been treated as a monetary item and is therefore shown at historical value.

5. Movement on reserves	Revaluation Reserve £'000	General Reserve £'000
Balance at 1st October 1975	1,350	1,243
Appropriation from total surplus for year	778	
Undistributed surplus		794
Balance at 30th September 1976	2,128	2,037

The balance on revaluation reserve at 1st October 1975 represents the surplus on revaluation of assets at that date on the bases set out in note 4.

The whole of the net surplus arising from the revaluation of assets in the year to 30th September 1976, has been transferred to the revaluation reserve. In the opinion of the directors, this transfer is advisable to preserve the capital employed in the business.

Exhibit 7(a) continued

7.3 THE HYDE GUIDELINES

ED 18 created a tremendous amount of discussion concerning both its suitability and the way that it had dealt with points of detail rather than concern itself with principles. Although both the ICAEW and the ACCA accepted it in principle at their respective Annual General Meetings, resistance quickly built up against the proposals. The ICMA in a submission to the ASC stated that they would prefer a simplified version which only involved depreciation and cost of sales adjustments. The CIPFA made statements that the ED 18 proposals appeared irrelevant as far as local authority accounts* were concerned and were also doubtful about the benefits to non-trading entities of implementing CCA. Accordingly, it wanted local authorities and non-trading entities to be excluded from any eventual standard or the introduction of ED 18 to be delayed while further discussion took place.

By 10 June 1977 Chris Westwick, then the IASG Secretary, stated that over 500 comments concerning ED 18 had already been received. Meanwhile, at the grass roots of the ICAEW, Martin Haslam and David Keymer were working to obtain sufficient support to force the Institute to call an extraordinary meeting to debate ED 18. This led to a meeting on 6 July 1977 at which a large majority of the Institute's members present voted against the acceptance of ED 18. John Addison was also working to obtain support from the ACCA members to call a similar meeting to vote on the withdrawal of ED 18 or for the Association to press for the retention of HCA side-by-side with CCA. However, this proved unnecessary for at its meeting on 27 July 1977 the ASC set up a sub-committee under the chairmanship of William Hyde to look further into the problems relating to the introduction of CCA. The terms of reference of this sub-committee were to produce an interim statement on inflation accounting which would have simplicity as its aim. This was to be achieved by simply considering the cost of sales and depreciation adjustments. These adjustments were to be based on indexes rather than valuations. On 4 November 1977 *Inflation Accounting—an Interim Recommendation* was published and has become popularly known as the 'Hyde Guidelines'.

Basically the Hyde Guidelines avoided the detail of ED 18. They recommended that three adjustments be made to financial results prepared on the traditional HCA basis, these being for (a) depreciation; (b) cost of sales; and (c) gearing. It recommended that companies listed on the Stock Exchange should show these adjustments as a prominent separate statement for accounts prepared for periods ending from 31 December 1977 but urged that these recommendations should have a wider adoption 'in the interests of more informative reporting'.[2]

---

* Note that the ASC is now issuing guidance on the application of CCA to entities such as local authorities and on the application of SSAP 16 to specific industries such as the oil industry.

Examples of Accounts showing the Hyde Guidelines Adjustments: Samuel Osborn and Co. Ltd and Allied Breweries Ltd

Soon after the publication of the Hyde Guidelines, firms started to include statements for the recommended adjustments in their published accounts. Exhibit 7(b) provides an example of a statement of these adjustments for Samuel Osborn & Co. Ltd's accounts for the year ended 30 September 1977 and Exhibit 7(c) shows them as reported for Allied Breweries Ltd's accounts for the year ended 24 September 1977.

Inflation accounting

Since the end of the Company's financial year an interim recommendation on this subject has been published by the Accounting Standards Committee of the professional accountancy bodies. The recommendation has the merit of simplicity. However, in its present form it fails to recognise and isolate specific raw material cost increases which may not be sustained and may not be dependent on the general level of inflation; particularly the cost of alloys of the kind incorporated in many of the Group's products. Accordingly, the Directors believe that the recommendation is not appropriate to all of the Group's business.

Subject to the above comments, the recommended calculation would reduce the Group profit before taxation for the year as follows:—

	£'000
In respect of additional depreciation	711
In respect of increase in cost of sales	2,422
	3,133
Less: gearing adjustment	1,034
Reduction in Group profit before taxation	2,099

Exhibit 7(b) Samuel Osborn & Co. Ltd: current cost statement for year ended 30 Sept. 1977 based on the Hyde Guidelines

7.4 CURRENT COST ACCOUNTING: FROM ED 24 TO SSAP 16

The Hyde adjustments only applied to an organisation's profit and loss account. Therefore, the ASC continued with its task of developing a more comprehensive system for adjusting financial statements prepared on an historic cost basis. On 30 April 1979 a new exposure draft was produced on current cost accounting, ED 24. With apparently little controversy, this became SSAP 16 during March 1980. Essentially these two documents followed the same approach to CCA as that taken by Sandilands and ED 18, which also provided the conceptual basis for the Hyde Guidelines. However SSAP 16 recommended that any adjustments made to the HCA statements to allow for changes in price levels should be incorporated in a supplementary statement. This was perhaps the most fundamental difference between ED 18's proposals for CCA and SSAP 16. The Hyde type of adjustments were to continue and to be extended to the balance sheet. Nevertheless there were some major developments. Whereas the Hyde gearing adjustment was originally shown as a single computation there was now to be a

Current cost statement

52 weeks ended 24th September, 1977

	£m	£m
Turnover		1,105·9
Profit before tax as in historical cost accounts		77·2
Adjustments—depreciation	22·2	
—cost of sales	11·3	
	33·5	
—less gearing	10·4	23·1
Adjusted profit before tax		54·1
Tax on profit		10·4
		43·7
Minority interests	0·8	
Preference dividends	0·4	1·2
		42·5
Foreign currency (losses)	(0·1)	
Gains and losses arising other than from trading	3·7	3·6
Adjusted profit available for ordinary dividends		46·1
Ordinary dividends		20·7
Adjusted retained profit		25·4

The adjustments have been calculated in accordance with the interim recommendations of the Accounting Standards Committee.

In the U.K. buildings have been revalued by the group's own professional staff.

No depreciation is provided on licensed and other properties which are freehold or held on lease for a term of and exceeding 100 years unexpired.

Plant and machinery and stocks have in the main been valued by reference to specific asset indices issued by the Central Statistical Office.

Overseas companies have used the best equivalent index for their revaluation.

The gearing adjustment has been calculated on a group basis.

Tax has been provided on the basis of the application of ED19.

Exhibit 7(c) Allied Breweries Ltd: current cost statements based on the Hyde Guidelines

two-part adjustment to show the effect of price level changes on monetary assets and liabilities. There was also to be CCA information on earnings per share.

Comments on ED 24 had to be sent to the ASC before 31 October 1979, and it was hoped to issue an SSAP on CCA as soon as possible after that date, so that the resultant standard could be effective for annual financial statements relating to accounting periods starting on or after 1 January 1980.

ED 24 appears to have had a favourable reception both from the accounting profession and other interested parties. This is perhaps surprising as it was probably just as complex as ED 18. However, a number of separate factors may have contributed to its relatively easy acceptance.

Firstly, the ASC appear to have learned that long, bulky documents are unpopular.* Secondly, following from the publication of ED 18 and the Hyde Guidelines, members of the profession had gained experience of CCA and may have been less worried about the mechanics of implementation of some form of CCA by the time ED 24 was published. Thirdly, there appeared to be a general acceptance that some form of inflation accounting had become inevitable and the apparent simplicity and the limited applicability of ED 24 probably came as something of a relief to many practising accountants. This relief may have been heightened by the realisation that ED 24 applied only to large companies.† Finally, and perhaps most importantly, SSAP 16 allowed the current cost adjusted accounts to be published as supplementary statements.

An Example of Accounts Based on ED 24: British Airways Board

Quite quickly after ED 24 had been published a number of organisations produced financial statements with a component which complied with the requirements of this document. One of the first to do this was the British Airways Board, and the appropriate section from their annual report and accounts for the year ended 31 March 1979 is shown as Exhibit 7(d).

7.5 SSAP 16

After a less heated debate than that which followed the issue of ED 18, ED 24 became SSAP 16 in March 1980.

---

* ED 18 had 93 pages and its Guidance Manual 278, whereas although its pages were unnumbered, ED 24 has only 32 and its Guidance Notes 46.
† With the wisdom of hindsight it is possible that in the future some accountants will regret not having taken a 'stronger' stand against ED 24. SSAP 16 which evolved from it, may well prove to be just as complex as ED 18. Even if the rules covering its applicability are not changed inflation will reduce the thresholds in real terms unless they are reviewed from time to time.

The basic objective of SSAP 16 is to make possible the production of financial statements which are of more help to users of accounts in making decisions about organisations than are existing HCAs. It seeks to achieve this objective by specifying procedures for calculating the profit of the organisation such that the capital, measured in terms of the net operating assets, is maintained intact and by requiring that the assets of the organisation should be shown at their current values in the balance sheet.

There are two essential features of the CCA approach as included in SSAP 16. One is to charge the current costs of resources used at the time the transactions took place against revenue for profit and loss account purposes, rather than basing the costs of resources used on their historic costs. The second is to extend this approach by using current values in the balance sheet. The major difficulty with these ideas, which are attempting to help maintain the substance of an organisation in real terms, lies in the definition of the substance of the business.

The Basic Principle of 'Value to the Business'

SSAP 16 used Sandilands' basic principles of valuing assets at their value to the business.* The value of an asset to a business is likely to be its net replacement cost. Although, if the benefits expected from an asset in the future are lower than its net replacement cost, then either the net realisable value or the economic value of the asset can be brought into the analysis, the procedure being to take the higher of these. The economic value of an asset, as was seen in the previous chapter, is defined as the present value of the asset's potential future earning power. However, SSAP 16 departed from this approach of using an asset's value to the business in the case of intangible assets, especially goodwill. Depending upon the availability of information and the type of asset involved, methods of finding the value of an asset to a business include the use of both internal and external valuers, suppliers' price lists, the examination of the prices found in recent transactions, use of indices, including those computed by organisations themselves, and externally by Government departments for groups of assets or industries.

The Requirements of SSAP 16

SSAP 16 requires the profit and loss account to be in two parts. The first shows the current cost (CC) operating profit/loss. This is calculated by making the so-called depreciation, cost of sales (COSA) and monetary working capital adjustments (MWCA) to the historic cost (HC) profit/loss. Of the three adjustments only the MWCA is new to ED 24 and hence

---

* The concept of 'value to the business', which is the basic principle behind CCA, was discussed in detail in Chapter 6 pages 124 and 125.

Group current cost statements
for the year ended 31 March 1979

These statements have been prepared in line with the proposed Statement of Standard Accounting Practice ED 24 on Current Cost Accounting issued by the Accounting Standards Committee on 30 April 1979

Current Cost Profit and Loss Account

	£m	1979 £m
Turnover		**1,640**
Historic profit before cost of capital borrowings and taxation		**110**
Additional depreciation *note 3*		**(55)**
Current cost profit before cost of capital borrowings and taxation		**55**
Cost of capital borrowings		
Gearing adjustment note 5	**16**	
Interest	**(25)**	
Currency profits	**6**	
		(3)
Current cost profit before taxation		**52**
Taxation and minority interests		**(13)**
Current cost profit attributable to British Airways		**39**
Proposed dividend		**(15)**
Retained current cost profit of year		**24**

Current Cost Balance Sheet

	1979 £m	1978 £m
Net assets		
Fixed assets *note 1*	**1,213**	1,041
Investments *note 1*	**26**	20
Net current liabilities	**(54)**	(4)
	1,185	1,057
Funds		
Public dividend capital	**150**	300
Capital maintenance reserve *note 6*	**546**	344
Other reserves *note 7*	**132**	107
	828	751
Capital borrowings	**337**	298
Exchange equalisation	**18**	7
Minority interests	**2**	1
	1,185	1,057

Return on net assets

Mean net assets	£1,121m
Current cost profit	£55m
Return on net assets	4.9%

Exhibit 7(d) British Airways Board: group current

Notes on the current cost statements

1 Assets have been revalued on the following bases:

a where new aircraft of the same or similar type are still being purchased, at net current replacement cost;

b where aircraft will be replaced by different types, at the net current cost of a replacement aircraft after allowing for differences in aircraft capacity and technology;

c property, at current market value on an existing use basis;

d equipment, by applying factors taken from the Wholesale Prices Index to the net historic cost;

e investments in associated companies and trade investments, at Directors' valuation taking account of the applicable proportion of the historic cost net assets of each company, the differences from their current cost amounts being considered immaterial.

2 Concorde assets have been excluded in both years in view of the agreement reached with HM Government (see Note 7 on page 49).

3 The current cost charge for depreciation is based on current cost asset values using the same asset lives as those in the historic cost accounts or longer in the case of aircraft whose lives have expired or substantially expired but the aircraft are expected to continue in service for a limited period.

4 As stocks are not generally held for resale no adjustment has been made for cost of sales and the monetary working capital adjustment is included in the calculation of the gearing adjustment.

5 The gearing adjustment has been made in 1978/79 only and is based on the proportion which capital borrowings, including borrowings from the National Loans Fund, and net current liabilities bear to the total funds required to finance assets (other than current assets) revalued at current cost.

6 **Capital Maintenance Reserve**

	£m	£m
Balance at 1 April 1978		344
Adjustment to reflect the write-down of Concorde assets in the historic cost accounts at 31 March 1979		136
		480
Surplus on revaluation		
Fleet	61	
Property	14	
Equipment	6	
Investments	1	
		82
		562
Gearing adjustment		(16)
Balance at 31 March 1979		546

7 **Other Reserves**

Balance at 1 April 1978 in the historic cost accounts	222
Cumulative additional depreciation of fixed assets required at beginning of year	(115)
	107
Current cost profit of the year	24
Capital reserve movement	1
Balance at 31 March 1979	132

cost statements for year ended 31 March 1979 based on ED 24

SSAP 16. The MWCA allows for the impact of changing prices on the monetary items included in working capital.

Recognising the circulating nature of working capital the Standard concedes the possibility of merging the COSA and the MWCA into a single adjustment. Having determined the CC operating profit SSAP 16 requires the calculation of CC profit attributable to shareholders to be made. This latter figure recognises the significance of capital structure and is arrived at by adding back to CC operating profit a proportion of the other three adjustments based on the proportion of debt included in the total capital structure. Interest on debt capital is then deducted to arrive at CC profit attributable to shareholders. The adjustment made to CC operating profit in arriving at CC profit attributable to the shareholders is referred to as the *gearing adjustment* and has its origins in the Hyde Guidelines. It should be noted that the SSAP 16 profit and loss adjustments concerning monetary items differ from Hyde in that they are split up into components for a MWCA and a gearing adjustment.

To complement the CC profit and loss account a CC balance sheet is required. SSAP 16 requires that the majority of assets owned by the business should be included on the CC balance sheet at their current value. However, certain assets, for example, cash and debtors and liabilities such as loans, overdrafts, etc. whose value is fixed in money terms, will not be revalued in the CC balance sheet.

In addition to any reserve shown in the HCAs there will be a Current Cost Reserve (CCR) which will be credited with all realised and unrealised revaluations of assets, and incidentally providing backlog depreciation.

The overall financial statements must include a Statement of Source and Application of Funds drawn up using the accounting conventions underlying the preparation of the main accounts. As these may be in either HC or CC form it follows that if the main accounts are HCAs there will be no necessity for a flow of funds statement in CCA form. Explanatory notes must also be used to indicate the bases and methods on which the CC adjustments have been made.

In all this the other SSAPs will be followed unless there are any conceptual differences between the HCA and the CCA systems which are likely to make their use cause conflict.

Other points to note are: there must be CC Earnings Per Share (EPS) calculations which have been made on a basis which is consistent with the way in which these have been expressed in the HCAs; group CCAs should also be prepared as is appropriate; and preceeding periods' corresponding amounts should be shown, although it is realised that a series of such figures will not be comparable on an inter-temporal basis as they are not expressed in constant prices.*

---

* *Corresponding Amounts and Ten Year Summaries in Current Cost Accounting: a Discussion Paper*, Accounting Standards Committee, 1982, suggests ways of dealing with this problem.

The application of SSAP 16 is only compulsory for companies which are listed on the Stock Exchange or for those entities which go through two of three 'gateways'. These gateways are that they have:

(a) a turnover which is greater than £5 million;
(b) fixed and current assets valued at more than £2½ million (current assets to be before the deduction of current liabilities);
(c) on average more than 250 employees.

The Standard can be complied with in one of three ways.* That is by having:

(a) HCAs as the main accounts and CCAs supplementary to these;
(b) CCAs as the main accounts and HCAs supplementary to these; or
(c) CCAs as the only accounts, but accompanying these with adequate HC information.

It is not appropriate to go into the mechanics of CCA computations or into more detail about the application of SSAP 16 here. There are many sources which enable the reader interested in the application of SSAP 16 to follow this up.†

Examples of Accounts Based on SSAP 16: ICI and British Gas

Many organisations produced financial statements soon after SSAP 16 was issued.‡ Examples of these are included in Exhibit 7(e) for ICI where the HCAs were the main accounts and the CCAs are supplementary, and Exhibit 7(f) for British Gas Corporation. Based on the CCAs being the main and only accounts where only sufficient HCA information has been provided.

7.6 DIARY OF EVENTS IN THE DEVELOPMENT OF ACCOUNTING FOR PRICE LEVEL CHANGES WITHIN THE UK

A summary of the major documents issued within the UK which have led to the production of SSAP 16 is provided in Exhibit 7(g).

---

* The Companies Act 1981 also allows the use of CCA through the Alternative Accounting Rules (page 145).
† For example *Current Cost Accounting: An Introduction to SSAP 16*, Mike Harvey and Fred Keer, Certified Accountants Education Trust, 1981.
‡ Some organisations refused to produce and include CCAs in their Financial Statements, including Allied Plant Group PLC, Crown Paints PLC, Dixons Photographic PLC, Grindley's Bank Ltd, Mann Egerton Ltd during the 1981 to 1982 period.

Date	Document
1973 17 January	ED 8 Accounting for Changes in the Purchasing Power of Money
1974 May	(P)SSAP 7 Accounting for Changes in the Purchasing Power of Money
1975 4 September	Inflation Accounting. The report of the Inflation Accounting Committee (Sandilands)
1976 January	Inflation Accounting Steering Group set up under the chairmanship of Douglas Morpeth
1976 30 November	ED 18 Current Cost Accounting
1977 4 November	Inflation Accounting; An interim recommendation (Hyde Guidelines)
1979 30 April	ED 24 Current Cost Accounting
1980 March	SSAP 16 Current Cost Accounting

Exhibit 7(g) Issue dates of key documents on accounting for price level changes

7.7   A COMPARISON OF CPP AND CCA

The publication of the Sandilands Report added fresh fuel to a controversy that had already continued over many years. Since its publication with the recommendation of CCA the pendulum has begun to swing back towards some of the features of (P)SSAP 7 that were argued against and omitted from Sandilands. Thus it is worth comparing both methods advocated to deal with accounting for price level changes before looking at the current situation. One question is whether the adjustments should be made to accounts based on general or relative price increases. Thus a major part of the debate is couched in terms of whether a general or specific index should be used—a contentious issue. Both arguments have their advocates.

Among the most spirited proponents of the use of specific indexes has been Professor Gynther.[3] He argues that the most important use of accounts is by the management of the firm (in the broadest sense) to guide them in their investment and dividend policies. In this case he suggests that it will be necessary to show changes in the firm's real position on the assumption that it is to continue more or less in its present form, as a going concern. Furthermore, due to the size of many modern corporations and the highly specialised nature of much of their equipment, realisation of non-monetary investments is rarely a serious commercial proposition. Hence many businesses are effectively 'locked into' their relevant industry. From this it can be seen that, for example, it would not be possible for the Ford

Group accounts (current cost)

Profit and loss account
for the year ended 31 December 1981

1980 £million	1980 restated in 1981 £'s £million		1981 £million	1981 Percentages of profits to related average assets	1980
5,715	6,395	**Sales**	6,581		
93	104	**Trading profit** (Note 5)	111	2·0%	1·9%
26	29	Share of profits less losses of principal associated companies and income from other trade investments	27		
119	133	**Profit before financing costs and taxation**	138	2·0%	1·9%
(46)	(51)	Interest and other financial items	(54)		
(110)	(123)	As in historical cost accounts	(142)		
64	72	Gearing adjustment (Note 6)	88		
73	82	**Profit before taxation** (Note 6)	84		
				Pence per £1 Ordinary stock	
(123)	(138)	Taxation	(111)		
(11)	(12)	Minority interests	(14)		
(61)	(68)	**Loss attributable to parent company** (Note 6)	(41)	(6·9p)	(10·4p)
(173)	(194)	Extraordinary items	(6)		
(234)	(262)	**Loss attributable to parent company after extraordinary items** (Note 6)	(47)	(7·9p)	(39·8p)
(101)	(113)	Dividends	(113)	19·0p	17·0p
(335)	(375)	**Deficit met from reserves**	(160)		
(188)	(210)	**Deficit met from reserves under ICI's gearing method** (Note 6)	(221)		

Balance sheet
at 31 December 1981

	1981 £million	1980 restated in 1981 £'s £million	1980 £million
Assets employed			
Fixed assets excluding those under construction (Note 7)	5,264	4,759	4,253
Government grants (Note 4)	(679)	(744)	(665)
	4,585	4,015	3,588
Stocks	1,298	1,229	1,098
Trading debtors	1,361	1,230	1,099
Trading creditors	(1,011)	(911)	(814)
Net assets employed in manufacturing and trading activities	6,233	5,563	4,971
Fixed assets under construction, less capital creditors	264	935	836
Trade investments	660	628	561
Total investment	7,157	7,126	6,368
Financed by			
Preference share capital	9	10	9
Loans	1,497	1,462	1,307
Advance proceeds from oil sales	67	96	86
Liquid resources less short-term borrowings	(130)	(163)	(146)
Taxation and other non-trading provisions (net)	346	299	267
Total non-equity finance	1,789	1,704	1,523
Capital and reserves attributable to minorities	476	412	368
Capital and reserves attributable to Ordinary stockholders	4,892	5,010	4,477
Issued capital	594	664	593
Reserves (Note 8)	4,239	4,313	3,854
Provision for second interim dividend	59	33	30
	7,157	7,126	6,368

Exhibit 7(e) CCAs for Imperial Chemical Industries PLC based on SSAP 16 where the HCAs were the main accounts and the CCAs supplementary

Notes relating to the CCA results

1 The accounts prepared on a Current Cost Accounting (CCA) basis include allowance for the impact of price changes on the funds needed to carry on the business and maintain its operating capability. Under the provisions of Statement of Standard Accounting Practice No. 16 (SSAP16) this is achieved by making adjustments to the holding values of assets employed and to the historical cost trading profit to take into account the current levels of construction costs and of raw materials and other operating costs. The profit before taxation further includes a gearing adjustment which represents the inflationary benefit to the stockholders from loan finance, and partially offsets the cost of loan interest. The presentation of the accounts has been designed to separate trading items from items associated with finance and to demonstrate the relationship between the profit and loss account and the balance sheet (see also Note 6 – gearing adjustment).

2 The accounting policies adopted in the historical cost accounts, set out on page 25, apply also to the CCA accounts, except for modifications required to comply with SSAP16.

3 In order to provide a more useful comparison between 1980 and 1981, the results for 1980 have been shown both in 1980 £'s and re-stated in 1981 £'s. For this purpose the movement of 11.9 per cent in the average UK retail price index between 1980 and 1981 has been taken to represent the general rate of inflation.

4 The bases for the current cost adjustments are:

(a) Fixed assets and depreciation–

(i) In general, indices of the cost of chemical plants, and

(ii) Asset lives which are approximately one third longer than those applied in the historical cost accounts (see page 25). Based on reviews of asset values and lives which have been undertaken as part of the Group's consideration of the current cost basis of accounting, the Group believes that it is appropriate for CCA purposes to use longer lives from within the range of possible lives.

(b) Stocks and the cost of sales adjustment – actual movements in costs, using the averaging method.

(c) Changes in the requirements for monetary working capital (trading debtors less creditors) – movements in appropriate specific indices.

(d) Government grants – indices of the cost of chemical plants; grants have been brought into profits over the lives adopted for CCA accounts. In the balance sheet a deduction is made from fixed assets in respect of the current value of grants attributable to the residual value of the assets.

5 Trading profit

Current cost adjustments reduced the historical cost trading profit as shown below:

	1981	1980 restated in 1981 £'s	1980
	£million	£million	£million
Trading profit – historical cost accounts	425	372	332
Cost of sales adjustment	(119)	(122)	(109)
Monetary working capital adjustment	(52)	(3)	(3)
Supplementary depreciation	(185)	(185)	(165)
Indexation of government grants	42	42	38
Trading profit – current cost accounts	111	104	93

The amounts of depreciation charged and government grants credited in the current cost accounts were:

	1981	1980 restated in 1981 £'s	1980
Depreciation	533	510	456
Government grants	65	66	59

6 Gearing adjustment

The gearing percentage, being the proportion of average non-equity finance to average total investment, was 24.5% (1980 22.8%).

Under SSAP16 the gearing adjustment in respect of fixed assets is related to the charge for supplementary depreciation (after making allowance for the difference between historical and CCA asset lives). The adjustment thus excludes revaluation surpluses not yet treated as realised. ICI believes that this results in mis-stating the amount by which the interests of the equity stockholders have been affected by loan and other external financing, the interest on which has been charged against profits.

Under ICI's method, the gearing adjustment represents the total holding gains less losses for the year on assets effectively financed by borrowings less cash. The exchange gains or losses on the non-sterling part of these net borrowings are then added to or deducted from the adjustment; in the event that the forthcoming UK accounting standard on foreign currency translation contains concepts on matching borrowings and assets which do not accord with this treatment, some future modification of the method may be appropriate.

The cost of interest and other financial items calculated in accordance with ICI's method would be:

	1981	1980 restated in 1981 £'s	1980
	£million	£million	£million
As in historical cost accounts	225	96	86
Gearing adjustment	(188)	(123)	(110)
Exchange gains (losses) on financial items	132	96	118
As in current cost accounts – ICI's method	(105)	105	94

On this basis results would be:

	1981	1980 restated in 1981 £'s	1980
Profit before taxation	33	238	213

Profit (loss) attributable to the parent company:

	1981	1980 restated in 1981 £'s	1980
before extraordinary items	(102)	96	86
after extraordinary items	(108)	(97)	(87)
Deficit met from reserves	(221)	(210)	(188)

Exhibit 7(e) continued

7 Fixed assets

| | 31 December 1981 | | | 1980 restated in 1981 £'s | 1980 |
	Gross £million	Depreciation £million	Net £million	Net £million	Net £million
Land and buildings	2,314	1,035	1,279	1,124	1,004
Plant and machinery	10,627	6,341	4,286	4,647	4,153
	12,941	7,376	5,565	5,771	5,157
Under construction	(301)		(301)	(1,012)	(904)
	12,640	7,376	5,264	4,759	4,253

8 Reserves

	1981 £million	1980 restated in 1981 £'s £million	1980 £million
At beginning of year	3,854	4,077	3,643
Inflation and exchange adjustments	536	576	515
Revaluation surplus on:			
Fixed assets	247	665	594
Government grants	(28)	(94)	(84)
Investments	65	90	81
Stocks	123	85	76
Monetary working capital adjustment	49	(3)	(3)
Gearing adjustment	(82)	(65)	(58)
Exchange adjustments	162	(102)	(91)
Deficit for year	(160)	(375)	(335)
Share premiums	1	35	31
Other movements	8	—	—
At end of year	4,239	4,313	3,854

Exhibit 7(e) continued

Consolidated current cost profit and loss account

for the year ended 31st March 1982

£ million

	Notes	1982	1981
1 Turnover	1	5 235·3	4 295·4
2 Current cost operating profit	2	310·8	381·1
3 Taxation	6	(190·6)	(227·2)
4 Net interest receivable	7	23·4	2·2
5 Current cost profit retained		143·6	156·1
6 Retained profits at 1st April 1981		1 105·1	949·0
7 Current cost profit retained		143·6	156·1
8 Retained profits at 31st March 1982		1 248·7	1 105·1

Return on average net assets at current cost

		£ million	%
(i)	Average net assets at current cost	10 513·1	
(ii)	Current cost operating profit	310·8	
(iii)	Return		3·0
(iv)	Current cost profit retained	143·6	
(v)	Return		1·4

Financial target

The Financial Target set by H.M. Government for the Corporation for the three year period 1980/81 to 1982/83 is an average annual return of 3·5% of current cost operating profit on average net assets at current cost. The actual return in 1981/82 was 3·0% (line (iii) above). The cumulative average return for the two year period covering the financial years 1980/81 and 1981/82 is 3·5%.

Exhibit 7(f) British Gas Corporation accounts based on SSAP 16 where the CC

Current cost balance sheets

at 31st March 1982

£ million

	Notes	British Gas Corporation 1982	British Gas Corporation 1981	Consolidated 1982	Consolidated 1981
Net assets					
1 Fixed assets	Sch 3	9 582·7	8 935·0	9 946·6	9 246·0
2 Investments	9	209·3	213·9	·0	·0
3 Deposits with the National Loans Fund	10	300·0	300·0	300·0	300·0
4 Net current assets	11	746·3	567·7	708·8	524·8
		10 838·3	10 016·6	10 955·4	10 070·8
Financed as follows					
5 Capital liabilities	12	386·5	420·8	386·5	420·8
6 Current cost reserve	13	8 999·4	8 197·5	8 923·0	8 158·4
7 Retained profits		1 126·1	1 063·1	1 248·7	1 105·1
8 Deferred taxation	15	322·6	335·2	370·4	364·1
9 Provision for site restoration costs	16	3·7	—	26·8	22·4
		10 838·3	10 016·6	10 955·4	10 070·8

Denis Rooke   Chairman

W G Jewers   Managing Director, Finance

are the main accounts with only sufficient HCA information being provided

Notes to the Accounts

(a) Basis of accounting
The consolidated accounts of the British Gas Corporation and its subsidiaries for the year ended 31st March 1982 have been prepared under the current cost accounting convention, in accordance with Statement of Standard Accounting Practice Number 16 (SSAP 16). Under this accounting convention, provision is made in the accounts for the effects of specific price changes on the resources necessary to maintain the operating capability of the business.

SSAP 16 requires that Nationalised Industries, in view of the special nature of their capital structures, should not make a gearing adjustment in their profit and loss accounts. At the Government's request, however, the effect of a gearing adjustment is shown in Note 2 (b) to the Corporation's accounts.

(b) Fixed assets
Fixed assets are stated in the balance sheets at their value to the business, being current replacement cost less accumulated depreciation. Additions to fixed assets are included at actual cost, after deducting grants and contributions from customers.

The balance sheets include the value to the business of all fixed assets in use by the Corporation and its subsidiaries, although certain assets of undertakings taken over in 1949 (pre-vesting assets) had previously been written out of the Corporation's historical cost accounts.

The value to the business of fixed assets has been assessed on the following bases:

(i)   land and buildings—valuation by the Corporation's professional surveying staff;

(ii) regional mains, services, meters and gas storage—application of calculated industry average unit replacement costs to the physical distances or quantities in use;

(iii) all other fixed assets, including the national transmission system—indexation of historical costs using appropriate indices.

The assessment of value to the business involves certain estimates being made. These may be subject to continuing revision in future years as more information becomes available and as a result of further research into current cost accounting.

(c) Depreciation
The assets referred to in sub-paragraphs (i) to (iii) below are subject to straight line depreciation, while the assets referred to in sub-paragraphs (iv) and (v) below are subject to throughput depreciation:

(i)   Freehold land is not depreciated, but the value to the business of buildings standing thereon is depreciated over varying periods, depending on the type of construction, with a maximum of fifty years.

(ii) The value to the business of leasehold premiums is depreciated over the period to the next rent review. Specialist leasehold buildings are depreciated over the term of the lease or fifty years, whichever is the shorter.

(iii) The regional distribution systems and all other fixed assets of the Corporation, apart from the national transmission system, are depreciated at rates sufficient to write off the gross current cost of individual assets over their estimated useful lives. The depreciation periods for the principal categories of assets are as follows:

    40 years—mains, gas holders and brick or concrete storage tanks.

    25 years—service pipes.

    20 years—meters, metal storage tanks and plant and machinery.

    10 years—electronic and electrical control equipment.

    5 years—mobile plant and machinery, furniture, fittings and office machinery and motor vehicles.

(iv) The present estimated cost of the national transmission system, including estimated expenditure to completion in current cost terms, is depreciated on the throughput basis by reference to the volume of gas passed through the system each year compared with the estimated recoverable reserves of natural gas from contracted and near-contracted gas fields. Both the estimates of recoverable reserves and the estimated cost of the completed system are reviewed annually and the rate of depreciation (1982 4%; 1981 4%) adjusted accordingly.

(v)   Expenditure on the development of natural gas and oil fields is not depreciated until such time as production commences from the fields concerned. When production has commenced, the present estimated cost of the field developments, including estimated expenditure to completion in current cost terms, is depreciated on the throughput basis by reference to the volume of gas and oil produced each year from the fields, compared with the total estimated recoverable reserves of those fields. Both the estimates of recoverable reserves and the estimated cost of the completed developments are reviewed annually and the rates of depreciation adjusted accordingly.

Exhibit 7(f) continued

The Corporation charges the cost of replacing certain categories of fixed assets (principally mains, services and meters) as a trading cost, capitalising only that expenditure which represents an extension to, or a significant increase in, capacity of its fixed assets. This replacement expenditure, together with historical cost depreciation and supplementary depreciation, represents the total current cost depreciation charge.

(d) Working capital adjustments
The cost of sales adjustment (COSA) is the difference between the current cost at the date of sale and the historical cost of stocks sold. It is calculated by applying indices, to reflect increases in input costs, to average stocks of gas, appliances and installation materials.

The monetary working capital adjustment (MWCA) represents the change in working capital attributable to increases in input prices during the year. The MWCA has been calculated using indices and average monetary working capital during the year. Monetary working capital comprises debtors and payments in advance, accrued revenue for gas, hire purchase and deferred payment accounts and sundry stocks, less creditors (excluding creditors for fixed assets) and accrued charges.

(e) Site restoration costs
Operators of North Sea oil and gas fields are required to restore the sea bed at the end of the producing lives of the fields to a condition acceptable to the Department of Trade. Provision is made for site restoration costs, calculated field by field on a throughput basis similar to that used for depreciation. Estimates of such costs (based on price levels at the balance sheet date), which are subject to considerable uncertainty, are reviewed periodically.

(f) Stocks of gas, appliances and stores
These are valued at current cost less provision for deterioration, damage and obsolescence.

(g) Deferred taxation
(i) Corporation tax
   Deferred taxation, in respect of accelerated depreciation and other timing differences, is provided except where such timing differences are expected, with reasonable probability, to continue in the foreseeable future.

(ii) Petroleum revenue tax
   Deferred taxation, in respect of accelerated depreciation, is provided except where such timing differences are expected, with reasonable probability, to continue in the foreseeable future. The taxation benefit of uplift allowance is spread over the shorter of (i) the life of the field and (ii) the expected period of ownership of the field. Uplift is amortised in accordance with oil production. Credit for safeguard and oil allowance is recognised in the accounting periods in which they are effective.

(h) Foreign currencies
The Corporation's foreign currency loans have all been guaranteed by H.M. Treasury as to payment of interest and principal and are subject to special exchange cover arrangements, whereby H.M. Treasury insures the Corporation against exchange rate fluctuations. The loans are stated in the balance sheets at their original sterling proceeds.

(i) Research and development expenditure
Expenditure on research and development is written off when incurred.

(j) Exploration expenditure
Expenditure on exploration for natural gas and oil is written off when incurred.

(k) Investment in subsidiaries
The Corporation's interest in shares in subsidiaries is included in its balance sheet at the Corporation's share of the book amount of the net assets, expressed on a current cost basis, of those subsidiaries.

Exhibit 7(f) continued

Motor Corporation to move into anything other than automobile manufacture in the foreseeable future. Therefore Ford must survive in the motor industry or not at all. If it were to liquidate, both the nature of its assets and the economic implications of its closure would ensure that the monies realised would be sufficiently small to render closure an unattractive proposition to both its management and owners. In this situation for profit to have any meaning the capital maintained needs to be the specialised physical capital necessary to a motor vehicle manufacturer. Maintenance of purchasing power would have little relevance.

Obviously the case for the use of specific indices is weakened as the firm becomes more diversified. In the extreme case, for a completely diversified firm the choice between specific or general indexes will make little difference since the general index is simply a weighted average of all specific indices. Hence corporate profit for a very widely diversified firm would not differ greatly whichever system were employed (although profits reported by different divisions could show significant differences depending upon the capital maintenance concept used). On the other hand, Professor Baxter,[4] has maintained that the most important users of published accounts are outsiders (including the shareholders) who will be more interested in changes in the value of the firm in general purchasing power terms. In addition, while liquidation of the whole concern is rarely a viable proposition the realisation of a relatively small shareholding frequently is. Although whole corporations cannot switch in and out of industrial sectors at will, individual shareholders can. Accordingly, since shareholders are interested in the consumption potential that their shareholdings bring and that consumption is of a general nature then they are interested in profits in general purchasing power terms.

The ASC implicitly claimed for CPP accounting the objectivity advantage of HCA when in (P)SSAP 7 it said that the historical cost convention 'has the advantage that the recorded historical cost is derived from factual monetary transactions, and its use helps to limit the number of matters within the accounts which are subject to the exercise of judgement'[5] and stated that CPP 'does not suggest the abandonment of the historic cost convention, but simply that historical costs should be converted from an aggregation of historical pounds of many different purchasing powers into approximate figures of current purchasing power and that this information be given in a supplement to the basic accounts prepared on the historical cost basis'.[6] In fact ED 8 from which (P)SSAP 7 came was even more explicit, saying that CPP 'helps to limit the number of matters within accounts which are subject to the exercise of judgement' while producing figures that are 'reasonably comparable between companies and over time', and according to ED 8 current value accounting* can only exist 'separately

---

* The concept of current value accounting has been discussed for many years and the Sandilands form of CCA is only one specific version of this.

from the concept of general price level adjusted accounting'. In other words it is being suggested that CCA is not an adjustment for inflation at all but rather adjustment for relative price changes due to changes in technology or market pressure. (P)SSAP 7 was superseded by the report of the Sandilands Committee which rejected CPP adjustments in favour of CCA. However, Sandilands recognised that CPP had widespread support. In fact 65 per cent of the respondents to Sandilands' own questionnaire considered CPP useful for a defined list of purposes and 63 per cent of quoted companies considered the proposals in ED 8 preferable to any alternative method of accounting for price level changes. Nevertheless, the Sandilands Committee put aside this evidence of support in the (unsubstantiated) belief that it arose from the fact that at the time of the questionnaire CPP was the only form of inflation accounting defined in a single, readily available document, namely (P)SSAP 7.

An important advantage of CPP, particularly from the viewpoint of practising accountants is the relative arithmetic certainty of one independently produced and verifiable index. Thus CPP combined the objectivity of HCA with the objectivity of the RPI. This is obviously important for auditing and may account for the popularity of CPP with the audit profession.

The Sandilands Report then goes on to criticise CPP on a number of grounds. The first and perhaps most important criticism is that it draws attention to the fact that the adoption of CPP accounting involves moving away from money as the unit of measurement in accounts and adopting a new measure—a 'unit of current purchasing power'. The Committee believed that the principal criteria for a unit of measurement underlying an accounting system should be:

1. The unit should be equally useful to all users of accounts.
2. The unit should not change from year to year.
3. The unit should be the same for all enterprises presenting financial statements.
4. The unit should preferably be a physical object which could be exchanged by users of accounts.
5. The unit should represent a constant value through time.[7]

The monetary unit meets the first four of these criteria but fails to meet the fifth when the value of money is changing. However, according to the Sandilands Report, the 'unit of current purchasing power' fails to meet the first four criteria. Although the first criterion (based as it is on the RPI) may be a useful measure of purchasing power for those shareholders whose consumption pattern is similar to that on which the RPI is based, it will be less useful to shareholders, such as institutional shareholders, whose consumption pattern is significantly different. Regarding the second criterion, as accounts will be drawn up in terms of units of current purchasing power at the appropriate year end, the unit of measurement will change from year to year. Since different businesses have different accounting periods then even within the same calendar year different sets of accounts will be based on different units. Thus the third criterion is not met. As far as the fourth criterion is concerned, as the unit of current purchasing power is obviously an abstraction and does not exist in a physical form, it cannot be exchanged by users of accounts.

As evidence of the confusion that exists with respect to accounts based on units of current purchasing power the Committee note 'that a number of companies already publishing CPP statements have suggested in their annual reports that the profit figures contained in these statements are 'higher' or 'lower' than the profit figures shown in the basic accounts'. The Report continues 'This can only be true in numerical terms. The profit figure in a CPP supplementary statement is the same as the profit figure in the basic accounts, converted into different units of measurement'.[8]

The second major criticism that Sandilands made of CPP is that restating asset values at the current purchasing power equivalent of historic cost still does not result in the balance sheet giving an accurate picture of the value to the business of the various assets and liabilities owned and owed by the firm. Increases in the general price level are usually only one of the causes of the discrepancy between historic cost and the value of assets to the business.

The third criticism is that the Committee believed that current operating profit, i.e. the difference between current revenues and the current cost of the assets used up in generating those revenues, is a useful measure in determining the efficiency with which the affairs of the business have been conducted. They argue that including holding gains and gains and losses on monetary items as part of a single total profit figure reduces the usefulness of profit as a measure of managerial efficiency. Finally there are a number of practical difficulties associated with the use of CPP among which they include the difficulty of making the distinction between monetary and non-monetary items.

In consequence of their criticism of CPP Sandilands recommend that accounts should be based on a form of current value accounting—CCA. They claim for this the advantages that it is simple to understand and that adjustments are based on changes in the money value of the actual assets employed. In this they recommend that operating profit should be separated from holding gains and that no cognisance should be taken of gains and losses on monetary items in the accounts proper.

The Sandilands proposals have been criticised. Members of the profession are particularly concerned at the discretion that must inevitably be given to directors in determining the 'value to the business' of the various assets that their organisations own. This is a marked movement away from the need for objective evidence which has hitherto been a cornerstone of conventional accounts. A second important criticism is that by initially excluding gains and losses on monetary items from the accounts proper (which the

Method (based on)	CCA (Sandilands Recommendations)	CPP (P)SSAP 7
Status of financial statement provided	A single adjusted statement (book values still to be shown)	Normal historic cost statement with supplementary statement of adjusted figures
Objective of adjustment	To maintain productive capacity and real capital (i.e. inward looking)	To maintain purchasing power on the parts of the investors (i.e. outward looking)
Inflation index used	Specific indexes	General indexes (RPI)
Monetary items	Not adjusted	Adjusted
Presentation	See Exhibit 7(f)	See Exhibits 6(a) & 6(b)

Exhibit 7(h) CCA and CPP compared

ED 18 supplementary statements did) the proposals ignore the very real benefits from owing money in a period of high inflation.*

The argument of Sandilands which carefully considered this point, was that implicit in its suggested adjustments was an allowance for this aspect of the effect of changing price levels on published financial statements. However, adjustments to monetary items can sometimes give extraordinary results, e.g. particularly where companies are highly geared. This can affect the accounts of property companies or firms with large property holdings such as breweries, retailing or entertainment and leisure organisations which typically have large amounts of debts in their capital structures, as seen from Exhibit 6(f) on page 131.

One important point to note is that, as Professor Baxter has pointed out many times, any system developed for price level change accounting must also be capable of dealing with periods of deflation as well as inflation. He says about CCA that 'Lack of caution in bad times seems one of CCA's worst features yet it has attracted little or no attention'.[9]

To help a comparison of the major divergencies between CCA and CPP and the effects of these on financial statements, the differences between the two systems are set out in Exhibit 7(h).

The Advantages of SSAP 16

Whatever the relative merits of CPP and CCA it is clear that the ASC has become convinced that CCA is the superior system. As part of its attempt

---

* Although the ED 18 supplementary statements did this, SSAP 16 takes some cognisance of monetary items through its MWCA and gearing adjustments.

to convince the accounting profession that this is the case it set out the following 'advantages' of CCA in the introduction to ED 18.

(a) Calculating *depreciation* based on the value to the business of fixed assets provides a more realistic measure of the resources used in a period.

(b) Calculating the *cost of sales* on the basis of the cost of replacing goods at the time they were sold helps maintain the value of the entity in real terms.

(c) The introduction of the *appropriation account* brings together revaluation surpluses and current cost profit, which helps directors in their retention and dividend decisions.

(d) Assets would be shown at their *current values* in the balance sheet.

(e) A statement of the change in *equity interest*, after allowing for changes in the value of money, shows how the company has performed in real terms during inflationary periods.

(f) The effect of holding *monetary items* in terms of gains or losses would be highlighted.

(g) Both management and users of accounts would be provided with more *realistic information* on such things as the value of assets, costs and profits, and thus on real returns on assets and capital.

(h) It would clearly distinguish between gains made from *operations* and gains made from *holding assets*.

ED 18 stated that all these advantages would help in the appraisal of an organisation by both its management and outsiders, with managers being able to evaluate the performance of departments, products, etc. and the people responsible for them. Also both management and outsiders would be able to evaluate the performance of companies and industries on an Inter-Divisional (Departmental) Comparison (IDC), Inter-Firm Comparison (IFC) and Inter-Temporal Comparison (ITC) basis.

7.8   THE DEBATE CONTINUES

During the middle of 1982 Martin Haslam and David Keymer stepped up their continuing rebellion against current cost accounting. In 1977 they had been successful in persuading the membership of the ICAEW to vote against the acceptance of ED 18, which was subsequently withdrawn. In 1982 they proposed a motion calling for the immediate withdrawal of SSAP 16. The view of the other accounting bodies, and other interested parties such as the Stock Exchange and clearing banks, was that it should be allowed to

---

* While ED 18 was subsequently withdrawn, the essential ideas contained therein form the basis of SSAP 16. It is apparent that the ASC, at least, has not changed its mind on the merits of the two systems.

finish the three year trial period which had been agreed for it when it was issued in March 1980. After that time it should be carefully evaluated by the CCA sub-committee of the ASC—which, no doubt because of the emotive connotations of current cost accounting, had its name changed during 1982 to the Inflation Accounting Sub-Committee. On Thursday 29 July 1982, after two months of debate on the subject, the ICAEW held a special meeting to vote on the Haslam – Keymer motion for the withdrawal of SSAP 16. With some 40% of the membership voting, including proxies, the motion was lost by a narrow margin of 933 votes; 14,812 votes (48.47%) had been cast in favour of withdrawal, and 15,745 (51.53%) against.

Thus support for CCA as enshrined in SSAP 16 is not complete, and no doubt the ASC will have to carefully consider the benefits that it is felt to give and the problems that organisations have come across as they implemented it. It seems that some changes will have to be forthcoming if a Standard to deal with the undoubted problems caused by the effect of inflation on financial statements is to survive in the UK.

7.9   CONCLUSIONS

Although the arguments still rage, a working consensus has now been reached on how to adjust financial statements for changing price levels. SSAP 16 probably represents a compromise between those who advocate the complete abandonment of HCAs and the traditionalists who see no viable, objective alternative to them. Presumably neither group is completely satisfied and it is unlikely that those who favour CPP accounting have yet given up the fight. It would be rash indeed to suppose that the issue is now decided. However what does seem clear is that some form of price level adjustment is here to stay. Just as yesterday's revolutionary becomes today's establishment figure, so yesterday's innovation is today's accepted practice.

It seems likely that as more experience is gained in operating a system of CCA then the requirements of SSAP 16 will be refined and built upon. Certainly it seems inevitable that they will be extended to cover a wider range of organisations than they now apply to. The question of how to adjust accounts for changing prices is no longer simply one of academic interest, the formal requirements to do so now exists. Those who must keep pace with the development that must surely come will be better able to do so if they are equipped with an understanding of what has gone before.

REFERENCES

1. ED 18 *Current Cost Accounting* ,Accounting Standards Committee, 30 November 1976, paras. 76 to 79 explain these statements and p. 82 provides examples of suggested layouts for them.

2. *Inflation Accounting—An Interim Recommendation*, Accounting Standards Committee, 4 November 1977 (Hyde Guidelines), para. 4.
3. Gynther, R.S., *Accounting for Price Level Changes: Theory and Procedures*, Pergamon Press 1966.
4. Baxter, W.T., 'General or specific index?—capital maintenance under changing prices', *Journal of UEC*, No. 3., September 1967.
5. (P)SSAP 7, *Accounting for Changes in the Purchasing Power of Money*, Accounting Standards Steering Committee, May 1974.
6. *Ibid*, para. 3.
7. *Inflation Accounting: Report of the Inflation Accounting Committee*, Cmnd 6225, HMSO, September 1975 (Sandilands) paras. 149 and 407.
8. *Ibid*, para. 417.
9. Baxter, W.T., 'Accountants and inflation', *Lloyds Bank Review*, October 1977, p. 12.

QUESTIONS AND DISCUSSION PROBLEMS

1. Describe the major adjustments required to be made to the profit and loss account by SSAP 16.
2. Compare the advantages and disadvantages of adjusting financial statements prepared using the historic cost convention with the concepts underlying CPP and CCA.
3. From ED 8 to SSAP 16 has been a long haul. (i) Briefly discuss the major milestones along this road; (ii) Carefully examine the point at which the UK accounting profession has arrived.
4. Originally, Sandilands recommended a single adjusted current cost statement with book values of assets still to be shown. However SSAP 16 provides for the use of one of three alternative methods to show CCAs. Critically discuss the three ways allowed in SSAP16.
5. If there have been any developments to 'accounting for price level changes' since this book was published, briefly outline these.

CHAPTER 8
Towards Accounting Standards

8.1 INTRODUCTION

The aim of this final chapter is to draw together the previous sections where the emphasis was on the development of accounting theories and discuss these in relation to reported value and income. The purpose of the financial accounting system is to provide financial information in quantitative form for both internal and external users of the accounts. Therefore it is important to know precisely what information is needed and to what use it will be put. Financial accounts are basically a measurement device and a major problem in accounting is that there has been a tendency to develop the measuring device before asking the questions 'What is being measured?' 'For what purpose?' and 'For whom?'

It is not normal to think of choosing devices to measure inanimate objects before deciding upon what is required in their measurement. For example, an exporter may have chosen scales to measure cargo by weight only to find later that the shipping company did not measure by weight but by volume. The calibrations of measuring devices must also be known—unlike the case of a builder in America who assumed the architect's plan for a house to be built in Palm Beach, which did not state a scale, was drawn in inches and built accordingly, only to find later that the scale was, in fact, based upon centimetres.

8.2 USERS OF FINANCIAL STATEMENTS AND THEIR OBJECTIVES

For discussion purposes users of accounts will be grouped into a number of major headings under which requirements for each group will be considered.[1]

(a) Management
Obviously an enterprise's management will be the major user of the information generated by the organisation's accounting system. However, as

they have complete and immediate access to financial information within their firm they do not need to wait for, neither are they limited by, the information contained in the published accounts. Furthermore, since organisations' major financial accounts tend to be produced annually, and have a lag between their appearance and the operations upon which they report, they are of little more than academic, historic interest to management. Nevertheless, management know that published financial statements will provide information on their own ability to manage as these statements indicate to other user groups how successful the organisation has been. Thus although for their day-to-day decision-making and operational control purposes management will be using information about revenues and expenditures immediately the information is generated, they will still want to keep an eye on the potential reactions of other user groups to the published accounts and reports of their organisation.

(b) Investors

Under this heading the investor group will be widened to embrace both the current and the potential shareholders of an organisation and investment analysts.* Basically this group will be interested in the dividends that are paid. Investors will also be concerned with the organisation's prospects. As the mainstream financial statements are produced after the economic events that they report, and are produced in terms of the historic cost figures applicable at the time the various business transactions concerned took place, then the traditional published financial statements provide little indication of the future prospects of an organisation. Perhaps the best that can be said about a series of published accounts of a firm is that they may indicate its continued progress and it may (or may not) be a fair assumption that this progress can be extrapolated into the future. However, the published accounts do indicate whether the stewardship requirements are being met, even if only at the basic level of listing the assets owned by the organisation and providing information on its liabilities.

It is interesting to note that today organisations' published financial and annual reports are quite glossy affairs. No doubt this is to inspire the confidence of the lay investor and readers. Currently, published accounts contain much information which not long ago management would never have agreed to include. They also provide the organisation's Chairman with the opportunity to state his views on the future prospects of his enterprise. For the Chairman's report is generally the only information to be found in financial statements that is indicative of the firm's future (even if usually rather nebulous).†

---

* Investment analysts could be classified as a separate user group.
† See the section Forecasts and Budgetary Disclosure on page 174 for a debate about the disclosure of forecasts.

(c) Long-term debt holders
An organisation's long-term debt holders (and potential debt holders)
include debenture holders and those providing long-term loans, for example
the banks. The long-term debt holders are mainly interested in ensuring
that they will get the interest payments due to them and that these will be
received on time. They are also concerned with the security of their capital.
Perhaps this class of user is reasonably well served by the published financial
statements currently issued, since these statements, being prepared with
the stewardship function in mind, are drawn up on the basis of prudence.
In addition, this group's ability to evaluate the organisation as a going
concern has been improved now that flow of funds statements have become
general.*

       However, it should be noted that flow of funds statements do no more
than reassemble existing figures and provide no additional information to
user groups. Thus their basic purpose is to highlight the liquidity position
of the organisation. Previously this could have been, and probably was,
done by informed readers of accounts, who have now been saved from the
necessity of compiling this statement themselves.

(d) Employees
Included in this category will be both individual employees and groups of
them represented by trade unions. In the latter case the trade union group
will probably have an additional role as investors, for example through
their pension funds. However, all employees will have an interest as far as
both their future employment and income prospects are concerned. Today,
many companies produce an 'employee report'.† This is to provide
employees with financial information about their employers in a more
readable form and thus, it is hoped, lead to better understanding of the
business by employees. It should be noted that the employee report does
not have statutory standing and thus is not restricted by audit requirements
in any way. An interesting point is that in current thinking the employee
report remains an optional extra and the idea of it being compulsory
commands little support from the Government or accounting bodies.

       Financial statements are only helpful to employees in so far as they

---

* Such a statement is now required by SSAP 10, *Statements of Source and Application of Funds*,
  which was issued by the ASC during July 1975, for all businesses with a turnover of
  £25,000 or more.
† This is not the same thing as the 'employment statement' introduced by the Companies
  Act 1967 which directed that certain information concerning employees must be provided
  in financial statements, nor the more far-reaching suggestions for the disclosure of information on: numbers joining and leaving; training policies; recognised unions; employment
  participation arrangements; days lost through strikes; pension and sick pay arrangements;
  and numbers of disabled employed, in the employment statement to be found in *The
  Future of Company Reports*, Cmnd 6888, HMSO, July 1977, para. 21.

indicate that they are unlikely to be facing the possibility of redundancies because their employer appears to be in a buoyant position—which may also indicate that the time is ripe to put in another wage demand!

(e) Suppliers

The supplier group has a number of reasons for being interested in the firms which are its customers. These interests include knowing whether any goods that they may supply on credit are likely to be paid for. With respect to this interest, a problem arises in that, since accounts are likely to be prepared well in arrears, the information contained in them is likely to arrive too late to help suppliers stop supplying customers with developing cash flow difficulties.

The suppliers are also interested in the future prospects of their customers. However, it has already been noted that the published accounts provide very little information about an organisation's future prospects, unless of course they show that the firm with a proven track record is likely to at least maintain its past performance. Probably suppliers are more likely to get information on future prospects of customers through informal contacts and talks between the executives of the parties involved.

(f) Consumers

This group contains the final and the industrial consumer both of whom are interested in the firms from which they make purchases, for a number of reasons. Most important among these is concern with continuity of supply. For example both sorts of consumers make purchases of items which require after sales service, in the form of maintenance and repairs, and want to know that they will be able to obtain this. The industrial consumer wants to know about the continuation of sources of supply of raw materials and components. Consumers also want to know whether monopoly situations exist and if so whether they are likely to be exploited. Ways are being developed to provide final consumers with the sort of information about enterprises that would be useful to them. Current developments in social accounting show an interest and awareness of the importance of this user group.

(g) The Government

The Government and government departments require accounting information for revenue, that is, taxation, and economic planning purposes. Accounts based upon historic information are really only helpful in as far as the revenue function is concerned, for they enable a tax demand to be raised. However, in the case of the government formulating their economic plans it would be information concerning such things as the enterprise's intentions about their investment and activity plans that would be more helpful. This sort of information tends to come from other sources such as censuses, planning agreements, and so on, rather than published financial statements.

(h) Society
The public and society are a relatively new addition to the list of users of accounts. People, especially those affected by an organisation operating in their local area, want to know how the firm is likely to fare in the future. This is especially so when its operations have an effect on the local economy. Society is also concerned with many environmental aspects of the organisation. This may be with respect to factories producing effluents which pollute the environment or the organisation's concern with conservation. However, how well the firm's published accounts can provide information which will help this user group is questionable, although some Chairman's Reports make the right noises about their organisation's social responsibilities.

Professors Nicholas Dopuch and Shyam Sunder have suggested that before objectives for financial accounting can be discussed the definition of these must be clear. They suggest that objectives can be classified as functional, common and dominant group ones.[2]

Functional Objectives

These are the objectives of a social activity* in a functional sense, and the union of individual objectives can be ascertained by observing the social activity without having to find out what the motives of the individuals involved in it are. Thus the activities of accounting such as systematically recording, classifying and reporting on business transactions; helping to monitor an organisation's and its management's performance; attempting to maximise the shareholders' wealth; and so on are functional objectives as they are all legitimate objectives for individuals or one or more of the user groups.

Common Objectives

Common objectives are those where individuals' objectives overlap. Therefore by definition the number of objectives in this group must equal or be less than the number of functional objectives. It is likely that individuals or organisations in each user group will have common objectives, but the objectives of different user groups are unlikely always to be common.

Dominant Group Objectives

These come about when an individual or group is able to impose his objec-

---

* Accounting is a social activity in which social groupings of managers, accountants and auditors, employees, the government and its agencies, and so on engage.

tives on others involved in the same activity. If for example, the ICAEW dominated the ASC membership, and the ASC were dominated by the large professional firms, the latter's own objectives might dominate the profession as a whole.

In the past the investor user group probably dominated accounting objectives, but over the past century, this dominance has diminished. Today the dominant objectives emerge through consensus between the various user groups.

8.3   DISCLOSURE DEVELOPMENTS IN PUBLISHED FINANCIAL STATEMENTS

The question of how much information should be disclosed is frequently a major issue in any new development of published financial statements. Initially accounts only involved the keeping of records of assets owned, which led on to the development of bookkeeping. Landlords wanted records of what property they owned and how this was being used. Thus the first development of accounting was for what has become termed the '*stewardship*' function—the idea of keeping records by the steward. Then came the duality of double-entry bookkeeping which is generally credited to Fra Pacioli, an Italian who wrote his famous treatise on the subject during the fifteenth century.[3] In this, full instructions for the preparation of a profit statement, with surpluses transferred to a capital account, were given. This is the system which is fundamental to late twentieth century computerised bookkeeping. The stewardship function continued to be the main principle underlying the development of accounts well into the Industrial Revolution. Accounts for partnerships and the original joint stock companies were also to ensure that the owners' assets were being properly used, and not misappropriated by servants of the organisation.

However, for a variety of reasons, the emphasis in the accounting statements prepared has changed from time to time. In the nineteenth century stress remained upon the balance sheet. This was because of the development of the idea that the principal function of company accounts was the protection of creditors, the people who had lent the organisation funds, and the providers of capital. In the twentieth century, the purpose of the statements moved away from stewardship towards that of measuring the performance of management in relation to the funds under their control. Thus the profit and loss account, which was slow to develop as a published statement has become an important part of the accounts to help the user groups whose interest in published accounts is acknowledged to have multiplied. An additional financial statement, the source and application of funds statement,* which is designed to help in evaluating the organisation's liquidity position, has increased in importance.

---

* SSAP 10, *Statements of Source and Application of Funds*, which was issued July 1975 requires

Essentially individuals are interested in what they or their investments have earned during a period, the value of their assets and their future income and value prospects. To provide information about past earnings and current value for all user groups, financial reports are prepared for all types of organisations, from the giant trading enterprises to non-profit making clubs and charities.

Level of Disclosure

The question of how much information should be disclosed has always been a very controversial one. Academics, possibly to help them in their research through empirical surveys which hopefully lead to the development of theories, have always been strongly in favour of a much freer disclosure of information in company financial statements. Controversy has raged on this subject for over half a century now, with strong arguments provided both for and against disclosure every time it is suggested that even more information should be forthcoming in accounting reports.[4]

Advantages of disclosure
A number of advantages are suggested for greater disclosure in financial statements. These include:

(a) It helps to maximise economic welfare, since the more information people have the more likely they are to make optimal decisions regarding the allocation of resources within the economy.

(b) The more 'opportunity cost' information that can be provided about the current value of an organisation's resources, the less likely it is to get into a takeover situation which may be unfavourable to the company's investors. Once investors know the true value of the assets that they own they are more likely to make correct decisions about their use.

(c) It will help to motivate management. The greater the level of information management have to provide the more they will want to be seen to have performed well.

(d) As business enterprises provide the wealth from which social services can be provided, the way in which the business is conducted has implications for society as a whole. Therefore information must be provided to enable judgements to be made about their efficiency and whether they are fulfilling their social responsibilities.

---

these statements for enterprises with a turnover or gross income of £25,000 or more. *The Future of Company Reports*, Cmnd 6888, HMSO, July 1977 stated that 'the Government believes that a statutory requirement for a flow of funds statement would be a useful complement to this current development in accounting practice. It would require the statement to be included as part of the audited accounts and would specify in general terms the contents of the statement' (para. 24). However the Companies Act 1981 ignored such a development in company law.

Disadvantages of disclosure

The arguments against greater disclosure follow. However, our own prejudice which we freely confess, is that these are not particularly persuasive for the reasons stated.

(a) Disclosure provides too much information to rivals. This factor has always been important in arguments against any additional disclosure of financial information. It could be suggested that the disclosure required by legislation puts nobody at a competitive disadvantage because everybody has to provide the information. However, there may be a danger if one country forces more and more disclosure on its commercial and industrial enterprises while others do not. This may give organisations operating from countries with fewer disclosure requirements a competitive advantage.

(b) Great volumes of information, it is said, will cause confusion amongst those trying to digest it. However, it could be argued that the investment analysts will be able to find a way through this jungle of information on behalf of investors.

(c) Producing more and more information is costly. However, the fact is that management have usually already produced the information for their own use. Thus as the sort of information users require should be available anyway, any cost associated with putting it into publishable form is likely to be marginal.

(d) The question is frequently raised as to whether the various sectors of the population can be trusted with additional information. For example, it is suggested that if investors saw information about an organisation's budget which showed that it was going into decline, they may be tempted to withdraw their funds transferring these to an enterprise which apparently has more favourable prospects. This would then cause the decline of some firms to be even faster. Or employees on seeing budgets showing a profitable period ahead for the organisation may try and take such a large share of the expected additional cake that these profits will be wiped out even before they were made, causing the firm to ultimately do rather badly.

Whatever the antagonists of greater disclosure argue, it appears that the demands of society are for even greater disclosure.[5] One area in which major controversy over greater disclosure has developed and continues is that of disclosing company forecasts and budgets.

Forecasts and Budgetary Disclosure

Possibly the next major development in additional information to be disclosed will be the disclosure of companies' budgets or cash flow forecasts. Professor Harold Edey feels that investors require an estimate of the cash flows that they can expect to receive from their investment. Such flows will be defined to include both dividend and the ultimate return to the investor when the investment is eventually disposed of. He also suggests that people want an indication of the liquidity of their investment, and in this he is intimating that information on liquidity will provide a measurement of the risk of the investment.[6] The advantage to the investor receiving details of the patterns of firms' cash flows would be that these could be converted into net present values using his own time preference discount rate. This is probably what many investors attempt to do today although perhaps only on an intuitive basis as they have insufficient information about companies' future prospects.

However, could a company be expected to publish a series of cash flows for a number of years ahead? The proponents of the idea seem to minimise the forecasting difficulties involved. If this did happen, a major problem for the investors would be to try and ascertain the reliability of these forecasts. However, undoubtedly the investor would like to have information on an organisation's future potential as indicated by its expected cash flows. Both Professor Yuji Ijiri[7] and Professor Cyril Tomkins[8] have proposed ways in which the major objection to the publication of budgets, namely the difficulties of auditing them, can be overcome.

In company accounts today the brief statement by the Chairman, which has already been discussed, usually makes a vague statement along the lines that things may become better if the economic environment conditions improve. However, rarely do they make an attempt to quantify any possible changes in performance. The Chairman's report is the only forward-looking statement available to outside appraisers of financial statements, yet it is not really sufficient. It does seem possible that in the not too distant future when the accounting profession has digested the problem of accounting for price level changes it will move on to tackle this particular area. Then, perhaps, even if companies do not have to publish budget or cash flow forecasts, the Chairman's statement may have become more formal and possibly some attempt will have to be made to quantify the organisation's future prospects.

Mr A.M.C. Morison in an article written in 1970 on this subject[9] said 'I therefore expect that companies will regularly publish their profit forecasts for the coming year on their annual reports, together with a comparison between last year's forecast and the actual results achieved, and that these forecasts will be covered in the auditor's examination. Much kudos—and no doubt an improved market rating—awaits the first large concern that is prepared to take the plunge'. Mr Morison continues that by making the publication of such forecasts a regular thing they would attract less ballyhoo. They would also be prepared and issued at a time when reliable audited figures were available, rather than at the drop of a hat, so improving the firm's forecasting procedures and helping the auditor in his examination of them. Eventually, users of the statements could attach a level of reliability to various concerns' forecasts, for example discounting ones which were continually optimistic and enhancing the pessimistic ones.

In fact a consultative document in the form of a Green Paper entitled *The Future of Company Reports* which was presented to Parliament by the Secretary of State for Trade stated, 'The information given in a company's annual report and accounts is, by its nature, largely historical. Shareholders, employees, creditors and others concerned with the company are, however, also interested in its prospects, but there are limits to the extent to which historical information in the annual report can be used as a reliable guide'.[10]

Although favourably disposed to the publication of forecasts this Green Paper shows awareness of the potential dangers associated with their being too optimistic, which may make them misleading. So it suggests that the same principles should apply to the preparation of these forecasts as in the cases of forecasts for prospectuses and take-over bids. It recognises the possibility of delays if these principles are followed and the associated costs. It also recognises that forecasts which originally had a sound basis may be overtaken by changing exogenous environmental influences which may invalidate the assumptions initially underlying them.

The Green Paper continues that because of these difficulties financial forecasts would have to be ruled out for the time being, but nevertheless the publication of any information that could throw light on a company's future outlook and prospects, even on a general basis, should be encouraged. It provides examples of the sort of general information that might be disclosed including: orders in hand, projected new investment projects and development; short term borrowings; and such things as the expiration of patents or licences. The Green Paper concludes on this matter 'The Government believes that it would be a useful development for companies to publish more information about future prospects ... but considers that further study is necessary before any decision could be taken as to whether to introduce detailed guidelines covering a formal requirement for a statement of future prospects'.

The European Economic Community (EEC), Fourth Council Directive[11] which covers accounting matters requires that an indication of a company's likely future development be given. However, the enabling legislation for this appears to be found in the Director's Report requirements of the Companies Act 1981 which has been framed in rather broad terms, saying that this should contain:

(i) particulars of any important events affecting the company or its subsidiaries which have occurred since the end of the year;

(ii) an indication of likely future developments in the business of the company and of its subsidiaries;

(iii) an indication of the activities, if any, of the company and its subsidiaries in the field of research and development.[12]

This information should be audited because later, it says, 'it shall be the duty of the auditor of the company in preparing the report on the company's accounts to consider whether the information given in the directors' report relating to the financial year in question is consistent with the accounts'.[13]

It does seem reasonable to conclude that as shareholders are trying to predict the future cash flows of companies, although still requiring an indication of past trends, profitability and current asset values to help them in their predictions, more help needs to be given to them in this area.

Legal and Other Requirements in the Presentation of Accounting Information[14]

In the preparation of company accounts there are a number of legal and quasi-legal requirements. The legal requirements are contained in the Companies Acts 1948 to 1981. These cover the general provisions as to the form of accounts, including the balance sheet and profit and loss account, and the requirements for additional information required to supplement these statements. For example, it is necessary to include a director's report. Special cases, such as group accounts are also covered. European Economic Community requirements for the harmonisation of company accounts contained in the Fourth Council Directive[15] have also now been enshrined in company law through the Companies Act 1981. These various regulations have to be followed although their development appears to have been more dependent on expedience than on any logical extension of accounting or economic theory. In addition to the legal requirements the Stock Exchange has its own disclosure requirements for listed companies. While there is no legal backing for these requirements there are effective sanctions to ensure adherence to them, such as withdrawing the listing of companies who do not comply with them. There are also the Statements of Standard Accounting Practice which will be discussed in detail in the next section. Although SSAPs do not have the force of law* the Explanatory Foreword to them states that where members of the professional bodies supporting the ASC are associated with certain financial statements they must use their best endeavours to ensure that the Standards are complied with and disclose and explain any significant departures from them showing the material effects of these. They must also ensure that non-members who are also responsible for the financial statements that members of the accounting profession are involved with also understand the implications of the Standards.†

The major points relating to the Companies Acts and Stock Exchange requirements for financial statements are summarised in Appendix A and

---

* In the Argyll Foods case the courts have appeared to take the view that non-conformity with accounting standards is a crime. 'Unfair accounts—Argyll directors summoned', *Accountancy*, Aug. 1981; and 'After Argyll Foods what is a "true and fair view"?' by P. Bird, *Accountancy*, June 1982.

† See the Explanatory Foreword to SSAPs, ASC, January 1971, revised May 1974, para. 4.

B, respectively, of this chapter. SSAPs and EDs extant at 31 January 1983 are listed in Appendix C. There are also certain conventions as to the style and form of published accounts concerning the grouping and marshalling of items for easy reading and assimilation. However, any flexibility in the presentation of accounts has been reduced by the prescriptions for format found in The Companies Act 1981.[16]

8.4   THE POSSIBLE PROGRESSION FROM THEORY TO STANDARD

The first chapter of this book discussed the construction of a theory in relation to financial accounting, and in this drew heavily from the discipline of economics. To draw further from this area, a discussion on the methodology of theory construction is provided in Professor Richard Lipsey's *Positive Economics* at a very early stage.[17] In this, Professor Lipsey takes an approach towards the construction of a theory in social sciences from which Exhibit 8(a) has been developed. Here a number of stages can be discerned, these are to:

1. carry out empirical observations and make other investigations of activities in the real world relating to the area being considered;
2. analyse these observations to assist the formulation of hypotheses about behaviour in the area;
3. carefully state any assumptions made;
4. examine the implications of the theory by using it to make predictions;
5. test these predictions by further observations and find out whether they are consistent with the facts.

At the crucial fifth stage the theory will either be accepted or rejected. If the predictions made by the theory are reasonably consistent with observation, it may be concluded that the theory is reasonable and can be used until a better one is developed. If not, it is rejected and either discarded and replaced by a new theory or amended and the circular process continues.

It is interesting to note that recently in the development of a theory for accounting for price level changes, academic accountants went through this process a number of times. They came to no single conclusion and so were not able to develop a single theory for this area of accounting. The professional accountants then took up the cudgels through the Accounting Standards Committee. Initially they selected what could loosely be called a theory of 'accounting for price level changes' in an SSAP with this name which was issued as a provisional statement (P)SSAP 7. This was based on current purchasing power (CPP) accounting which was felt to be the best way of dealing with the problem at the time. However, shortly afterwards this approach was discarded by the Report of the Committee on Inflation Accounting, Sandilands, who replaced CPP with current cost accounting

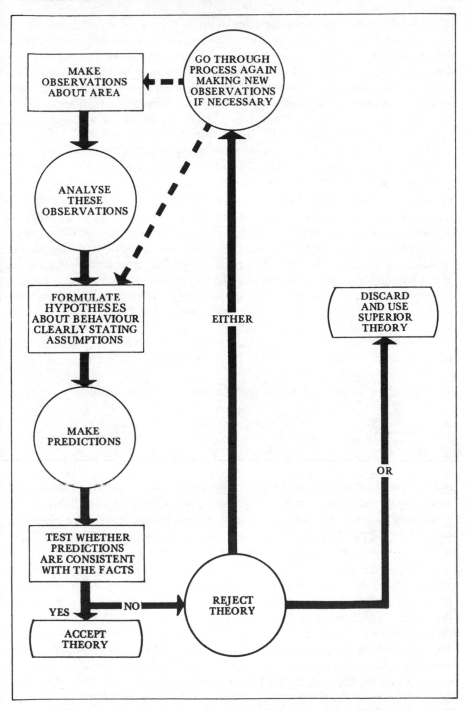

Exhibit 8(a) Stages in the development of an accounting theory

(CCA), which is supposedly superior to the previous theory. When ED 18, *Current Cost Accounting*, was produced the hue and cry from the profession, although not resulting in CCA being discarded, necessitated going through the process again with the Hyde Guidelines and a further time with ED 24 before temporarily coming to rest in SSAP 16. This provides a good example of the application of methodology towards the development of accounting theory; a more detailed examination of the development of accounting for price level changes was provided in Chapter 6.

In the development of theories for accounting for post balance sheet events and contingencies, and providing a practical application of these, the profession had to go through the process only once to obtain an acceptable recommendation in the form of SSAP 17 and SSAP 18. There are other examples where the procedure was followed more than once, such as in the area of foreign currency translation where ED 21 *Accounting for Foreign Currency Transactions* was issued on 29 September 1977 to be withdrawn and replaced by ED 27 on 27 October 1980. The problem was to agree upon the method of translation to be used for currencies from overseas subsidiaries' financial statements. Two possibilities were considered, the *temporal* and *closing rate* methods. The *temporal* method is where assets, liabilities, revenues and expenses are translated using the exchange rate ruling on the date when the amounts recorded in the financial statements were established, with closing assets and liabilities being re-translation at the rate on the balance sheet date. The *closing rate* method is where revenue items are translated using the average exchange rate of the period, and assets and liabilities by using the closing rate. The choice between the two is influenced by how hard the domestic currency is. For example, in the US where the currency is hard FAS 8 chose the temporal method to produce acceptable results. Initially in the UK, ED 21 allowed either method. ED 27 is based on the *net investment* concept, which is concerned with the effective stake in both share capital and reserves in a foreign subsidiary. Where assets and liabilities are translated at the closing rate, exchange differences which cause cash flows are to be reported in the profit and loss account, those resulting from re-translations, and not giving rise to cash flows being shown as reserve movements. This approach is now felt to be more appropriate to the British scene.

In all this it can be seen that the basic stages are firstly for the ASC to describe and formulate the problem that it is felt an accounting standard for the area would help to overcome. Secondly there should be a reasoned discussion of the problem based on the fundamental theory of the area associating possible 'hows' and 'whys'. Finally a prescribed solution is issued in the form of an accounting standard which tells the profession what to do.

This all shows the benefit to the practising accountant of understanding the method of development of accounting theories. A knowledge of this will help in understanding what lies behind the various accounting standards and will often help overcome any conceptual problems associated with their acceptance and application.

8.5   INTERNATIONAL APPROACHES TO THE SETTING OF ACCOUNTING STANDARDS COMPARED

This section examines the approaches taken to the setting of accounting standards in the USA, the UK and internationally. Firstly, though, it looks briefly at the stages in the development of an accounting theory into its practical, or part practical application as an accounting standard.

The USA

On the academic front at the beginning of the twentieth century the US academics established a body called the American Accounting Association (AAA). Later, membership of this body was widened to include practising accountants. One objective of the AAA, amongst others, is to encourage research in accounting and it publishes a quarterly journal, the *Accounting Review*. In 1966, one of the AAA's committees carried out research into accounting theory and published a paper on this entitled *A Statement of Basic Accounting Theory* (ASOBAT).[18] Amongst the discussions to be found in this paper is one of the main concepts that should be used in the preparation of accounting reports. These are: relevance; verifiability; freedom from bias; and quantifiability. At that time the concept of relevance was rarely considered. This was because many 'relevant' items could not be objectively verified. Even when current values were more relevant than the historic costs, the 'objectivity' of the latter was sufficient to ensure that accounts continued to be drawn up on that basis. ASOBAT suggested that relevance should take precedence over any of the other concepts it had suggested.

It also recommended the use of multi-value accounting statements, that is, different statements for different users.* This seems an admirable approach as a single set of figures which tries to meet the needs of all users and their accounting objectives tends to end up being inappropriate for most purposes and so satisfies nobody. There was no immediate follow up to ASOBAT by the accounting profession in the USA.

On the professional front the American Institute of Certified Public Accountants (AICPA) issued a Statement of Accounting Principles in 1938 which they had commissioned three people to write. In 1939 it charged its Committee on Accounting Procedure (CAP) to issue Accounting Research Bulletins (ARBs). The Committee had only 20 part time members and carried out little research into the areas on which ARBs were issued. Many of these allowed a number of accounting bases, and there was no way of ensuring ARBs were complied with. In spite of this within 12 years CAP had issued about 40 ARBs and by the time it was replaced in 1959, 51 ARBs had been issued including No. 43 which consolidated the previous ones.

---

* The FASB's FAS 33 on inflation accounting takes a multi-column statement approach.

The CAP was disbanded on 1 September 1959 and the Accounting Principles Board (APB) established to replace it. Following research it aimed to limit the number of allowable accounting bases and over its life time issued some 31 'opinions'. However, dissatisfaction grew against this body with its large membership dominated by the profession and in 1973 it was disbanded.

The Financial Accounting Standards Board (FASB) which is independent of the AICPA replaced the APB. The FASB has a full time membership of seven people drawn from widely different backgrounds. Well financed, it can carry out appropriate research before issuing Exposure Drafts for comment and then finally produce standards as felt appropriate.

The UK

During the Second World War, partly because of the dearth of fully qualified accountants, as many were conscripted for war service, the ICAEW announced that it had charged its Taxation and Financial Relations Committee to make recommendations on accounting practices. In its publication of this development[19] in 1942 it was at pains to point out these recommendations were not to be compulsory.

For many years the ICAEW continued to issue recommendations on accounting principles[20] and statements on auditing. By the late 1960s because of concern expressed in government and other circles, the accounting profession felt that it needed to put its own house in order. This concern was partly due to some apparently dubious practices found in takeover situations. For example, an organisation's assets may be recorded in historic accounting terms at a much lower value than their true value. This could result in its being taken over at a value much less than its true worth. Then the enterprise taking over the assets would indulge in the practice of what was termed 'asset stripping'. Although asset stripping might have seemed unpalatable to many, it was argued by others that it helped to ensure that the country's resources were being used more efficiently. However, a major argument against asset stripping is that frequently no new economic resources are created nor does the redistribution of old resources take place, it simply causes the price of the existing assets to rise. For example, property would be acquired and rented out at a higher rate, or sold off at inflated values.

Accounting Standards Committee

During 1970 the ICAEW issued their *Statement of Intent on Accounting Standards in the Nineteen Seventies*.[21] This statement had a number of aims including to: encourage uniformity of practice in accounts; ensure the disclosure of accounting bases; disclosure any departure from an accounting base or policy; use an exposure draft principle, where suggested standards would be exposed to the profession and other interested bodies for comment before a definitive standard was introduced; continue encouragement to improve legislation and regulations, for example on the City Code on Takeovers and Mergers and the Stock Exchange requirements.

The outcome of this statement was the establishment of the Accounting Standards Steering Committee (ASSC) during 1970. Although initially formed by the ICAEW, its membership was eventually widened to include members from the various UK and Irish professional accounting bodies with the ICAS and ICAI becoming members later in 1970, the ACCA and ICMA joining in 1971 and CIPFA in 1976. The ASSC became the Accounting Standards Committee on 1 February 1976, when it was reconstituted as a joint committee of the six member bodies who act collectively through the Consultative Committee of Accountancy Bodies (CCAB) which had been formed about two years previously during June 1974. The ASSC soon began to issue exposure drafts (EDs); the first one ED 1, *Accounting for the Results of Associated Companies* was issued on 26 June 1970. Within six months, on 1 January 1971, this ED became the first Statement of Standard Accounting Practice, SSAP 1, with the same name as the ED. Since then many exposure drafts and standards have been issued. A list of those which are extant at the time of publication will be found in Appendix C to this chapter.

A Basic Grouping for Accounting Standards

SSAPs and EDs have been usefully divided into four types by Professor Harold Edey.[22] Basically his classification scheme shows that SSAPs are attempting to provide answers to four questions which are asked in the following order as financial statements are prepared:

(a) What are the recommended methods of asset valuation and income measurement? That is, *valuation and profit measurement* (Edey's type 4).
(b) Which principles have been followed in the preparation of the financial statements concerned? That is, *description* (Edey's type 1).
(c) What items are to be disclosed? That is, *disclosure* (Edey's type 3).
(d) How are the items to be presented? That is, *presentation* (Edey's type 2).

When attempts are made to classify SSAPs and EDs into these four types it will be found that some of the pronouncements overlap into more than one group. In the following classification, where the overlap has been felt to be important an item has been included under more than one heading.

Valuation and Profit Measurement (Type 4)
These establish procedures for the measurement of value or profit in particular circumstances. The EDs and resultant SSAPs which fall into this grouping are likely to be extremely controversial. This is because in many of the areas concerned arguments about the underlying theory have not been satisfactorily resolved. Consequently the measures selected may

appear to be rather arbitrary and are frequently based on little more than current practice. SSAPs and EDs that could fall into this grouping include: SSAP 1, SSAP 2, SSAP 4, SSAP 9, SSAP 12, SSAP 13, SSAP 15, SSAP 16, SSAP 19, ED 3, ED 27, ED 29, ED 30 and ED 31.

Description (Type 1)

These require the disclosure of the methods and assumptions used in the preparation of financial reports. Thus they are less likely to attract controversy unless they include statements of general policy. SSAP 2 falls into this category although the list of fundamental accounting concepts contained in this SSAP would more likely come under type 4. Few fall into this classification, those which do include: SSAP 2 and SSAP 12.

Disclosure (Type 3)

These require the disclosure of specific items either because they are subject to a particularly high degree of estimation (as in the case of depreciation) or because their accounting treatment is based on convenience of uniformity or prudence rather than on finer points of theory.[23] For example R and D expenditure of a general nature, which is 'expensed' under SSAP 13, is required to be separately disclosed. This type also encompasses 'exceptional' and 'extraordinary' items (for which the appropriate presentation is classified in Type 2) and the 'explicit' disclosure of information already largely implicit in the income statement and balance sheet.[24] Therefore this grouping would include source and application of funds and post balance sheet events. This grouping could include: SSAP 3, SSAP 6, SSAP 10, SSAP 12, SSAP 13, SSAP 14, SSAP 15, SSAP 17, SSAP 18, ED 16, ED 26, ED 28, ED 29, ED 30 and ED 31.

Presentation* (Type 2)

These are concerned with standardising the methods of presentation of items in financial statements. For example, SSAP 6 requires prior year items to be shown as an adjustment to the opening balance of retained earnings. SSAPs and EDs that would currently fall into this grouping include: SSAP 5, SSAP 6, SSAP 8, SSAP 16, ED 16, ED 27 and ED 28.

SSAP 2: Disclosure of Accounting Policies

One statement, SSAP 2, sets the ground rules for accounting in the UK

---

* In some countries, such as France and Germany, their accountants favour standard layouts, whereas in the past in the UK and the US the standardisation of the presentation of accounts has been felt to impose another straitjacket onto the profession, likely to stop it experimenting. Nevertheless, the Companies Act 1981 produced enabling legislation for the Fourth Directive, so prescribed the form in which financial statements must be presented in great detail.

and this standard is worth further examination. It deals with the fundamental accounting concepts, accounting bases and accounting policies. It considers the words 'principles', 'rules', 'conventions', 'methods' and 'procedures' as all being synonymous and uses the word 'practices' as the generic term to cover them all. It lists the fundamental accounting concepts as: going concern; accruals; consistency and prudence. It is interesting to note that the first International Accounting Standard, discussed in a later section of this chapter, uses only the first three of these as fundamental accounting concepts.

Accounting bases

The ASC recognises that accounting bases may be numerous, and that there may be more than one way of dealing with a particular item. For example, depreciation may be dealt with using the straight line, reducing balance or other methods as is appropriate. Charging out the consumption of stock may be dealt with using the 'IFO' family, or any of the average methods and so on. In fact in many other areas of accounting, including: the amortisation of intangible assets; the way in which contracts are dealt with; how leasing, rental and HP agreements are shown in the accounts; the conversion of foreign currencies; the way in which repairs and renewals are covered (especially where there is any capitalisation aspect because of improvement); the way in which warranties are dealt with; it is possible to have more than one accounting base.

Accounting policies

The statement continues to say that when there are a number of possible accounting bases for an area, organisations should select and use one of these in the preparation of their financial statements. However, this does not limit an organisation to the use of a single base. For example in selecting the methods of depreciation, different ones could be used for various classes of assets. Nevertheless standards will be found to limit the number of bases that can be used to deal with any specific item so that not every possible way of dealing with it would be permitted.

The standard also states that an organisation has to disclose the bases that it used and that these will be referred to as its accounting policies. If its policy is changed so that a different accounting base is used for any classification of items this would have to be disclosed and the organisation would have to make a statement of the effect of this change in quantified terms. This means that an organisation will not be able to change the accounting bases that it uses at will.

It should be noted that SSAP 2 gives no guidance concerning the selection of an accounting policy when more than one accounting base is allowable, whereas its international equivalent, IAS 1, does, as will be seen in the next section on International Accounting Standards.

Exhibits 8(b) and 8(c) provide examples of statements by Coats Patons

Accounting Policies

Consolidation

The main accounting policies of the group are described below. Fiscal and company legislation affecting some foreign subsidiaries prevents them from conforming with these policies and in such cases adjustments are made on consolidation in order to present the group accounts on a consistent basis. All subsidiary accounts are prepared for a calendar year and their accounts are closed on 31st December.

Foreign exchange

Profits in foreign subsidiaries and associates are converted to sterling at the rates of exchange ruling at the year-end. Fixed assets in foreign currencies are converted at the rates of time of purchase. Current assets and liabilities are converted at the rates ruling at the year-end. All exchange differences on the conversion of balance sheet items after any related tax adjustments are transferred directly to reserves.

Associated companies

These are listed on page 32 and meet the following conditions:—

(a) that the group has a beneficial interest of at least 20% in the equity capital and

(b) the group is able to exercise significant influence over the company.

The proportion of the profits for the year relating to the group is included in the profit and loss account and the proportion of the investment relating to the group is shown in the balance sheet at directors' valuation or, where listed, at market value.

Stocks

Stocks of goods are valued at the lower of cost or net realisable value relating to each main product group. Costs are established on the basis of existing levels of production in each manufacturing unit and include appropriate production overheads.

Depreciation

Fixed assets excluding land are depreciated evenly over their estimated useful life. Assets qualifying for United Kingdom investment or regional development grants are depreciated on the basis of full cost. As certain overseas subsidiaries are required to charge fiscal depreciation in their accounts, adjustments are made on consolidation to conform with group policy.

Research and development

This expenditure is written off in the year in which it is incurred.

Taxation

Provision for United Kingdom and overseas taxation on the profits of the year is based on the Statement of Standard Accounting Practice No. 15, providing for deferred tax to the extent that a liability is expected in the foreseeable future. No provison has been made for taxation that will arise on the remittance of profits by overseas subsidiaries after the close of the accounts.

Investment grants

Investment or regional development grants receivable in respect of each year's capital expenditure are credited, net of any necessary tax adjustments, to the profit and loss account evenly over a period of ten years.

Source and utilisation of funds

The statement of source and utilisation of funds on page 18 is prepared on the basis of the Statement of Standard Accounting Practice No. 10 and also shows expenditure on replacement of fixed assets together with the estimated additional working capital required on account of inflation as a first charge against funds.

Exhibit 8(b) Accounting policies for Coats Paton PLC for the year ending 31 December 1981

PLC, Debenhams PLC, Thorn EMI PLC and Tube Investments PLC within their annual report of their respective accounting polices. These are typical of such statements currently found in companies' annual reports, and cover such aspects of accounting policies as stocks, depreciation, research and development, and so on.

Accounting Policies

Basis of accounts and consolidation
The accounts are prepared under the historical cost convention, supplemented by the revaluation of certain assets. The accounts of subsidiary companies are consolidated for the 52 weeks to 30th January 1982.

Sales
The sales figure is the total amount receivable for goods and services supplied to customers outside the Group, excluding value added tax.

Stock
Stock is stated at the lower of cost and net realisable value which is generally computed at selling price less appropriate trading margins.
The valuation of stock includes overhead expenses where appropriate.

Depreciation on fixed assets
The principal annual rates of depreciation on a straight line basis are as follows:

Properties	See below
Building services	4%
Fixtures and fittings	10%-15%
Floor coverings	15%
Motor vehicles	20%
Display equipment	33⅓%

The structure of freehold and long leasehold buildings (other than investment properties) is depreciated at the rate of 1% per annum or over the life of the lease, if less than 100 years. Depreciation on the original cost of freehold and long leasehold properties (other than investment properties) continues to be charged within trading profit, whereas depreciation on the revaluation surplus is charged within Other items. The figures for last year have been restated on a comparable basis. Depreciation is provided on short leasehold properties having a life of 50 years or less so as to write off the cost over the remaining period of the lease.

Disposal of properties
Where the Group disposes of substantially all its interest in a property, the profit or loss, being the difference between the net proceeds of sale and historical cost, is taken to profit and loss account and included in Other items. Where the Group retains a material disposable interest in the property, no profit or loss is recognised and any adjustment to valuation is taken direct to reserves.

Deferred taxation
Provision is made for deferred taxation except where a liability is not expected to arise in the foreseeable future.

Exchange rates
Profits, assets and liabilities denominated in foreign currency are translated at the rates of exchange ruling at the balance sheet date. In accordance with the provisions of ED27, translation differences relating to the Group's equity investments in foreign subsidiaries are taken to reserves.

Pensions
The Group operates a number of externally funded retirement benefit schemes for employees. These schemes are set up under irrevocable trusts and their assets are completely separate from those of the Group.
The annual funding cost of pension benefits is charged in the profit and loss account and is determined in accordance with actuarial principles. The schemes are subject to a regular actuarial review procedure independent of the Group.

Interest
The financing cost of major developments is capitalised into the cost of the project. This financing cost is calculated to the date of opening for trading. Prior to the Finance Act 1981 this cost was charged in the profit and loss account within Other items. The figures for the 52 weeks to 31st January 1981 have been restated.

Exhibit 8(c) Accounting policies for Debenhams PLC for the year ending 30 January 1982

International Accounting Standards

In 1973 following the International Accounting Congress at Sydney, the International Accounting Standards Committee (IASC) was set up on 29 June 1973. The founder members of this Committee were accountancy

Accounting policies

Basis of consolidation The consolidated accounts comprise the accounts of the holding company and all subsidiaries made up to 31 March 1982 and have been prepared in compliance with Section 152A of the Companies Act 1948 and Schedule 8A to that Act. The results of subsidiaries sold or acquired during the year are included up to or from the respective dates of sale or acquisition.

Goodwill arises from the excess of the consideration paid over the values attributed to net tangible assets acquired and is written off against reserves in the year of acquisition.

Foreign currencies All amounts denominated in foreign currencies have been translated into sterling at rates ruling at 31 March 1982. The adjustments to investments in overseas subsidiaries at the beginning of the year resulting from exchange movements during the year are dealt with through reserves.

Associated companies are those other than subsidiaries where the Group has a beneficial interest of at least 20% in the equity share capital and is in a position to exercise significant influence. The investment in associated companies is stated at cost less provisions plus the Group's share of the post-acquisition reserves.

The results of associated companies taken into the trading profit are those for the year to 31 March 1982, based on unaudited accounts to that date where necessary.

Depreciation of television and video equipment on rental Rental equipment is depreciated to a nil residual value by the application of basic depreciation rates from month of installation on a graduated basis so that a relatively high charge is borne in the early years. Depreciation periods used for the year ended 31 March 1982 have been: colour sets—6 years (overseas 5 years), monochrome sets—3 years (overseas 1 year), video equipment—4 years.

Depreciation periods and written down values are reviewed annually and additional provisions as deemed necessary are made.

Depreciation of fixed assets is calculated on cost or valuation at rates estimated to write off the relevant assets by equal annual amounts over their expected useful lives; effect is given where necessary to commercial and technical obsolescence.

The annual rates used are:

Freehold buildings and long leasehold property 2%.

Short leasehold property over period of lease.

Plant, machinery and furniture at rates ranging from 10% to $33\frac{1}{3}$%.

Motor vehicles 25%.

Exhibit 8(d) Accounting policies for

bodies from: Australia, Canada, Eire, France, Germany, Japan, Mexico, Netherlands, UK and the USA.

The IASC's Constitution was revised on 10 October 1977, and many other countries' professional accounting bodies in Bangladesh, Belgium, Brazil, Cyprus, Denmark, Fiji, Finland, Ghana, Greece, Hong Kong, India, Israel, Italy, Jamaica, Korea, Luxembourg, Malaysia, Malta, New Zealand, Nigeria, Norway, Pakistan, Panama, Philippines, Portugal,

Reorganisation costs The costs of reorganisation (redundancies and other rationalisation costs) to recognise the effect of changing business conditions are provided when a reorganisation decision has been made in principle. The costs relating to the reorganisation of continuing businesses are charged against trading profit and those relating to the withdrawal from the businesses concerned are charged as extraordinary items.

Government grants in respect of capital expenditure are applied in reduction of the cost of the assets and depreciation is calculated by reference to net cost.

Patent income arises from licenses granted to third parties. Where the licensee pays a lump sum instead of a continuing royalty for the use of a patent that lump sum is apportioned on a straight-line basis over the estimated life of the patent.

Stocks and work in progress are stated at the lower of cost and realisable value, less progress payments on uncompleted contracts and provisions for expected losses. Cost includes manufacturing overheads where appropriate. A conservatively estimated profit element is taken during the course of long term contracts.

Films, television and video productions and rights therein are stated at cost less sales, advance payments and provisions for any estimated shortfall in revenue. No production profit is taken before full recovery of all relevant costs.

Deferred taxation is provided to the extent that it could become payable in the foreseeable future. Accordingly, in normal circumstances, no provision is made in respect of UK tax deferred by accelerated allowances on fixed assets and stock appreciation relief. However, provision is made at the current rate of tax (52%) for cumulative accelerated allowances on UK television and video equipment on rental and other timing differences.

Full deferred tax provision is maintained in respect of overseas subsidiaries.

No provision is made for potential tax liabilities which might arise on the future disposal of property at the revalued amounts at which they are included in the accounts.

Guarantee provisions Many products carry formal guarantees of satisfactory performance for varying periods following purchase by customers. Provision is made at accounting dates for the estimated cost of honouring unexpired guarantees.

Research and development expenditure, and the expense of establishing and protecting patent rights in respect of inventions derived therefrom, are wholly written off as incurred.

Recording and associated costs in adding to the permanent catalogue of recorded music, and administrative and technical expenses in maintaining and developing the copyright interests in music compositions, are also written off as incurred.

Thorn EMI PLC for the year ending 31 March 1982

Rhodesia, Sierra Leone, Singapore, South Africa, Spain, Sri Lanka, Sweden, Trinidad and Tobago and Yugoslavia have since become members. The business of the IASC is now conducted by a Board, whose membership today is comprised of the Founder Members' Bodies and not more than two other Member Bodies.

The IASC was to use the same procedures as the ASC of issuing exposure drafts and, after a reasonable time had been allowed for comment, to issue

Accounting policies

Basis of consolidation
The consolidated accounts set out on pages 20 to 37, which are prepared under the historical cost convention, incorporate the accounts of Tube Investments plc and its subsidiaries. New subsidiaries are included from their respective dates of acquisition during the year. The results of subsidiaries disposed of during the year are included to the date of disposal.

Year end dates
The year end date of the financial statements of UK and overseas subsidiary companies is 31st December, except for some small overseas subsidiary companies whose results are not material in relation to the consolidated accounts.

Associated companies
The Group's share of profits or losses and interests in associated companies included in the Group accounts is calculated from audited accounts to 31st December except in one case where the year end is 30th September.

Treatment of a company as an associated company has regard to the Group's holding of at least 20% of the equity capital, representation on its board of directors and participation in policy-making including dividend policy. However, in certain cases overseas where there are significant constraints on the rights of non-resident shareholders and/or on remitting dividends, the policy is to treat these holdings as trade investments.

Foreign currencies
Assets and liabilities stated in foreign currencies together with the trading results of overseas subsidiary and associated companies are translated into sterling at the rates of exchange ruling at 31st December.

Exchange differences arising from the translation into sterling of the net equity interest in overseas subsidiary and associated companies are treated as movements in reserves together with exchange differences on translation of foreign currency borrowings which finance overseas investment.

Research and development
Expenditure on research and development is written off in the year in which it is incurred except for the costs of major prototypes which are capitalised and written off over three years or, if shorter, the period of their useful lives.

Intangible assets
Expenditure on patents, trade marks and goodwill is written off in the year in which it is incurred.

Cost of acquisitions
The difference between the cost of shares and the fair value of net assets attributable to such shares at the dates of acquisition of subsidiary and associated companies is now written off to reserves in the year of acquisition. Prior year figures have not been restated since the amounts are not material.

Exhibit 8(e) Accounting policies for

Depreciation
Depreciation of fixed assets is mainly on the straight line basis and is charged
generally as follows:
(a) freehold land nil,
(b) freehold buildings over fifty years,
(c) leasehold land and buildings over fifty years or over the period of the lease if less
than fifty years and
(d) plant, machinery and equipment at $7\frac{1}{2}\%$ per annum.

Deferred taxation
UK deferred taxation relating to capital allowances and other timing differences is
provided in the accounts only in so far as a liability is likely to arise in the
foreseeable future.
Advance corporation tax paid and payable in respect of dividends is written off,
except to the extent that set-off against the corporation tax liabilities is expected to
be available.

Pensions
It is the policy of the Group to provide for pension liabilities by payments to trusts
or insurance companies independent from the finances of the Group and
contributions by companies are charged against profits. Liabilities which relate to
past service are being funded over a period of years.

Repairs and renewals
Repairs and renewals are charged to revenue in the year in which the expenditure
is incurred.

Stocks
Stocks and work in progress are valued at the lower of cost, including an appropriate
proportion of overheads, and net realisable value.

Capital grants
Capital grants are credited to profit and loss account over the useful lives of the
relevant fixed assets and the balance is included in deferred liabilities and credits in
the balance sheet.

Leased assets
Fixed assets acquired under finance leasing contracts are recorded in the balance
sheet as fixed assets at their equivalent capital value and are depreciated over the
useful life of the asset. The corresponding liability is recorded as a deferred
obligation and the interest element of the finance charge is charged to the profit
and loss account over the primary lease period.

Tube Investments PLC for the year ending 31 December 1981

a standard. The definitive standards will be published in the English language and the member bodies would have the responsibility for translating standards into their own language. This might cause some difficulties as some accounting terms do not have exact equivalent translations. Already a number of International Accounting Standards (IAS) have been issued, and these are listed in Appendix D to this chapter.

IAS 1: Disclosure of Accounting Policies

The first International Accounting Standard, IAS 1, *Disclosure of Accounting Policies* was agreed in November 1974 and published during January 1975. This concerns the preparation and presentation of financial statements (balance sheets, income statements, profit and loss accounts, notes, etc.) and it is worth examination in detail to enable it to be compared with its UK equivalent, SSAP 2. It can be seen from IAS 1 that already through the use of the two terms 'income statement' or 'profit and loss account', the IAS is finding it difficult to agree on the use of either US or UK terminology. In this case it has played safe and used both. Although in other cases, such as through the use of the term 'balance sheet' they have selected one country's semantics for certain aspects of accountancy. The fundamental accounting assumptions are stated in IAS 1 as: going concern; consistency; accrual.

The standard states that accounting policies could encompass accounting principles, bases, conventions, rules and procedures. It goes further than its UK counterpart SSAP 2 because it provides some ground rules for the selection of an accounting policy when more than one accounting base is involved. This is by stating that judgement will be required in the selection of an accounting policy based upon an organisation's circumstances. Three criteria were given to help in this selection. These were:

(a) *Prudence*, which has been relegated from being the fundamental accounting assumption it was in the UK standard;
(b) *Substance over form*,* meaning that the substance and financial reality, not merely the legal form of the accounts, should be considered.
(c) *Materiality*.

With the help of these criteria, organisations would be able to select the most appropriate accounting policies to suit their circumstances.

IASs are aimed at helping multi-national organisations acquire some consistency in the preparation of the accounts for their various component organisations operating from different countries.

---

* It should be noted that although not using the term 'substance over form' the Companies Act 1981, Part 1, Section 1, implies the use of this concept in the preparation of financial statements under its requirements by saying that the Act should be overridden if this is necessary to enable the financial statements to show a 'true and fair view' of the company's affairs.

International vis-à-vis UK Standards

On the list of extant IASs provided in Appendix D the UK standards, which if followed ensure compliance with an international standard, are shown as appropriate. Sometimes the international standard provides more information to help in its application than the UK equivalent. For example, in the area of stock valuation IAS 2, in stating the lower of historic cost and net realisable value rule provides fairly detailed guidance to help in the ascertainment of both these values. Therefore it could be considered to be more helpful to its users. In other cases the UK standard could be judged to provide more information to help in its application. Although IASs are aimed to help in the development of consistency in the preparation and presentation of the multi-national enterprise's (MNE) financial statements, it will be beneficial for any accountant involved with the preparation of financial statements to look at them.

Financial or General Standards

It should be noted that the IASs are clearly for *financial* statements. The American FASB also shows that its standards are clearly applicable to *financial* accounts, whereas in the UK the term 'financial' is not introduced as a limiting influence and SSAPs are simply 'accounting standards'. In fact, in ED 18, the Morpeth Committee's exposure draft on current cost accounting, the introduction mentions the use of the standard for management accounting as well, an approach also taken by SSAP 16 the definitive standard on the subject. However, it seems unnecessary to formally introduce a new set of users to published financial accounts—management—who, because they have access to all the information within the organisation that they require, are already catered for. Introducing the management user group means trying to make the single statement cover the needs and accounting objectives of an even wider range of users. Clearly, SSAP 16 implies that current costs should be used at all levels in the preparation of accounts; the question remains whether in fact they are still appropriate for management decision making in the planning and control areas as current cost information need not necessarily provide relevant information to decision takers.

8.6   SETTING ACCOUNTING STANDARDS: THE FUTURE

The ASC set up a task group during January 1978 to review the accounting standards setting process. This group was chaired by Mr Tom Watts, the ASC Chairman. In May 1979 it submitted a draft consultative document to the ASC, which was adopted and published during September 1979 for public comment. This document had a rough ride, and it did not receive the unanimous support of the governing bodies, i.e. the Councils of the

CCAB. Nevertheless, it was published in January 1981 as *Setting Accounting Standards: A Report and Recommendations*[25] by the Accounting Standards Committee because they felt that action needed to be taken. This document is worth studying because it provides a view of how the ASC see the standard setting procedures and mechanisms developing in the future.

Conclusions of the Report

The report concluded that accounting standards are necessary to complement legislation and will continue to be necessary. However, a main aim should be to narrow the choice of accounting bases so that financial statements have a 'common language' and are reasonably comparable. It emphasises that the standards should not be considered to be 'bench marks' from which any deviation should be disclosed, but definitive principles. Therefore material departures from them should only be permitted if *to do so* would enable the financial statements to provide a more 'true and fair' view of the enterprise's operations and financial position. In this it suggests that the reason for a departure and the financial effects of this should be disclosed in the notes to the accounts. No doubt reacting to the criticism concerning the volume of standards being produced it says that no more of these than necessary should be produced, and future ones must not be issued faster than the profession can absorb them.

It suggests for practical reasons some standards will have to be confined to large enterprises, but other firms outside their application should disclose whether they have not complied with them or have done so on a voluntary basis. The ASC also feels that special standards should only be issued to deal with special accounting problems of major specific industries.

About the standard setting mechanism it says this should be retained by the profession and not move to the Government or one of its agencies. Hence, not surprisingly, it suggests the continuance of the ASC. A widening of its membership is suggested to include some non-accountants,* although accountants are to dominate.

The standard setting procedures should continue to involve the widest and most open consultation. An innovation will be for discussion papers to be published early in the development of a standard. Consultative groups should be more closely involved, and the ED procedures will be continued. However, the ASC's own meetings are still to be held in private.

The possibility of the major countries setting conflicting standards must be avoided, but where there are any necessary significant differences between other countries and UK equivalent standards, this must be made clear.

Where appropriate, non-mandatory guidance notes, rather than recommendations will be issued as adjuncts to complex standards, but for existing

---

* Note the FASB in the US includes non-accountant members.

less complex standards, it will be better to amend them rather than issue authoritative interpretations. Also in response to general enquiries, the ASC staff will continue to give oral guidance as far as is practical.

The report suggests that the supervision of the application of accounting standards should also remain in the private sector, but that as well as a qualified audit report, a supervisory body is necessary in the form of a joint panel of the CCAB and CSI to review any non-compliance for the listed companies.

The ASC recognises that there is a heavy cost associated with this: the whole process could eventually cost up to £400,000 per annum in January 1981 prices, including a new post of 'director of accounting standards', and more technical staff support. The possibility of the Chairman* being remunerated was raised. The estimated cost is double that budgeted for that purpose by the CCAB at the time the report was issued. The ASC also felt that it should provide further resources to research into the possibility of developing an agreed conceptual framework. Some of these conclusions were then hardened into the form of recommendations. From this it can be seen that the accounting standard setting process and the mechanism underlying it is likely to continue to gain momentum for some time.

Has the Process of Producing Accounting Standards Slowed Down?

Not all agree with the speed and the present way standards are being produced. For example, some of the membership of the ACCA felt that the process of producing accounting standards should be slowed down. Even the new chairman of the ASC, Mr Ian Hay Davison, warned the IASC to slow down, saying that not all standards will work in the UK.[26] Teddy Boyd, the president of the ICAS in 1982, has also called for fewer standards.[27]

Professor Baxter[28] would prefer to see SSAPs being produced in terms of normal behaviour, the normative approach to theory discussed in Chapter 1, where a rule was devised to fit the facts. Then he suggests that on the publication of this rule the SSAP should limit itself to a bare statement concerning what the rule is all about rather than discussing principles and then pronouncing on them.

Professor Baxter also feels that it would be beneficial if the people involved in the production of a standard sign their names to it with dissenters also being cited. He holds the view because institutions appear to be credited with wisdom, and their pronouncements, even in an area where there may be cause for dispute, appear accepted as if they give a seal of approval to particular theories, whereas it is more readily accepted that individuals can err. He is also for deviating from a standard where justified, that is, to enable a 'true and fair' view being presented, but for any such deviation to be disclosed. Nevertheless, Professor Baxter feels it inevitable that the profession should progress from having gentle guide lines, to firm rules, which will ultimately be backed by sanctions.

8.7 CONCLUSIONS

This book has provided an introduction to the theory and framework of financial accounting. It has also considered the development of standards underlying the preparation of financial accounts. It has discussed why accounts are prepared and shown why considerable importance is attached to accounting profit and that there are other definitions of profit.* We hope it will have been shown why it was said in the preface 'in our view the quest for "true profit" has much in common with the quest for the Holy Grail'. Also by discussing the various user groups—management, investors, debt holders (both short- and long-term creditors), employees, the government and society, and their requirement from financial statements—it provides an indication of the difficulties likely to be found in trying to fulfil the needs of them all in a single all-embracing accounting report. To add to the problems it was seen that accounting concepts, principles and practice are various, that these sometimes conflict and that frequently even when an SSAP is produced and there is 'standardisation', the multiplicity of accounting bases, the different accounting policies chosen from these can lead to different reported incomes and financial statements. It is important that as soon as possible in a study of financial accounting, accounting entries should be related to accounting concepts and policies. This requires a knowledge of the current SSAPs issued by the ASC and an appreciation of the theoretical principles, if any, that underlie them.

However, it must be remembered that overall constraints are placed upon the way in which published accounts can be produced by the laws of a country.

REFERENCES

1. For a different discussion on user groups and their requirements, see *The Corporate Report*, Accounting Standards Steering Committee, July 1975, for a UK view and *Objectives of Financial Reporting and Elements of Financial Statements of Business Enterprises*, Financial Accounting Standards Board, 29 December 1977, for an American view.
2. Dopuch, N. and Sunder, S. 'FASBs statements on objectives and elements of financial accounting: a review', *The Accounting Review*, Vol. LV, No. 1, January 1980.

---

* Mr R.M. Morison said that 'In accountancy the term profit has no absolute meaning. It is simply a measure of the success or failure of a business to achieve what it sets out to achieve. The measurement is a subjective one insofar as it depends upon the view taken as to what the business has in fact set out to achieve. Thus the term profit as used by accountants can never have that absolute meaning which lawyers, economists and Revenue Officials seek to attribute to it'. R.M. Morison, 'A critical review of recognised accounting conventions', *The Accountant Magazine*, September 1962.

3. Fra Pacioli, *Double-entry Bookkeeping*, translated by Pietro Crivelli, Institute of Bookkeepers, 1924.
4. Rose, H., *Disclosure in Company Accounts*, Eaton Paper No. 1, The Institute of Economic Affairs 1965, provides one view on possible future areas of disclosure in published accounts.
5. For an example of suggestions for even more disclosure coming from Government quarters, see *The Future of Company Reports*, Cmnd 6888, HMSO, July 1977.
6. Edey, H.C., 'Accounting principles and business reality', *Accountancy*, November and December 1963.
7. Ijiri, Y., 'On budget principles and budget-auditing standards', *The Accounting Review*, October 1968.
8. Tomkins, C., 'The development of relevant published accounting reports', *Accountancy*, November 1969.
9. Morison, A.M.C., 'The role of the reporting accountant today', *Accountants Magazine*, January 1970.
10. *The Future of Company Reports, op. cit.*, paras. 48–51.
11. *Fourth Council Directive*, Official Journal of the European Communities, No. L 222/11, 14 August 1978, Article 46.2(b).
12. *Companies Act, 1981*, Part 1, Section 13 to become Section 16 of the 1967 Act.
13. *Companies Act, 1981*, Part 1, Section 15(2) to become Section 23A of the 1967 Act.
14. *Guide to the Accounting Requirements of the Companies Acts*, Institute of Chartered Accountants in England and Wales and Gee & Co., January 1982, provides a useful summary of the statutory requirements contained in the 1948, 1967, 1976, 1980 and 1981 Acts relating to the production of annual accounts of companies.
15. *Fourth Council Directive, op. cit.*, Article 46.2(b) 54(3)(g).
16. *Companies Act 1981, op. cit.*, Schedule 1, Part 1, Section B, 'The required formats for accounts'.
17. Lipsey, R.G., 'An Introduction to Positive Economics' 2nd edn. Weidenfeld and Nicolson 1966, Chap. 1.
18. *A Statement of Basic Accounting Theory*, American Accounting Association, 1966.
19. See *The Accountant*, December 1942, page 354.
20. See for example the 1975 edition *Recommendations on Accounting Principles*, ICAEW, 1975.
21. *Statement of Intent on Accounting Standards in the Nineteen Seventies*, Institute of Chartered Accountants in England and Wales, January 1970.
22. Edey, H.C., 'Accounting standards in the British Isles', in Baxter, W.T. and Davidson, S. (eds), *Studies in Accounting*, 3rd edn, Institute of Chartered Accountants in England and Wales, 1977.
23. Edey, *op. cit.*, p. 296.
24. Edey, *op. cit.*, p. 297.
25. *Setting Accounting Standards*, Accounting Standards Committee, January 1981.
26. *The Accountant*, 7 October 1982, p. 2.
27. *The Accountant*, 29 November 1982, p.3.
28. Baxter, W.T., 'Accounting standards—boon or curse?', *Accounting and Business Research*, Winter 1981, page 9.

QUESTIONS AND DISCUSSION PROBLEMS

1. Distinguish between the major groupings of users of accounts. What requirements do each of these groupings have from published financial statements? Do you feel that these requirements are currently being met?

2. There are many advantages and disadvantages to greater disclosure in accounting reports. Appraise these advantages and disadvantages and state whether you feel that more or less disclosure would be beneficial.

3. 'Although (relevance is) not sufficient as the sole criterion, it represents a necessary characteristic for all accounting information', from *A Statement of Basic Accounting Theory* (American Accounting Association 1966). Consider whether, and if so how, relevance is taken into consideration in the preparation of financial statements in the UK.

4. Briefly explain the stages in the production of a statement of standard accounting practice, in relation to one standard with which you are familiar. Do you feel that this process ensured that the best possible standard was produced?

5. What are the objectives of accounting standards? Have the SSAPs issued to date helped to achieve these objectives?

6. Discuss areas so far void of SSAPs where you think that these would be beneficial. Consider whether it is likely that standards will be developed for these areas in the near future.

7. The accounting policies used by four PLCs appear on pp. 186 – 191. State any additional information about the accounting policies of one of these companies that you would like to have. Why would this information be helpful in the appraisal of that company's accounts?

Appendix A

COMPANIES ACT REQUIREMENTS FOR THE PRESENTATION OF ACCOUNTING INFORMATION

This Appendix will outline the main requirements of the Companies Acts 1948 to 1981 with respect to published financial information. Of course the basic requirement contained in Section I of the 1976 Act is that the directors shall prepare a set of accounts for each accounting reference period, lay them before the company in general meeting and file a copy with the Registrar of Companies. The accounts must be audited and signed by two directors. The company must keep adequate accounting records to enable the requirements of the Act to be met. All shareholders, member and debenture holders are entitled to receive copies of the accounts.

The further requirements of the Acts will be considered under three headings, namely:

Accounting principles
The form and content of accounts
The disclosure requirements

It should be noted that certain classes of companies may be exempt from the more onerous requirements of the 1981 Acts.

Accounting Principles

The 1981 Act, which is not a consolidating Act, reaffirms the fundamental 'true and fair' requirement of Section 149 of the 1948 Act. Furthermore it specifically states that the true and fair principle shall have predominance over any other requirement of the Act. However, the 1981 Companies Act goes further than its predecessors in that it sets out in statute the accounting principles to be applied in preparing accounts. It gives statutory force to SSAP 2 and contains two alternative sets of rules for the valuation of assets—the so-called historic cost accounting rules and the alternative rules.

Sections 39 and 40 of the 1980 Act contain detailed rules on distributable profits.

The Form and Content of Financial Statements

The other major departure of the 1981 Act to previous Acts is that the format of accounts is now prescribed. Schedule 1 of the Act contains two balance sheet formats and four profit and loss account formats. The formats specify both the information to be disclosed and its order. Directors are required to choose one of the formats for both the profit and loss account and the balance sheet and to use it consistently.

FATS - N

199

The Disclosure Requirements

Balance sheet

The balance sheet will provide the following information:

Authorised and issued share capital.

Details of any movements on reserves will be shown, classified under appropriate headings.

Liabilities and provisions will be classified as appropriate unless particular groupings are immaterial.

Information about debentures, including dates of redemption, reissue, etc.

The aggregate totals of bank loans and overdrafts.

Any other borrowings, classifications of which may be aggregated.

Corporation Tax and its computations.

Inter-group debts.

Dividends including recommended dividends.

Details of contingent liabilities by way of a note.

Assets, classified under appropriate headings as between fixed and current assets.

In the case of fixed assets, their cost or valuation and details of any provisions for depreciation, etc. must be given.

Where fixed assets have been revalued, the year of the valuation must be stated and if this revaluation has taken place during the period the accounts cover, the name of the valuers and their qualifications must also be provided.

Intangible assets such as goodwill payments and trade marks will be stated at their book value, less any amount written off.

Investment, classified as between listed and unlisted.

Loans to employees, including officers of the company.

The basis for the conversion of foreign currency.

Profit and Loss Account

The profit and loss account will provide the following information:

Information on the company's turnover and how it was computed in the case of companies whose turnover is greater than £1 million per annum.

Income from rents or investments must be stated separately.

Information on directors' emoluments, including past director pension and compensation paid to directors. The number of directors whose emoluments fall into bands of £5000 per annum will be given although where combined directors' emoluments do not exceed £40,000 per annum there is no need to fulfil this requirement. Similar information must be given for employees earnings over £20,000 per annum.

Chairman's emoluments must also be shown separately.

Auditor's fee, classified as an expense, will be stated.

Any interest payable will be shown separately.

Information on depreciation, including details of provisions for depreciation.

Information on taxation showing UK Corporation Tax, UK Income Tax and Overseas Tax in separate categories.

The aggregate amounts of dividends including dividends proposed.

Any items concerning transactions not usually undertaken by the organisation and which are of an exceptional or non-recurring nature. A note of any changes in the basis of accounting policies used.

Additional Information Required
The following additional information is required as notes to the accounts:

For subsidiary companies the name of their holding company, and its country of origin.
Details of investments in subsidiaries and other companies.
Where a company has a 10% investment in another non-subsidiary company its country of incorporation and the nature of the shareholding. If the holding is 20% or more it must also disclose the aggregate amount of shares and reserves of that company and the profit or loss of that company for the immediate preceding financial year.
Recommended dividends and proposed transfers to reserves.
Any significant changes in fixed assets of the company.
Information on the issue of shares, debentures, etc.
Analysis of turnover and profit or loss before taxation, including the proportion of turnover amongst various classes of business, and information on the extent to which, in the directors' opinion, each class of business has contributed to the profit or loss of the company before taxation.
The average number of employees per week, and information on the remuneration paid to employees.
In the case of groups, group accounts will be required in the form of consolidated accounts.

Directors' Report
The general requirement is that the report will provide 'a fair review of the development of the business of the company and its subsidiaries during the year and its position at the end of the year'. In particular the report should give information on important events that have affected the business since the end of the accounting year, likely future developments and information on Research and Development activity. The following information should also be disclosed:

The names of the directors must be listed, together with any material information, as far as their interest in contracts of other organisations with the company are concerned, rights to acquire shares or debentures, changes in their holdings of shares, etc.
The principal activities of the company.
Information with respect to arrangements for ensuring employees' health, safety and welfare at work.
Information on contributions to political organisations and donations to charitable bodies.
Any information on any other matters which are material to the members' appreciation of the company's position.

Miscellaneous
It should be noted that there are certain special classes of company which have special arrangements under the Companies Acts, these include banking and discount companies, insurance companies, shipping companies and certain overseas companies. Unlimited companies are not required to file accounts.

Appendix B

STOCK EXCHANGE REQUIREMENTS FOR THE PRESENTATION OF ACCOUNTING INFORMATION

The Stock Exchange also has certain disclosure requirements under their 'Listing Agreement—Companies'. Obviously there is no legal backing to these requirements but listed companies are required to sign a general undertaking to adhere to them and, if they do not follow them, would be in danger of having their quotation suspended. This additional information includes:

When statements of standard accounting practice have not been followed, reasons must be given for the alternative basis used to prepare the accounts.

Turnover and trading results analysed geographically for operations outside the United Kingdom.

The principal countries in which the company has subsidiaries.

Interests of each director in the share capital, and any substantial interests held by people other than directors.

Any information on contracts the directors are materially interested in and information such as waivers of emoluments by directors or waivers of dividends by shareholders.

Information on each company in which an investment of over 20 per cent of the equity is held.

Appendix C

STATEMENTS OF STANDARD ACCOUNTING PRACTICE AND EXPOSURE DRAFTS

The objective of this Appendix is to provide a list of all the Statements of Standard Accounting Practice and Exposure Drafts.

Statements of Standard Accounting Practice (extant at 31 January 1983)

		Date issued
SSAP	*Explanatory Foreword* (Revised May 1975)	January 1971
SSAP 1	*Accounting for the Results of Associated Companies* (Amended August 1974)	January 1971
SSAP 2	*Disclosure of Accounting Policies*	November 1971
SSAP 3	*Earnings Per Share* (Revised August 1974)	February 1972
SSAP 4	*The Accounting Treatment of Government Grants*	April 1974
SSAP 5	*Accounting for Value Added Tax*	April 1974
SSAP 6	*Extraordinary Items and Prior Year Adjustments* (Revised April 1975, Part 5 added June 1978)	April 1974
SSAP 7	(Provisional) *Accounting for Changes in the Purchasing Power of Money* (withdrawn January 1978)	May 1974
SSAP 8	*The Treatment of Taxation under the Imputation System in the Accounts of Companies* (Appendix 3 added December 1977)	August 1974
SSAP 9	*Stocks and Work-in-Progress*	May 1975
SSAP 10	*Statements of Source and Application of Funds* (Part 4 added June 1978)	July 1975
SSAP 11 Withdrawn	*Accounting for Deferred Taxation* (amended October 1976)	August 1975
SSAP 12	*Accounting for Depreciation*	December 1977
SSAP 13	*Accounting for Research and Development*	December 1977

SSAP 14	*Group Accounts*	September 1978
SSAP 15	*Accounting for Deferred Taxation*	October 1978
SSAP 16	*Current Cost Accounting*	March 1980
SSAP 17	*Accounting for Post Balance Sheet Events*	August 1980
SSAP 18	*Accounting for Contingencies*	August 1980
SSAP 19	*Accounting for Investment Properties*	November 1981

Exposure Drafts Issued But Not Yet Converted into SSAPs (extant at 31 January 1983)

ED 3	*Accounting for Acquisitions and Mergers*	20 January 1971
ED 16	Supplement to *Extraordinary Items and Prior Year Adjustments*	11 September 1975
ED 27	*Accounting for Foreign Currency Transactions*	27 October 1980
ED 28	*Accounting for Petroleum Revenue Tax*	6 March 1981
ED 29	*Accounting for Leases and Hire Purchase Contracts*	October 1981
ED 30	*Accounting for Goodwill*	October 1982
ED 31	*Accounting for Acquisitions and Mergers*	October 1982

Appendix D

INTERNATIONAL ACCOUNTING STANDARDS AND EXPOSURE DRAFTS

The Councils of the CCAB bodies have agreed that, as far as possible, IAS requirements will be incorporated in UK SSAPs so that only the latter have to be consulted. However, if certain provisions of the IASs are not acceptable to the CCAB bodies this may lead to non-compliance although SSAPs may have been followed. In such cases this should be disclosed by way of a note, although it is not necessary to quantify such non-compliance.

(a) IASs shown with an (a) have been adopted by the CCAB bodies and the SSAPs which incorporate them are indicated.

(b) Although some IASs have yet to be accepted and published by the CCAB bodies through the ASC, and are therefore technically not operative in the UK *International Accounting Standards*, a reprint of IASs by the ICAEW (IAS reprint) states in its introduction to each of the IASs shown in this Appendix with a (b) that compliance with company law and SSAPs will automatically ensure conformity with them.

(c) The IAS (reprint) states in its introduction to the IAS shown with a (c) that the requirements of IAS 4 accord very closely with the contents of SSAP 12 with the one exception of 'investment properties' which in SSAP 2 are explicitly required to be dealt with on the basis of annual valuations, and annual depreciation charges on them are not permitted. It is felt that the provisions of IAS 4 if applied to UK investment properties would be misleading in material cases.

(d) The IAS (reprint) states in its introduction to the IAS shown with a (d) that the requirement of IAS 9 accords very closely with the contents of SSAP 13 with the one exception that IAS 9 requires disclosure of the total of R & D costs, including amortisation of deferred development costs, charged as an expense which is not required in the UK at present because of the absence of an adequate definition of R & D costs.

International Accounting Standards Issued		Date of Approval	Date of Publication	UK and Irish Standards Incorporated in the International Equivalents	
IAS	Preface to statements of international accounting standards (superceding January 1975 publication)	October 1977	March 1978		
IAS 1	Disclosure of Accounting Policies	November 1974	January 1975	(a)	SSAP 2 Disclosure of accounting policies
IAS 2	Valuation and presentation of inventories in the context of the historical cost system	July 1975	October 1975	(a)	SSAP 9 Stocks and Work-in-progress
IAS 3	Consolidated financial statements	March 1976	June 1976	(a)	SSAP 1 Accounting for the results of associated companies and SSAP 14 Group Accounts
IAS 4	Depreciation accounting	July 1976	October 1976	(c)	SSAP 12 Accounting for depreciation
IAS 5	Information to be disclosed in financial statements	July 1976	October 1976	(b)	—
IAS 6 (withdrawn)	Accounting responses to changing prices (superceded by IAS 15)	March 1977	June 1977	(b)	—
IAS 7	Statement of changes in financial position	July 1977	October 1977	(a)	SSAP 10 Statements of source and application of funds
IAS 8	Unusual and prior period items and changes in accounting policies	October 1977	February 1978	(a)	SSAP 6 Extraordinary items and prior year adjustments

IAS 9	Accounting for research and development activities	March 1978	July 1978	(b)(d)	—
IAS 10	Contingencies and events occurring after balance sheet date	June 1978	October 1978	(b)	—
IAS 11	Accounting for construction contracts	November 1978	March 1979	(a)	SSAP 9 Stocks and Work-in-progress
IAS 12	Accounting for taxes on income	March 1979	July 1979	(b)	—
IAS 13	Presentation of current assets and current liabilities	June 1979	November 1979	(b)	—
IAS 14	Reporting financial information by segment	March 1981	August 1981	(b)	—
IAS 15	Information reflecting the effects of changing prices	June 1981	November 1981	(b)	—
IAS 16	Accounting for property, plant and equipment	October 1981	March 1982	(b)	—
IAS 17	Accounting for Leases	March 1982	September 1982		
IAS 18	Revenue Recognition	June 1982	December 1982		
IAS 19	Accounting for Retirement Benefits in the Financial Statements of Employers	June 1982	January 1983		

Glossary

A LIST OF ABBREVIATIONS USED IN THIS BOOK

ACCA	Association of Certified Accountants
AIA	American Institute of Accountants
AICPA	American Institute of Certified Public Accountants
ASC	Accounting Standards Committee
ASSC	Accounting Standards Steering Committee (Later to become the ASC)
CAP	Committee on Accounting Procedure (of the AICPA)
CC	Current Cost
CCA	Current Cost Account(s)/Accounting
CCAB	Consultative Committee for Accounting Bodies
CCR	Current Cost Reserve
CED	Consumer Expenditure Deflator
CPI	Consumer Price Index (now known as CED)
CIPFA	Chartered Institute of Public Finance and Accountancy
CPP	Current Purchasing Power
COS	Cost of Sales
COSA	Cost of Sales Adjustment
ED	Exposure Draft
EEC	European Economic Community
EV	Economic Value
FASB	Financial Accounting Standards Board (USA)
FIFO	First In First Out (method to value or charge out stock)
HC	Historic Cost
HCA	Historic Cost Account(s)/Accounting
IASC	International Accounting Standards Committee
IASG	Inflation Accounting Steering Group
ICAEW	Institute of Chartered Accountants in England and Wales
ICAI	Institute of Chartered Accountants of Ireland
ICAS	Institute of Chartered Accountants of Scotland
ICMA	Institute of Cost and Management Accountants
IDC	Inter Divisional (Departmental) Comparison
IFC	Inter Firm Comparison
ITC	Inter Temporal Comparison
LIFO	Last In First Out (method to value or charge out stock)
MNE	Multi-national enterprise
MWC	Monetary Working Capital
MWCA	Monetary Working Capital Adjustment
NIFO	Next In First Out (method to value or charge out stock)
NRC	Net Replacement Cost
NRV	Net Realisable Value
PINCCA	Price Index Numbers for Current Cost Accounting
PLC	Public Limited Company
RC	Replacement Cost
RCA	Replacement Cost Accounting
RPI	General Index of Retail Prices/Retail Price Index
SSAP	Statement of Standard Accounting Practice

Index